M:

CUTTING SCHOOL

CUTTING SCHOOL

Privatization,
Segregation,
and the End of
Public Education

NOLIWE ROOKS

NEW YORK
LONDON

Requests for permission to reproduce selections from this book should be mailed to: Permissions Department, The New Press, 120 Wall Street, 31st floor, New York, NY 10005

Published in the United States by The New Press, New York, 2017
Distributed by Perseus Distribution

ISBN 978-1-62097-248-9 (hc)
ISBN 978-1-62097-249-6 (e-book)

The New Press publishes books that promote and enrich public discussion and understanding of the issues vital to our democracy and to a more equitable world. These books are made possible by the enthusiasm of our readers; the support of a committed group of donors, large and small; the collaboration of our many partners in the independent media and the not-for-profit sector; booksellers, who often hand-sell New Press books; librarians; and above all by our authors.

www.thenewpress.com

Composition by dix!
This book was set in Garamond Premier Pro

Printed in the United States of America

10 9 8 7 6 5 4 3 2 1

For my stepfather, Dedan Gills,
who knew I would understand him
perfectly
when he told me
to "stay out the filthy water."
For my father, Milton Rooks,
who knew I sometimes believed him
when he told me I could walk on top of it.
They both transitioned during the last few months
of my writing this book.
I hear them
still.

CONTENTS

PREFACE

I am the child and grandchild of educators on both sides of my family. My mother was born in Texarkana, Texas. Her great-aunt, a woman I grew up calling Grandma Isabelle, was raising my mother when she and her husband, Bill, decided to join the flow out of the South during the great migration. They settled in San Francisco in the late 1950s, my teenage mother along with them. My Grandma Isabelle did what she termed "maid's work," sometimes for white families, sometimes in hospitals, up until her death in the 1980s. Her husband, my "Uncle Bill," worked a variety of odd jobs. However, more than what he did to earn a living, what I most recall about him was how he was able to impose his will on the hard, rocky ground in the back of their small, two-bedroom, one-bath home in the Hunters Point area of San Francisco. In defiance of the sky that was often gray and the chill of the fog-kissed wind, he made a garden grow tomatoes and okra and collard greens and cabbage.

Neither Grandma Isabelle nor Uncle Bill graduated from high school. They never even went. In the 1930s at the intersection of rural Texas and Arkansas—two heavily white-supremacist and segregated states—funding, access, and support for Black education took a back seat to doing backbreaking work as the means of survival. For their only child, Isabelle and Bill thought the public schools of San Francisco were a yellow brick road toward a more economically and socially secure place in America. I cannot fully imagine what they must have thought when my mother, the first in her family to attend college, jeopardized her scholarly pursuits by immersing herself in the Black student protest movement at San Francisco State in the early 1960s. This was a movement formed in part to demand that both the state and federal governments honor their commitments to financially supporting education for the poor, people of color, and all disenfranchised students. For the movement, education was a political weapon in the cause for freedom. Members began tutoring programs in the ghettos of the Bay Area with a curriculum that linked individual educational freedoms to a collective narrative about justice and the role of knowledge in wresting loose the promise of the so-called American Dream for those who needed it most. For my mother's parents, educational access could lead to economic uplift and racial equity; for my mother and many others of her generation, the goal was to achieve more than equality—they were fighting for racial justice.

On the paternal side of my family tree, my grandfather was the principal at the segregated North Ward Elementary School in Clearwater, Florida, where my grandmother was a teacher. Though they met in Clearwater, they grew up in different parts of Florida where their families farmed. Because they had "bettered" themselves and their situation through education, they truly believed that it was a vehicle through which each subsequent generation could rise up through the ranks of a Black, middle-class, segregated society. Education had the potential to remake the future for their children.

At the time, the idea of fully integrating into white American society did not factor heavily into their thinking about the importance of upward mobility. While recognizing that they needed a certain amount of access to resources and opportunities guarded by white privilege and "anti-Black" Jim Crow–style racism, they did not imagine that such desires would necessitate leaving Black communities behind to live and work in white ones. They didn't think whites would ever allow full integration. Like many Black folks, they were also unsure that they, themselves, would want it.

In addition to his role as a principal, in the late 1950s my grandfather led a ten-year—and ultimately successful—effort to integrate the teachers' union in Florida. He wanted Black teachers to be eligible for benefits, to receive equal pay, and to have the opportunity for career advancement and job security. He paid a price for his organizing. He was shot at a number of times over the years. His home was firebombed. His life was repeatedly threatened, as were his job, the lives of his wife and son (my grandmother and father), and the lives of the teachers with whom he worked. He did not romanticize integration, but still saw education as being important for community self-reliance, uplift, and respect of Black Americans.

As for me, given my parents' custody agreement following their divorce, my school years were divided almost equally between the newly integrated schools in Florida—where my classmates where overwhelmingly white—and schools in San Francisco, where my classrooms were for the most part of color, or all Black. In both places, I lived in Black communities. That experience, and my family history, led me to understand the tremendous influence of the segregated history of American education on our educational present. In our current moment, the type of education, the quality of the school buildings, the experience of the teachers, and the ability to graduate are vastly different depending on the racial and economic makeup of one's community. It is apartheid—a system that is, at its core, organized by physically separating racial groups and then privileging one racial group over another (a construct that cannot be disentangled from social class). Educational apartheid has high social costs. As discussed in the pages that follow, we can right this wrong, but first we have to take full account of the ways in which race and profit-driven interests in education have negatively impacted the futures of so many of our nation's youth. This book is a step in that direction.

CUTTING SCHOOL

INTRODUCTION

The Segrenomics of American Education

> Simple justice requires that public funds, to which all tax-
> payers of all races contribute, not be spent in any fashion
> which encourages, entrenches, subsidizes, or results in . . .
> discrimination.
> —John F. Kennedy, 1963

The road necessarily traveled to achieve freedom and equality in the United States leads directly through public education. For American citizens who are neither white nor wealthy, the journey has often twisted and turned before leading back to the beginning, exposing the stark tensions between racial and economic integration as an educational strategy and the strategy that champions separate but equal schools as America's educational ideology of choice. Since the earliest days when tax-supported public education was conceived and implemented, there have been intractable tensions between how economics, or race—or both—determine the funding, form, and purpose of education in America. Schools that educate the wealthy have generally had decent buildings, money for materials, a coherent curriculum, and well-trained teachers. Schools that educate poorer students and those of color too often have decrepit buildings, no funds for quality instructional materials, little input in the structure or purpose of the curriculum, and they make do with the best teachers they can find. These differences based on color and class are an undeniable constant throughout the history of education in America, and still are today.

It is then not surprising that students educated in wealthy schools perform well as measured by standard educational benchmarks. Students educated in poor schools do not. While there have been times in our nation's history when we have acknowledged the damage inflicted by separate educational systems on our constitutionally enshrined rights of citizenship, with few exceptions we have found little incentive to commit ourselves to integrating both halves of this literal and figurative schoolhouse. Racial and economic integration is the one systemic solution that we know ensures the tide will lift all educational boats equally. However, instead of committing to educating poor children in the same way as we do the wealthy, or actually *with* the wealthy, we have offered separate educational content (such as a reoccurring focus on vocational education for the poor) and idiosyncratic forms of educational funding and delivery (such as virtual charter schools and cyber education) as substitutes for what we know consistently works. While not ensuring educational equality, such separate, segregated, and unequal forms of education have provided the opportunity for businesses to make a profit selling schooling. I am calling this specific form of economic profit *segrenomics*. Segrenomics, or the business of profiting specifically from high levels of racial and economic segregation, is on the rise. Educational practices based on segrenomic practices trickle downward from the wealthy and well connected to poor communities and those of color.

This book explores the social and economic forces, past and present, that have worked together to propose and maintain separate school systems that are organized very differently depending on the race and class of the children in the classroom. This separation is profitable. The dynamics that intertwine to make it so—segregation, poverty, race—are one area of exploration in this book. At the same time, while the educational prescriptions for the most disadvantaged in our society are often imposed "from outside," their success or failure often depends on their active acceptance or rejection by parents and other members in the community. Groups seeking the assurances of American citizenship, advancement, and employment have always believed that education is one sure path to get there. They are then willing to achieve it by any means necessary. The desire that some have to profit from racial and economic segregation in education, coupled with the active desire members of segregated communities of color have for quality education, has led to our current moment where quality education is for some a distant mirage, and the promise to provide it is profitable for others.

A close look at highly racially and economically segregated neighborhoods, communities, and indeed regions of the country illustrates how high levels of segregation, combined with economic vulnerability, can lead to corporate profit for those who promise to provide children in these circumstances an education. We have long known that there is an undeniable link between a child being undereducated and her future life chances. Children who live in segregated communities and are Native American, Black, or Latino are more likely to have severely limited educational options that consign them to the lower rungs of a racial and economic caste system from which the likelihood of escape becomes ever more dim. Given that racial and economic segregation almost always guarantees a lesser form of educational attainment, we as a nation need more, not fewer, plans or policies to aggressively integrate our classrooms as a means of equalizing education. In the absence of such a widespread commitment and effort, integration as a cure for the disease of educational racism is, in the twenty-first century, tantamount to a prescription that can't be filled.

Instead, in the last thirty years, government, philanthropy, business, and financial sectors have heavily invested in efforts to privatize certain segments of public education; stock schools with inexperienced, less highly paid teachers whose hiring often provides companies with a "finder's fee"; outsource the running of schools to management organizations; and propose virtual schools as a literal replacement for—not just a supplement to—the brick and mortar educational experience. The attraction, of course, is the large pot of education dollars that's been increasingly available to private corporate financial interests. The public education budget funded by taxpayers is roughly $500–$600 billion per year. Each successful effort that shifts those funds from public to private hands—and there has been a growing number of such efforts since the 1980s—escalates corporate earnings.

The bulk of the privatization efforts aimed at America's public school system are generally described by businessmen, civil rights leaders, and government officials alike as the most successful means by which poor and working-class parents of color can exercise "choice" in their children's education, and as a powerful means by which to address the deficiencies of the traditional public education system. Parents are told by these influential voices, often perceived as experts, that such alternative educational strategies are the best way to close the achievement and opportunity gaps between Black, Latino, Native American, and poor children and their wealthier white and Asian counterparts. Charter schools, charter management organizations, vouchers, virtual schools, and an alternatively certified, non-unionized teaching force represent the bulk of the contemporary solutions offered as cures for what ails communities that are upward of 80 percent Black or Latino and overwhelmingly likely to fall below federally set poverty levels. Yet the practices and approaches that mark these so-called solutions are rarely if ever prescribed as an educational panacea for white students, or for those with wealth, or for communities with high levels of either. Wealthy communities would exact a high political cost on any who tried to similarly experiment with the educational futures of their children.

While consistently and successfully educating children who are poor and of color has eluded the nation as a whole, the public funds earmarked for their education have been a prize of staggering economic value and social importance. This has been the case since the nineteenth century, when tax-supported and -financed education was first implemented in the former slaveholding South. The post-Reconstruction period birthed the basic structures of both the racial and economic relationships and the power struggles that play out in education today. It was a time that gave rise to the earliest union between America's wealthy elite—philanthropists—and a business interest in the education of poor children, or those of color. As a result, when looking at the recurring history of educational segrenomics from the nineteenth century through to today, I assert that the only way to end this particular manifestation of the educational caste system in this country is to penalize those who seek to—or happen to—profit from educational inequality if that inequality is linked to racial and economic segregation. In the absence of safeguards, the most pernicious forms of segrenomics will continue. There is simply too much money to be made for them not to.

There are myriad myths about the intersection of race, class, and education in America that taxpayer-funded profit streams rely upon. The first in need of revision is that Black people do not care about education. Another is that, in relation to quality education, poverty does not make a difference. What I learned writing this book is that parents in poor communities care so deeply about education that they are willing to go to almost any lengths, both tested and experimental, to find the silver bullet that might possibly provide their children with the educational access that has been so long denied. I also learned that the systemic undereducation of some communities is lucrative. There are educational entrepreneurs who see and seek profit from segregated communities precisely because they are poor, of color, or both. Segrenomics is as much a business strategy as it is an educational ideology.

That reality helps to explain in part how it was that, in 2009, a Black middle school student from a failing and decrepit school in the town of Dillon, South Carolina, found herself in Washington, D.C., as the guest of the new president, Barack Obama. She was there as justification for why Congress should support the president in his request to authorize billions of dollars in funding for low-performing public schools—the largest sum ever dedicated to addressing the undereducation of poor students in failing schools. Much of it was in the form of construction and infrastructure spending wrapped in a bill to stimulate the economy. None of it was earmarked to support or enhance educational integration. Ultimately, that student would become the face of one of the most expensive educational funding failures in the United States.

For that first address to Congress in 2009, newly elected president Barack Obama invited fourteen-year-old eighth-grade student Ty'Sheoma Bethea to sit in a place of honor next to First Lady Michelle Obama. When the president acknowledged her, the entire gallery rose as one to applaud. As the clapping intensified and then crested, the First Lady gathered the teenager close in a hug and smiled at Ty'Sheoma's mother, holding her palm up for a "five on the Black hand side" moment of solidarity with her fellow parent. Years later, Ty'Sheoma would reflect on the evening with wonder, saying, "The president knew who I was." [1]

These magical moments happened because Ty'Sheoma had written to the president when he was a candidate, urging him to provide money to repair her aging and dilapidated middle school. In her letter, she said she wanted him to know that though the students there were poor, they "weren't quitters," and she and her classmates wanted to be doctors and lawyers and presidents too. They "wanted to make a difference not just in South Carolina, but in the world beyond." She told him that the sorry state of the school building, with its peeling paint, nonexistent AC system, overcrowded classrooms, and dilapidated bathrooms, made realizing those dreams difficult to imagine. She described the hardship created by the fact that the school sat close to the railroad tracks, and, as a result, at least six times each day academic instruction had to cease throughout the whole building while the students waited for the trains to pass.[2]

Not only did Ty'Sheoma's letter lead to her trip to Washington, where she and her mother met the first family, but also, two years later, she attended the ribbon cutting to commemorate the opening of a newly built school that replaced the one about which she had written. The Obama administration had allocated economic stimulus funding to pay for the cost. In fact, the president proposed rebuilding as many as 1,200 schools nationwide, many in communities that had suffered declining access to employment as manufacturing jobs disappeared. Called the School Improvement Grants program, between 2010 and 2013 the Obama administration awarded billions of dollars to struggling schools, most of it stimulus funds from the American Recovery and Reinvestment Act of 2009. Stimulus funding linked to educational infrastructure seemed like a win-win situation. Communities got new schools and enough money to provide short-term jobs to help pull the country out of a deep recession. The resultant new buildings were sorely needed and showcased the administration's commitment to bettering the lives of poor children by providing equal educational facilities regardless of race. It was good politics and good business, if not necessarily a sound or transformational educational solution.

The School Improvement Grants program wasn't new. President George W. Bush had started it, but under the Obama administration, the funding was greatly increased from less than $1 billion per year to $7 billion spent between 2010 and 2015. Former secretary of education Arne Duncan said the grants "unleashed innovation" across the country. The money went directly to states to distribute to their poorest-performing schools, defined as those with "exceedingly low graduation rates, or poor math and reading test scores, or both. Individual schools could receive up to $2 million per year for three years, on the condition that they adopt one of the administration's four preferred measures," which included replacing the principal and at least half the teachers, converting into a charter school, closing altogether, or undergoing a "transformation," including hiring a new principal and adopting new instructional strategies, new teacher evaluations, and a longer school day. None were measures proven to boost achievement for struggling students. At the end of 2016 a federal analysis showed that test scores, graduation rates, and college enrollment were no different in schools that received money through the School Improvement Grants program than in schools that did not. What that means is while the money did help to stimulate the overall economy, it didn't actually do much to help Ty'Sheoma and the other students at the school realize their academic dreams.[3]

When Dillon, South Carolina's new school was completed, there were no more crumbling walls, broken windows, mold-infested bathrooms, or backed-up sewage streams bubbling up into school hallways. However, the shiny new structure was not a harbinger of higher academic performance for children in the state who were both Black and poor. For that group, academic achievement continued to lag far behind standard expectations. This was and is true in the state overall. According to the National Urban League's 2015 Report on the State of Black America, in 2013 only 13.8 percent of Black fourth graders in South Carolina scored proficiently or above in math, compared to 48 percent of white fourth graders. By eighth grade, the Black math-proficiency rate dropped to 10.5 percent compared to 44.6 percent for whites. According to the state's superintendent of education, Mick Zais, in 2014 about 38 percent of all the state's fourth graders were functionally illiterate. Three-quarters were able to read, but they did so well below grade level. Scores in Ty'Sheoma's hometown of Dillon were no exception to these trends. For poor students in America, solving the riddle of startlingly low achievement continues to defy both infrastructure and good intentions. We will never know what would have happened if those funds had been invested in providing proven educational strategies.[4]

The media coverage of how Dillon, South Carolina, got one new middle school was in many ways uplifting, if not fully heart-warming. On the one hand, we saw a moment when the highest reaches of the federal government indicated that it was their role and responsibility to both push for and fund buildings and infra-structure as a means of demonstrating their commitment to en-suring that all children, regardless of race and income, received an equal education. On the other hand, given the educational results, it is clear that more than a building was necessary to uplift the educational futures of children like Ty'sheoma. The reasons this was true were as much because of the district's past as its present.

Ty'Sheoma's school, J.V. Martin Junior High, lay in a genera-tionally impoverished region of rural South Carolina with histori-cally poor public school achievement. The whole area was referred to as the "Corridor of Shame" in a 2005 documentary about a lawsuit brought against the state of South Carolina on behalf of thirty-six similarly run-down rural school districts. Much like the historic *Brown v. Board of Education* case, the South Carolina case charged that the students in these districts were receiving a substandard education and attempted to argue that a massive in-vestment of time, resources, and creativity was necessary to stem this tide that so disproportionately impacted the state's children who were Black and poor. Taken together, the districts that made up the plaintiffs represented districts where 88.4 percent of stu-dents were of color in a state where only 48 percent of the residents were non-white; where 86 percent were poor enough to qualify for free lunch when overall only 55 percent of state residents did; and where 75 percent of schools ranked as unsatisfactory and below average in a state where only 18 percent of all public schools were so ranked.[5]

The suit, first filed in 1993, argued that the children in those communities were not receiving an adequate education and were in need of more than advice about boot strapping, grit, and hard work or a new building to fix what ailed them. Those schools needed funding for experienced teachers, buses, social workers, books, new curricula, health care, and, perhaps most important, a commitment to quality education. The case, *Abbeville County School District v. The State of South Carolina*, was older than Ty'Sheoma when she wrote to President Obama in 2009. It was the longest-running case in the history of the state, appeared before the State Supreme Court twice, amassed over twenty thousand pages of documents, and included a hundred witnesses. The proceedings took place in Clarendon County—the very same county where in the 1940s a case, *Briggs v. Elliott*, was brought that would eventually contribute to the landmark *Brown* decision on segregation. While some things changed between the mid-twentieth century and the early decades of the twenty-first, it is still the case that in the United States it is just not possible to fully understand the role, success, and proposed function of education without weaving a tale inclusive of how segregation, race, and economics have combined to become the story of public education in America.

A discussion of the meaning of, accomplishments in, and fight for an equal education by Black children and their parents in contemporary as well as in historically Black communities is one of the contributions this book makes to conversations about educational strategy and equity in the United States. In 1933, Carter G. Woodson wrote about Black Americans' chief difficulty with education in his classic text *The Mis-Education of the Negro*:

> Somebody outside of the race has desired to try out on Negroes some experiment which interested him and his coworkers; and Negroes, being objects of charity, have received them cordially and have done what they required. In fact, the keynote in the education of the Negro has been to do what he is told to do. Any Negro who has learned to do this is well prepared to function in the American social order as others would have him.

By 1980, another legendary Black educator, Marva Collins, would continue that line of reasoning, saying, "Our people have been guinea pigged. No one experiments on other children the way our children are guinea pigged. I want for our children what the best get." Educational experimentation is part and parcel of the educational history for the poor and children of color.[6]

Among other things, this book shows the connections between past and present business and philanthropic interests in the education sector and the necessity of having the high levels of racial and economic segregation consistently required for their often experimental educational strategies to be tested. There have been few periods in American history when the success of business and philanthropic interests in education did *not* rely on high levels of racial and economic segregation. A pattern of cyclical regularity has emerged wherein powerful interests "plunder" public education dollars earmarked for poor students of color in order to enrich certain powerful individuals and their business interests. That is then followed by a period during which those same funds are "hoarded" and primarily used to educate students who are white and relatively privileged. There have been moments when we have had the collective will, funding, and infrastructure in place at the same time to successfully educate non-white, non-wealthy children. However, those moments are few and far between.

From the nineteenth century until the early 1950s, the question of education in the South, the region of the country where a majority of Black people then still lived, centered most specifically on issues of funding, type, and its relationship to the economic health of the larger region. By the 1970s, those same concerns left the confines of the South, along with a migrating mass of Black people who were leaving for urban cities in the North, West, and Midwest in search of jobs and equal education. Once there, they found themselves overwhelmingly confined to racially and economically segregated urban ghettos with schools that were underfunded and many teachers no other district or school wanted. They were generally locked out of schools in white neighborhoods and affluent suburbs. Neither the funding for the public schools in the cities and suburbs nor the education on offer was in any way equal to what white areas enjoyed.

Once the Nixon administration passed a bill making it illegal to use federal funds to provide buses as transportation to students for the purposes of integration, the federal government basically announced that it was for the most part out of the business of funding integration. Black parents and community members opened scores of Black independent schools, many of which were peerless in terms of their ability to educate the Black children who traditional public schools said were impossible to educate to and through college. However, there were simply too few such schools to fill the totality of the educational mandate of schools across the country. As a result of both policy and individual bias, educational segregation hardened, and the educational achievement of poor students and those of color fell farther behind.

If we don't see much protest, or even public upset, over these levels of separation, it's certainly not because the positive social and educational effects of integrated schools are unknown. As education scholar David Kirp remarked in a 2012 *New York Times* opinion piece, between 1970 and 1990, the Black–white gap in educational attainment shrank in racially integrated schools, and yet this strategy is no longer discussed, and there is no "vocal pro-integration constituency" pushing for it. Research studies make it clear that Blacks and Latinos in integrated schools learn more, get better grades in college, graduate in larger numbers, and secure better jobs.[7]

In addition to us knowing about the benefits of racial integration in education, the majority of Americans actually believe in it. Up to 75 percent of whites support school-integration efforts and say they would be comfortable sending their children to schools that were up to 50 percent Black. The numbers, however, decrease when whites are asked about *how* to achieve racial integration. They do not support busing or any program that would deny their children access to the school of their choice. This may be key to explaining why there is not more of a focus on integration in public schools—we simply are not comfortable with what it might take to actually make it happen, whether it's working to also integrate our neighborhoods, reapportion state and federal tax dollars to support magnet schools, or even creatively reorganize our entire public-school system. Perhaps the communities with the most at stake should be given a seat at the educational table where policy conversations are taking place to help find solutions.

The answers to the question of school integration are big, messy, and hard. In fact, after decades of trying, we as a nation seem to have decided that it is neither possible nor desirable. But the current stagnation around integration only further exacerbates inequality. While we wait for a solution, the forces that benefit financially and socially from high levels of educational segregation gain even more ground. The connections between education, business, and economics are now so entrenched that many no longer primarily think of schools as anything other than being central to the economy of the nation as a whole. It is no longer a great equalizer that benefits the status or well-being of poor or disadvantaged people. The process through which this happened was not accidental.[8]

In 1981 President Ronald Reagan convened a task force to do an analysis of public education. The result was a report named *A Nation at Risk*, a scathing appraisal of public education. Its authors were leaders from government, business, and education, and they spent a full two years examining American schools before releasing their assessment. In short, they were appalled. They said that standardized test and SAT scores were falling and America's children were falling further and further behind other countries. The task force found that the public education system was so bad that not only were our youth unprepared to join an increasingly high-tech workforce, but also, they warned, almost 23 million Americans were functionally illiterate. And perhaps worst of all, they scolded, Americans were complacent as their schools crumbled. One of the most repeated lines in the report said, "If an unfriendly foreign power had attempted to impose on America the mediocre educational performance that exists today, we might well have viewed it as an act of war." In response, members of the Reagan administration said that the report made it clear that our very nation was at risk because we had spent too much time focusing on issues of educational equality, racial integration, and social equality. Now, the overriding purpose of public education had to be in service to the nation's economy and businesses. Apparently, we could focus on equity, inclusion, and economics all at the same time.[9]

That one report led to hundreds of reports written by a variety of state and national commissions, all offering similar assessments of the ills of forced integration and calls for social equity in public education and offering suggestions for how business leaders could play more of a central role in the schoolhouse. In 1989, the National Business Roundtable urged its state and local affiliates to work more closely with state governments to radically restructure the nation's public schools. The National Alliance of Business circulated pamphlets instructing CEOs and business groups on how to shape local school policy toward economic restructuring goals. President Reagan and his education secretary, William Bennett, were in full agreement with such sentiments. In regard to public schools, integration was out, business was in.[10]

The first Bush White House expanded the ideology born during the Reagan years. It supported the New American School Development Corporation, whose purpose was to raise private money to promote partnerships between corporations and schools. In addition, George H. W. Bush's administration crafted the National Goals 2000 program, which called for privatization, deregulation, and competition between schools. In the 1990s, President

Bill Clinton continued Bush's National Goals 2000 program, and advocated for more charter schools, while making it clear that he welcomed congressional lobbying on education policy by corporate allies. President Obama's administration turned many of these educational strategies into federal policy. The upshot of all this activity was that racial and economic inequality—and segregation—have essentially become the business partners of so-called public education in America.[11]

Black Lives—and Black Education—Matter

Much of our contemporary conversation around how and why Black Lives Matter has focused most specifically on the lack of judicial response to police murders of unarmed Black people and on the seemingly unchecked growth of the prison industrial complex in the United States. Yet there is another story to be told about the relationship between our broken educational system and larger issues of social justice. The most high-profile cases associated with the emergence and growth of the Black Lives Matter movement are synonymous with cities, towns, and states that either have aggressively fought desegregating their traditional public schools or have downsized their traditional educational systems and replaced them with a variety of alternative educational plans. This is slow murder by other means.

Florida, where teenager Trayvon Martin was murdered by neighborhood watch volunteer George Zimmerman, is the state with the largest number of virtual charter schools in the country. Ferguson, Missouri, is where eighteen-year old Mike Brown was shot by police officer Darren Wilson. At the time he was shot, his heavily poor and of color Normandy, Missouri, school district had gone bankrupt, had lost its accreditation, and was trying to arrange for suburban districts to educate their children. Ohio, where twelve-year-old Tamir Rice was killed at a playground by a police officer while playing with a toy gun, leads the nation in the rate of expansion of charter schools. In South Carolina, where Walter Scott was shot in the back by police officer Michael Slager, virtual charter schools educate increasing numbers of rural and poor children. In Detroit, where nineteen-year-old Renisha Mc-Bride was shot after knocking on a door to ask for help, there is a higher percentage of charter schools than in any other city in the country, save New Orleans. The list goes on.

Each of the states just referenced leads the country in some aspect of the profit-driven models of public education, and their records of providing a quality education to students at the inter-section of poverty and racial inequality within traditional public schools are dismal. The privatization of public education is a big business, especially in communities where residents are poor and lack the resources to hire the types of D.C. lobbyists so neces-sary to effecting governmental change. These are the strands that weave together the overall story to be explored here. This book is not a story of the thread, but rather the whole tapestry of just how fiscally lucrative racially and economically segregated com-munities have been and continue to be for those profiting off of them.

I will look at education debates from the nineteenth century up through the present, ending with a look at how community orga-nizations and traditional public school stakeholders are success-fully addressing these issues in a number of communities across the country. However, in order to have any hope of moving for-ward, we—communities both of and not of color; those of us with wealth and those of us lacking it—will have to learn how to pro-ductively include conversations about race, inequality, and the role of white supremacy, past and present, in our educational systems and thinking. Historically, we have not been very good at having these sorts of conversations across the lines that divide us.

At the very end of 2014, during NPR's annual end of the year interview with President Obama, reporter Steve Inskeep asked the president if he thought that America was more racially divided than it had been six years earlier when he first took office. The president optimistically responded that in day-to-day interactions he thought the country was actually less racially divided. Inskeep seemed a bit taken aback by the answer, coming as it did after the grand jury decisions in Ferguson, Missouri, and Staten Island, New York, which found no reason to file criminal charges against police officers who had killed unarmed Black men. These murders and others, along with a consistent disinclination to file criminal charges against police officers who killed unarmed Black American citizens, led to numerous national and international protests against police brutality. Inskeep pushed back with what he called a couple of "data points" that he said might not suggest that race relations were worse, but did point to a wide gulf in race-based beliefs regarding the very concepts of justice and freedom. The president responded by saying, "I think that the fact that there's a conversation about it, and that there are tools out there that we know can make a difference in bridging those gaps of understanding and mistrust, should make us optimistic."

Simply put, instead of acknowledging that there are differing experiences, or even vastly different views on race, racism, equality, and justice in the country, or even signaling an understanding of the deeply raced context within which "race talk" about the criminal justice system was then taking place, at that moment President Obama told us to feel optimistic because the murders and protests at least provided an occasion for conversation and reflection. His response illustrates one side of a binary for "race talk" within the realms of mainstream politics, entertainment, and public culture—and the delineation between the two sides is stark. On the side where Obama seems to speak from, race talk is an occasion for Black people to take personal responsibility for overcoming racism, perhaps for acknowledging how their personal behaviors elicited a racial response, and for initiating talk about systemic instances of racism.

Conversely, discussions about the dismantling of societal structures that in effect perpetuate inequality are often only present when the victims are white. That is what happened late in 2014 when *New York Times* columnist Nicholas Kristof ran a series of data-laden columns explaining the inequality gap between Blacks and whites called "When Whites Just Don't Get It." When interviewed by a reporter from the *Washington Post* about the responses he had received, he said he was surprised by how frequently readers urged him to focus more on the fact that Blacks needed to stop blaming others for racism and start taking personal responsibility for their behavior, and less on the data showing race-based inequality. Far too many people consider the act of talking about structural racism—analyzing it, discussing it, or just pointing out that it exists—to be racist in and of itself. As a result, when Black people point out racism, or racism against Black people is pointed out by others, the default response is often that it can most easily be solved by the victims, who simply need to change their beliefs, their frame of reference, and their behavior. Structural forces are largely overlooked.

Similar findings emerged in 2014 when MTV conducted an opinion poll with young people in their twenties and thirties asking how they are "experiencing, affected by, and responding to issues associated with race." Overall, the findings show that these millennials are much more likely to believe in racial equality than are previous generations, and a full 91 percent say that all people should be treated equally regardless of race. However, they also feel that racism is a thing of the past and are uncomfortable with actual conversations about race, and almost half of white people who were polled believe discrimination against white people is just as big of a problem as is discrimination against people of color. This last result meshes with a study done a few years prior by researchers at Tufts and Harvard universities who surveyed Blacks and whites about their views on racism. They found that a majority of whites now believe they have "replaced Blacks" as the primary victims of racial discrimination in contemporary America and that anti-white prejudice is a "bigger problem" than the prejudice that African Americans face. Yet evidence to the contrary abounds.

As James Baldwin once wrote, "Words like freedom, justice, democracy are not common concepts; on the contrary, they are rare. People are not born knowing what these are. It takes enormous and, above all, individual effort to arrive at the respect for other people that these words imply." This book makes just such an effort with respect to education. From the differences in quality, organization, and rationale for charter schools in white communities to the virtual absence of cyber schools as a primary form of education in wealthy communities to the differences in teacher experience and quality, a deeper look at how some of the aforementioned educational practices are accepted, debated, affirmed, or defeated helps to make clear both the racial divide in education and who actually benefits from some of the more controversial—and lucrative—practices adopted by school districts that primarily serve children who are poor and of color. I look at the organized resistance and pushback of Black communities to the privatization and educational reform efforts that they believe deny their children the chance for an equitable education, and at what happens when these same types of reforms are tried in communities that are white and wealthy. Indeed, social class and color matter even in relation to resisting privatization.

The shared cultural belief that America's public education system is an engine for social and economic mobility is central to the very construct of the American Dream. For most of our country's history, up through the twentieth century, the narrative around education as our most reliable fuel for igniting personal or even group opportunities for mobility and equality has defined the sense of the United States as a country without the social, class, and caste barriers marking other parts of the world. Here, we are told, if one works hard enough and is smart enough, the possibilities for personal gain, as well as for generational social and economic advancement, are endless. In the past few decades, as we collectively watched the widening gulf of income inequality become an oceanic divide, the connective tissue pulling tight the imagined relationship between education and social and economic uplift for all in American society has begun to fray, in part, we are told, because the system itself is broken. A system, once the envy of the world, that is now near the bottom in terms of academic achievement.

Fundamentally, this book argues that through a series of federally proposed and supported policy initiatives purportedly aimed at addressing race- and class-based educational inequality in urban areas, the United States is in the process of unraveling public education for Native American, Black, Latino, and poor youth in rural and urban areas while at the same time allowing others to engage in the plunder of dollars, and of individual futures as well. The consequences of these actions are potentially devastating and may result in the business-proposed "cures" for educational inequality causing much more harm than healing. As a result, this moment is as significant for making clear the twenty-first-century relationship between race, citizenship, economics, and segregation as was the twentieth-century moment when *Brown v. Board of Education* was decided.

This is particularly important now, because in the summer of 2014 we learned that our public schools would, going forward, be what is known as "majority-minority." We also learned that these minority students, now in the majority in our schools, would be poor. The demographic shifts were attributed to the fact that both the Latino and Asian populations in the United States had grown. At the same time, there was a steady decline in the number of whites in classrooms, even as the total number of public school students had increased. The projections from the Department of Education noted that, in 1997, the United States had 46.1 million public school students, of which 63.4 percent were white. While whites would still outnumber any single racial or ethnic group, going forward, their overall share of the nation's 50 million public school students was projected to drop to 49.7 percent. In twenty-one states, at least half of the public school children were eligible for free and reduced-price lunches. These numbers range from Mississippi, where more than 70 percent of students were from low-income families, to Illinois, where one of every two students was low-income. The composition of the private school student population was markedly different. In 2009, about 73 percent of the estimated 4.7 million children enrolled in kindergarten through grade 12 in private schools were white. As a result of these demographics, ending segrenomics is an urgent need. Understanding how and why this system was created and the ways that it benefits some and not others has the potential to provide much-needed context and perspective to current educational debates and strategies for addressing raced-based educational inequality. If nothing else, it will help us to fulfill America's educational promise to young women facing struggles similar to those of Ty'Sheoma.[12]

While I sincerely wished for a happier ending for her story, perhaps it should not surprise any of us that Ty'Sheoma didn't end up becoming a doctor, lawyer, architect, or engineer. Once her mother lost her job in South Carolina as a result of a local plant closing, the family moved to Washington, D.C., where Ty'Sheoma attended high school. She did end up graduating from high school, but she has yet to attend college. The college fund set up for her years earlier when her letter attracted so much attention had garnered only about $800 in donations. She became a rapper, released one CD, and appeared briefly on a reality show on Black Entertainment Television (BET). In 2015, the year she turned

twenty, she was working as an attendant at a Quick Trip conve-
nience store in Atlanta. Educational funding, segregation, and
access pose challenging questions as urgently in need of answers
today as they have ever been. Earnest efforts to find these answers
might just help us to better understand our divided society.[13]

1

RICH COLLEGE STUDENTS, POOR PUBLIC SCHOOLS

In the fall of 2010, when I was on the faculty at Princeton University, a student emailed me asking to meet in order to talk about my classes and community–university projects focused on race, inequality, and K–12 urban education. When she showed up, I learned that she wasn't particularly interested in taking a class with me, but rather wanted to talk about some of my views on the state of public education for students who were poor and not white. As we began our conversation, she said that she felt our nation's educational system was broken and failed too many students who were not wealthy. She believed that students like her, who had not grown up in poverty or with much exposure to communities that were not similarly white and privileged, had a duty to work to equalize educational opportunities for students who were currently being educated in failing schools. Making sure that students in poverty had consistent access to a quality education was, she exclaimed, *the* civil rights issue of our time. It was, she said, a stain on our country that a child's zip code could determine the quality of their education.

Her introductory remarks, though inarguably true, had by 2010 become fairly common talking points summarizing the educational agendas of groups, individuals, and organizations who wanted, in the vein of Silicon Valley tech entrepreneurs, to change or "disrupt" how education was financed, delivered, and imagined. They joined forces under the rhetorical rubric of "school choice." The "choice" was between underperforming traditional public schools and nontraditional public school options such as charter schools, vouchers, and online cyber schools, among other options. Those most in need of such alternative options were generally poor children and those of color, as communities with high levels of both generally had the lowest-performing schools. School choice advocates said that it was unfair that wealthy parents could either pay to send their children to higher-performing private schools or, if they found their community schools lacking, simply move from one school district to another. Poor parents did not have the same economic means to find suitable education for their children.

At the time this passionate Princeton student sought me out, there was little discussion among school choice advocates about strengthening traditional public schools. They focused their efforts on a relatively narrow range of reform efforts aimed specifically at the lowest-performing schools. Their views were very much in the news and circulating in popular culture. In November 2009, President Barack Obama had announced a new federal grant called Race to the Top. It was a $4.5 billion pilot program that, among other things, rewarded states for their efforts at educational deregulation and "urged collaborations between business leaders, educators, and other stakeholders to raise student achievement and close achievement gaps . . . by expanding support for high-performing public charter schools, reinvigorating math and science education, and promoting other conditions favorable to innovation and reform."[1] That same year, a heavily marketed documentary about race- and class-based educational inefficiencies and inequalities titled *Waiting for Superman* won a top award at the prestigious Sundance Film Festival and was in wide release across the nation. The film made many of the same points about racial and economic segregation as had the student who came to visit me that day and highlighted the pent-up demand within disenfranchised communities for more types of public school options.

Also in 2010, Facebook founder Mark Zuckerberg appeared on Oprah Winfrey's television show with Cory Booker, then mayor of Newark, New Jersey, and Governor Chris Christie of New Jersey to make an announcement about his $100 million matching gift to Newark in order to fix its long-troubled school system. Like many of the policy proscriptions found in the Race to the Top grants and championed in the film, Zuckerberg's gift urged the district to shrink the number of traditional public schools and expand the footprint of public charter schools. These were but a few of the ubiquitous cultural conversations taking place about the undereducation of America's poor, urban youth. Consistently, the proposed "fix" involved expanding charter schools, providing alternative methods for teacher assessment and evaluation, and putting an increased focus on raising test scores. In each instance, increasing the quality of education options was referred to as a pressing civil rights issue. Though I agreed that public schools serving poor children could use an overhaul, I did not agree with the proposed remedies. I had been vocal about my dissent in my classes.

I was thus not surprised when the student's questions turned to my lectures, teaching, background, and work in education. She said that I seemed to be somewhat out of step with mainstream philanthropic and educational organizations at the forefront of fighting for comprehensive change for disadvantaged students in urban communities. She wanted to understand why I asked students to think critically about popular reform measures like charter schools and teacher-training organizations such as Teach for America. These were the kinds of educational interventions she, the Department of Education, and many reformers thought of as being central to making sustainable change. She didn't understand why I seemed hesitant to enthusiastically embrace them. She also wanted to know why I urged students in my classes to include the parents and guardians of urban students in educational conversations. From her perspective, their input was not essential and was sometimes at odds with the educational interventions that "reformers" championed. She shared that she was curious to know exactly what I meant when I said that privileged students interested in educational change in poor communities of color should probably have a metric beyond scores on standardized tests as a standard by which to judge success. From what she knew, there really wasn't any other way than test scores to ensure accountability. Signaling that it was my turn to talk, she finally asked me the question that had brought her to my office, "What do you think you are up to?"

I told her that Black parents and caretakers cared deeply about Black children, and it was never a good idea to come into someone else's community and completely exclude them from collaborating on solutions. There were not a lot of examples of that type of engagement ending well. I explained that I took issue with standardized test scores as a primary evaluative tool for poor children of color because, for reasons many researchers had studied but didn't fully understand, that population simply did not do well on them. I told her that, to me, it seemed unfair to judge a group of people by a metric that privileged wealthy whites and Asians but not students who were poor, Black, and/or Latino. I told her that what I was up to was doing the best job I could to fully and comprehensively educate the students who came to my class and to expose them to thinkers, ideas, and people with whom they were probably unfamiliar. As I walked her to the door of my office, I said that working toward the goal of an equal education for all American children was a worthy one, and that there were many ways to get there.

That is what I said to her. What I didn't say was that part of my overwhelming interest in the topic of educational reform was in trying to understand why the group of educational reformers had arisen at that particular time. I was looking for ways to explain the relatively tight-knit backgrounds and relationships that defined the majority of high-profile players in "the movement."

Educational inequality was not new. Such a widespread concern about the undereducation of poor students of color on the part of students who were elite, wealthy, and unaffected, however, was. I knew money, or the lack of it, was often the focus when the conversation turned to ways to improve inner-city schools. I wondered about the extent to which money, or the vast amounts of it available to educational entrepreneurs, was part of the reason for what seemed to me to be an explosion of interest in the systemic undereducation of Black and brown children in those same schools. I wondered if money might also explain some of the burgeoning interest on the part of the privileged in the education of the poor. I wanted to understand what *they* were up to.

Though that conversation took place some years ago, I have often returned to that one student's question. I thought about it when piecing together the narrative about the symbiotic relationship between Wall Street, private equity, and college students. With the support of venture capitalists, hedge-fund investors, captains of industry, and corporate supporters, privileged students on elite college campuses have increasingly turned to the business of education as a career following their graduation from college. Most often, they joined one of a number of burgeoning businesses promising to better educate students in failing public schools that had high levels of both poverty and non-white students. While the long-term and scalable benefits and effects of their various educational businesses remain as yet unclear, what we do know for certain is that this partnership has become an economically beneficial model from which both college students and profit-seeking businesspeople consistently benefit.

The young woman who came to see me did so during a time when student interest in underperforming urban schools was publicly debated not only by politicians, filmmakers, elected officials, and billionaire tech entrepreneurs, but also by students at Princeton and on other college campuses. Indeed, not long before the autumn of 2010 two Princeton students founded a new educational venture called Students for Educational Reform (SFER). Begun in 2009 by Alexis Monin and Catherine Bellinger while they were still freshmen at Princeton, the organization was formed because, according to the organization's website, the founders "were frustrated with the slow pace of educational change" and decided to "set out to mobilize college students and get them to advocate for education reform in the voting booth and in state capitals." This is the niche SFER planned to help fill, and it recruited college students to help execute its business plan. In 2011, the co-founders of the organization took a leave of absence from Princeton to continue to grow their new business. They were immediately successful.[2]

Draper Richards Kaplan, a San Francisco Bay–area venture philanthropy group focusing on early-stage nonprofit organizations, provided the relatively new organization with a grant in the amount of $300,000 to allow it to explore the implementation of its ideas. That one award was just the beginning. In short order, SFER received $1.6 million from Education Reform Now, a group associated with well-connected educational lobbyists under the name Democrats for Education Reform (DFER). It also received funding from the Walton Foundation, which is the philanthropic arm of the family who made their fortune from the Wal-Mart chain of stores. Clearly impressed with SFER's business model, the foundation gave SFER $250,000 in 2012, $650,000 in 2013, $300,000 in 2014, and $450,000 in 2015.[3] SFER's growth continued apace and, according to the organization's Internal Revenue Service 990 reports, by 2014 over $6.7 million had flowed to SFER's coffers since its founding. Many of the students who run Students for Education Reform volunteer and are first-generation college students who attended community schools in neighborhoods like those SFER claims to want to reform. However, the group's board of directors comprises corporate executives and wealthy philanthropists. There are no teachers, students, or community members.[4]

As noble as SFER's rhetoric and cause were, it was notable that it wanted to lobby and advocate for changes to the education system without learning about the people who relied on it, and certainly without including the members of such communities in its decision making. While this is not necessarily a recipe for poor outcomes, educational historian Diane Ravitch has observed that while it is certainly possible that, overall, those involved with what they refer to as the educational reform movement think that they are working in a way that will lead to a much-needed overhaul at the systemic level, there may be a variety of reasons for their interest:

> Some sincerely believe they are helping poor Black and brown children escape from failing public schools. Some think they are on the side of modernization and innovation. But others see an opportunity to make money in a large, risk-free, government-funded sector or an opportunity for personal advancement and power. Some—a small but important number—believe they are acting rationally by treating the public education sector as an investment opportunity.[5]

Wherever they fell on that spectrum, it's likely that Catherine and Alexis knew that an organization with a similar plan, focus, and business model had grown to be quite successful: Teach for America (TFA). TFA was started almost twenty years before SFER, in 1989, by Princeton undergraduate Wendy Kopp. Today, that organization is a titan of the educational reform movement, and in 2016 it was worth almost $400 million. These two organizations, SFER and TFA, exemplify the ways that, in the business of education, the segrenomics of education are important. While far too frequently high levels of poverty in communities of color have come to equal poor educational outcomes for some, just as often that combination offers the potential to increase the profit margins of educational entrepreneurs such as Teach for America and Students for Educational Reform. Their business models simply do not work in the absence of racial and economic segregation. Teach for America and Students for Educational Reform—at least in part—represent ways for college students to participate in the business of education. As such, they are part of a longer-term business strategy over thirty years in the making. Beginning in the 1980s, the business of public education and the funds to be made from privatizing public schooling were regularly touted in the business world, though the lucrative link to college students was not then fully developed.

The Birth of a Notion:
Private Profit/Public Education

In the fall of 2000, a financial industries publication, the *Journal of Private Equity*, published an article titled "Investment Opportunities in Education: Making a Profit While Making a Difference." The article tracked the upsurge in Wall Street interest in education during the previous decade, saying that in the first ten years of the twenty-first century, private investment had increased from $2.5 million in 1990 to $4 billion in 2000. The publication saw no end in sight to the growth potential. For evidence, the article pointed to another publication, a then-recent article from *Business Insider* that proclaimed, "Although education is a huge part of the U.S. economy, until recently it wasn't much of a business . . . but as the millennium dawns, the private sector is poised to play a much larger role . . . fueled by an explosion in the money available to education start-ups." That was an understatement.[6]

Since the 1980s, various wealth-management organizations, philanthropies, and corporations have shown an increased interest in schools that educate poor children who are not white. Although for some this burgeoning interest is frequently dressed up in the language of corporate responsibility and pointed to as an example of their "giving back" and "good citizenship," some have turned to education simply to bolster their bottom line. For that group, by the late 1990s the potential profit was so well known that conservative think tanks, investment banks, and business magazines began discussing the profit potential of investing in schooling, pointing out that the public school system was a potential $600 billion investment opportunity and comparing it to both the health care industry and the defense sector. The 1990s marked the beginning of a twentieth-century era in which those with an interest in educational profiteering hit upon new and more innovative ways to aid their bottom lines. One such company, the Edison Project, led the way by offering cash-strapped and underperforming urban school districts their services as a for-profit (in business primarily to generate profit for shareholders) educational company. The company told state and local officials that they could educate poor children of color more cost-effectively than could their own municipal school systems. When launched, the Edison Project—later renamed Edison Schools and then Edison Learning—immediately attracted Wall Street's attention.[7]

In unveiling the Edison Project at a news conference at the National Press Club in Washington, D.C., in May of 1991, the founder, Chris Whittle, described his vision as an independent for-profit chain of schools that would break the mold of traditional education and outperform public schools across the country. According to Samuel Abrams's comprehensive history of the Edison Schools, *Education and the Commercial Mindset*, Whittle said that he chose the new organization's name because, just as Thomas Alva Edison decided against using candles to create the lightbulb, choosing instead to devise an utterly different approach to achieving a better and more cost-effective form of lighting, American educators had to break with past practices to develop a new school system. Whittle persuaded school districts and investors that Edison could provide effective and efficient administration and turn a profit by centralizing bureaucracy, scaling up or growing their model, and hiring nonunion teachers at a lower cost to districts than what they paid unionized teachers. At the same time that it wooed Wall Street, Edison also sought to increase its allure to both districts and parents by offering to buy laptops for each student, providing dual-language instruction, and promising increased parent involvement, longer school days, and year-round learning. Whittle said tuition would be less than the per-pupil expenditure cities and states then paid, and he forecast "dramatic growth: 200 schools with 150,000 students by 1996 and 1,000 schools with 2 million students by 2010." Whittle said he would need roughly $2.5 billion to $3 billion to open the first two hundred schools and that he would raise what he needed from private investors.[8]

Throughout the 1990s, Whittle's business model grew the company until it became the largest publicly traded educational-management organization ever founded. He wooed Benno Schmidt, who was then the president of Yale University, to be the company's CEO. The business continued to thrive, and at its height Edison Schools ran schools enrolling 132,000 students in twenty states. Its profit relied on receiving the same federal and state tax dollars for educating students enrolled in their schools as were paid to traditional schools on a per-pupil basis. However, unlike traditional public schools, the Edison schools also profited from the revenue generated by the fact that the company was publicly traded on the stock exchange. They were the first "experiment in corporations taking over public schools to run them for profit." The vast majority of schools and districts Edison was hired to take over were in working-class and poor communities. The company did not run many schools in communities that could be characterized as economically privileged.

Despite its popularity with investors, Edison lost a great deal of money. In December 1996, when Edison was running twelve schools, it predicted the company would become profitable once it had twenty-five schools. By 1998, Edison was running twenty-five schools but posted losses of $11.4 million on revenue of $38.5 million. By 1999, Edison was "running fifty-one schools and posted losses of $21.9 million on revenue of $69.4 million; by 2000 Edison was running seventy-nine schools and posted losses of $49.4 million on revenue of $125 million." No matter the losses, in 1999, Edison raised nearly $250 million from investors and went public. Its stock opened at $18 a share, and by 2001 its price had shot up to $38.75 a share. In interviews, Whittle claimed that "much as locally owned restaurants, hardware stores, clothiers, groceries, and banks had been replaced by national brands like McDonald's, the Home Depot, Gap, Safeway, and Bank of America, schools, too, could and should be run by major corporations."[9]

Even with Wall Street's continued support, the company never achieved either the promised profits or test score gains. In June 2002, when financial analysts discovered that Edison was overstating its revenues, its stock plummeted to $1.01. In addition to falling from favor with Wall Street, Edison also ran into trouble with winning over communities who depended on the school systems with which it had contracted. In Philadelphia, students, community members, and teachers' unions protested their taking over management of forty schools in the city saying the company's track record was so poor it could not be trusted. School officials in Georgia, Texas, Massachusetts, and Michigan terminated Edison contracts early because of the lackluster performance of the students in the schools it managed. With each financial and educational setback, Edison's stock price plunged. By October 2002, it was down to fourteen cents a share, and NASDAQ was threatening to delist them.[10]

Despite the fact that almost every school system with which the company contracted its services ultimately severed their ties with Edison due to its inability to adequately educate students in cities such as San Francisco, Boston, Baltimore, and Philadelphia, the business model proved to Wall Street investors that educational entrepreneurship was nonetheless potentially lucrative. By 2000, the popularity among venture capitalists in growth investments that "Make a Profit While Making a Difference" pointed those interested in the growing sector toward education as a socially acceptable cause, or investment vehicle, that fulfills a rising desire for "dual bottom line" investments that are both financially and socially profitable. What Whittle began to shape, define, and perfect relative to public/private educational relationships continued to grow and deepen.[11]

Essentially, those who championed the profit potential in the fields of "impact" or "dual bottom line" investing were looking for ways for their money to contribute to solving social issues and bettering society in some way. The field has exploded and today includes a variety of subgroups: venture philanthropists, think tanks, private businesses, lobbyists, advocacy organizations, and social entrepreneurs, to name a few. The Rockefeller Foundation is but one example, and in 2007 it began to investigate the amount of money needed to address social needs globally. Judith Rodin, then president of the Rockefeller Foundation, said that it "recognized, if you put a price tag on all the social and environmental needs around the world, it is in the trillions. All of the philanthropy in the world is only $590 billion. So, the needs far exceed the resources. The one place where there are hundreds of trillions of dollars is in the private capital markets. So, we, and others, began to wonder are there ways to direct private funding to some of these incredible needs."[12]

The synchronistic rise of organizations aimed at bettering the educational futures of poor children of color and investment strategies that championed a public good meant that during the period of time I was teaching at Princeton, the business of funding the business of education was thriving. While Chris Whittle's Edison School model of education reform relied on making money by offering to manage poor school districts of color, Wendy Kopp's Teach for America model found an equally lucrative niche in supplying creatively certified teachers to similarly cash-strapped and struggling school systems.

Even though Kopp, in the twenty-five or so years since Teach for America was founded, has rarely mentioned it, she was very well aware of the corporate interest in the business of education before she founded TFA. She knew about the goals of the education reform movement and its burgeoning business and corporate interests in the education of non-white children in poor areas, and in the double bottom line: investment opportunities that yielded both the profits and the "good works" investors were so interested in achieving. In a *New York Times* article from 1989 about Teach for America's founding, Kopp explains that she first thought about this at a 1988 meeting of business and student leaders to discuss ways to improve the schools. She said, "The idea just popped into my mind," and explained, "I realized that top students might go into teaching if we could find a way to recruit them. It seemed so simple. One problem with the education reform movement is that people don't talk to college students." Her identification of college students as a missing piece in a lucrative equation to privatize and reform public education would one day make her organization one of the biggest players in the field of educational reform.[13]

Teach for America: Rich Reformers, Poor Performers

While the differing stories of TFA and how and why it is important to teaching, education, and indeed the nation itself could surely take up the space of an entire book, what I want to highlight here is how its decision to focus on "fixing" struggling schools in economically vulnerable areas, and to use newly graduating college students as the primary agents to effect that change, truly cemented the relationship between college students and the wealthy business elite in the cause of educational entrepreneurship. As Kopp reflected on the genesis of the organization in the preface to her early memoir *One Day, All Children*, she recalled that

> The idea was to create a corps of top recent college graduates—people of all academic majors and career interests—who would commit to teach two years in urban and rural public schools and become lifelong leaders dedicated to the goal of educational opportunity for all. Called Teach for America, this corps would mobilize some of the most passionate, dedicated members of my generation to change the fact that where a child is born in the United States does a great deal to determine his or her chances in life. Schools in America's inner cities and poor rural areas have low academic achievement rates.

As she tells the story, the basic idea came to her as she struggled to come up with an idea for her senior thesis—a substantial research project all undergraduate students at Princeton have to complete in order to graduate. One morning while she was out jogging, her thoughts turned to the ways students who had attended East Coast prep schools or well-resourced, highly ranked public schools described the rigors of Princeton University as "cake." For them, college classes were relatively easy when compared to how hard they had been expected to work in their academically rigorous middle and high schools. Likewise, she knew that the students who came from poorer schools and neighborhoods did not have the same level of preparation. She saw that they struggled at Princeton. As she continued to reflect on those differing experiences, and with the looming reality of her impending graduation from college and her potential joblessness along with it, she hit upon the idea of adapting a previous proposal for a national teaching corps from the late 1960s. She decided to combine that idea with the basic structure of the Peace Corps and to name the whole thing Teach America (she added the "for" a few years later). As she saw the new organization, in addition to potentially helping students in less well-resourced schools, the new "teacher corps would provide another option to the two-year corporate training programs and grad schools. It would speak to all of us college seniors who were searching for something meaningful to do with our lives. We would jump at the chance." Given the rapid and lucrative growth of TFA, in hindsight it is clear that Kopp was right.

At the same time, it is hard not to notice that the organization focused on privileged college students and their futures almost to the exclusion of the children the college students would teach. Kopp believed that "the corps members' teaching experiences were bound to strengthen their commitment to children in low-income communities and spur their outrage at the circumstances preventing these children from fulfilling their potential." Though she couldn't know if it were true, she posited that "many corps members would decide to stay in the field of education. And those who would go into other sectors would remain advocates for social change and education reform." She goes on to add, "They would become business leaders and newspaper editors, U.S. senators and Supreme Court justices, community leaders and school board members. And, because of their experience teaching in public schools, they would make decisions that would change the country for the better." She concludes, "The teacher corps would make teaching in low-income communities an attractive choice for top grads by surrounding it with an aura of status and selectivity." The vision for the organization says more about how college students would benefit from associating with the nascent organization than about the good they would do in the classroom.[14]

Teach for America was clearly a savvy and successful educational and business gambit (the organization generally charges between $2,000 and $5,000 in finder's fees for each teacher they supply to a school district), yet it is telling that Kopp's most pressing priority before familiarizing herself with the systems, history, or creative possibilities for teaching children who were so far removed from her own background was to recruit others who clearly understood the business potential of education. Which is to say, perhaps more important than who Kopp met with are the people with whom she did not meet. As she began to flesh out the specifics of her new venture to educate children in rural and urban areas who were at the bottom of the economic and educational ladder, she does not say that she met with parents, guardians, educators, teachers, or any number of stakeholders in the communities most likely to be impacted. Instead, she chronicles her meetings with representatives in business and finance whom she asks to help her get TFA off the ground.[15]

Kopp spent the spring of her senior year contacting the CEOs of a number of corporations and philanthropic organizations. While CEOs did not offer her meetings, she did converse with high-level executives at Xerox, IBM, AT&T, and Metropolitan Life, as well as with Stanley Kaplan, the founder of the test prep company. The first company to offer her financial assistance was Union Carbide, a Fortune 500 company that had just recently decided to begin funding education reform businesses in urban school districts. The company offered her free office space. Her next coup was to secure a meeting with the CEO of Merrill Lynch, who, as she tells the story, offered her $25,000 and free office space, telephone service, and access to a copy machine for five years (an in-kind investment worth upward of $500,000 during that period of time). The space was located in the McGraw-Hill building in New York. Harold McGraw, the educational textbook company's chairman emeritus, was one of the first members of her formal advisory board. The next company to agree to help her was Mobil Oil, whose vice president of administration offered Kopp a $26,000 seed grant. By the end of the summer, Kopp had recruited a board of advisers composed of high-level corporate executives, all of whom had in the past few years begun to invest in the "dual bottom line" area of education reform and to explore ways that they could offer poor students of color more choices while increasing their own bottom

line. Kopp's fund-raising was successful in part because her thinking was in line with that of others who had access to great wealth
and political access. Once her business was up and running, she
also met with Chris Whittle, the Edison Schools founder, to ask
him both for business advice and to invest in her educational start-
up. He ended up trying to recruit her to come work for him. She
declined the offer.

Kopp surrounded herself with young men and women who
were all recent college graduates and as privileged as she was.
Many of those working with her would impact the educations
of poor, non-white children for decades to come. One of her
first recruits was her brother's roommate at Harvard University,
Whitney Tilson. Tilson worked alongside Kopp as a co-founder
of TFA for two years before decamping for a job working on Wall
Street, and then, roughly ten years later, started his own hedge
fund. However, he became and remained an outspoken advocate
of corporate-approved education-reform strategies of the type
TFA would come to exemplify. Unlike many of Wendy Kopp's
other "first hires," Tilson, though having little in the way of experience with teaching or struggling urban communities himself,
at least came from an "education family." Both his parents had
been public school teachers for a time in Connecticut, and his father had earned a Ph.D. in education from Stanford University
and spent most of his career doing teacher training and developing and managing educational projects in third world countries.
As a child, Tilson spent at least six years living in Tanzania and
Nicaragua. While his experiences with poor communities of color
in the United States was severely limited, he did at least have sustained international experiences on which to draw, as well as parents with some experience in public school classrooms. Few others
in the early group of TFA recruits could say the same. Most had
come of age in neighborhoods where poverty rates were low and
attended schools that were predominantly white and academically
rigorous. Though bubbling over with good intentions, they'd had

little opportunity to encounter dissenting views, research, personal experiences, or analysis.[16]

Others with Ivy League backgrounds joined the early group of entrepreneurs, one of whom, Richard Barth, Kopp would eventually marry. He was also a Harvard graduate and, after working with Kopp for a short while, left the organization to work with Chris Whittle's Edison Schools. Following his stint at Edison Schools, he later became the CEO of the KIPP (Knowledge Is Power Program) schools, founded by two early TFA corps members, Mike Feinberg and David Levin, both Yale University graduates.

Edison Schools pioneered a particular model of educational profiteering by offering to run failing urban schools and districts. TFA grew its business by promising to provide those same cash-strapped and struggling school districts with high-quality teachers. KIPP schools premised their business model on providing those districts with high-quality public charter schools. All of the players in these organizations were longtime friends and colleagues whose business interests were deeply intertwined. By 2006, they decided to join together to use their money and access to form an organization with the express purpose of lobbying politicians to ensure the federal government was more supportive and responsive to their educational businesses.[17]

By 2005, it was clear to many educational entrepreneurs that though the explosive growth in the business of segrenomic education had come to pass, it could not continue without policy changes at the state and federal levels. By that time, Wall Street's hedge fund industry was deeply entwined with public education via the charter school movement. As Justin Miller writes in his expansive article in the *American Prospect*, "Hedging Education," hedge fund "executives see charter-school expansion as vital to the future of public education. . . . Several hedge fund managers have launched their own charter-school chains and . . . You'd be hard-pressed to find a hedge fund guy who doesn't sit on a charter-school board." Whitney Tilson became involved with charter schools almost a decade after he left TFA to start his own hedge fund.

As he tells the story, his longtime friend and former employer Wendy Kopp invited him to visit one of the two original KIPP schools in the South Bronx, an area that was and remains one of the poorest congressional districts in the nation. According to his interview in the *American Prospect*, as soon as Tilson became acquainted with charter schools, he was immediately convinced that such schools were going to be the future of education. He started bringing many of his friends, most of whom were also Ivy League graduates and hedge fund investors, to the South Bronx to see the KIPP school. He says, "KIPP was used as a converter for hedge fund guys . . . it went viral." As Tilson explains, hedge fund managers almost exclusively come from well-off backgrounds and got the best educations in the world. Given that this was his background, as well as Kopp's, as well as that of the founders of Students for Education Reform, it is instructive that he says, "I personally never knew what the situation was like for families forced to attend their local school in the South Bronx, or Brooklyn. I didn't know of anyone who dropped out of high school or college—much less that there were high schools where half the students dropped out." Despite his ignorance of the people, situation, students, and successful schools functioning in such communities, Tilson and his friends decided to use their financial and political access and college networks to institutionalize their views of what change should look like. They resolved to change the political system to make it more sympathetic to the alternatively certified teachers from TFA and the burgeoning charter school movement so popular with Wall Street.

Dave Levin told Tilson that he was trying to open up more schools, but was running into political resistance from unionized teachers whom Levin believed felt threatened by the fact that KIPP was succeeding in educating students without them. He told Tilson that KIPP's lack of union involvement was also threatening to many in the Democratic Party as a whole, since union households had historically been part of the Democratic base. In the Miller interview, Tilson recalls he was shocked that anyone would try to impede the growth of KIPP and disappointed that Democratic politicians opposed the charter expansion he and his friends championed. In response, Tilson got together with a number of other "highly educated, wealthy investors to build a political instrument to simultaneously advance pro-charter education reform and beat back what they saw as oppressive teacher unions." He explained, "Our public-school system—including charter schools—is a governmental system, and that means at the end of the day, it's run by politicians." Tilson continued, "And politicians respond to votes and they respond to money. That means if you want to change a governmental system you've got to play the political game." Tilson named his new group Democrats for Education Reform (DFER). Tellingly, its mission was not to explore innovative ways to educate poor, disenfranchised students, but rather, its mission was "to break the teacher unions' stranglehold over the Democratic Party." Going forward, school choice efforts would have deep-pocketed, well-connected lobbyists.[18]

DFER's founders include executives working with successful Wall Street firms such as Anchorage Capital Partners (a group that manages/invests over $8 billion); Greenlight Capital (which manages $6.8 billion); and Pershing Square Capital Management, with $5.5 billion under its management. In terms of the difference it makes when political and educational reform is attempted by those with access to money and political power, if not hands-on experience, "DFER identified then-Senator Barack Obama and then–Newark Mayor Cory Booker as promising politicians willing to break with teacher unions." Of course, when Senator Obama became President Obama, DFER found that it had a seat at a much larger table. For starters, the group worked to convince him to appoint Chicago school superintendent Arne Duncan as secretary of education. DFER knew Duncan supported charter school expansion and that he wouldn't mind shrinking the influence of unions in public education. Once Duncan took over, DFER lobbied the administration to pursue favorable education policies like Race to the Top, which rewarded states willing to support both the expansion of charter schools and the employment of non-unionized teachers. As Tilson reported to Miller, "All of a sudden, there were politicians all over the country who were willing to back education reform. We were able to raise more money, but there were also a lot more fields to play on." [19]

All of this success for the largest players in the educational reform field (Teach for America, Edison Learning, and KIPP Schools) came from ventures promising to help poor children improve educationally and to narrow the achievement gap for students in areas that were highly racially segregated without addressing the poverty or segregation with which those students were surrounded. In some ways, it was a twenty-first-century, updated version of the separate but equal doctrine the Supreme Court had struck down in the mid-twentieth century. This is surprising, because the TFA founders were highly educated at the time they began their educational efforts, and there is an abundance of research proving that racial and economic integration is one surefire way to close the achievement gaps in which they were all so interested. We will never know what might have happened if, instead of deciding to bring young, motivated college students into the teaching profession, offering to run highly segregated school districts, supporting the proliferation of racially and economically segregated charter schools, or lobbying federal officials to expand funds for educational programs that depend on racial and economic segregation for their growth, they had all spent their time, contacts, and money on finding ways to pursue the integration of the schools, neighborhoods, and cities that others claimed could not be integrated. Though the means to do it is an intractable twentieth-century problem, integration is one of the few strategies that has made systemic progress toward bringing about the kind of educational change that the close-knit group of educational reformers say is their goal.

Integration: A Road Not Traveled

In his 2013 article for the journal *National Affairs*, Frederick Hess points out what he describes as a single-minded focus on the creation of "90/90/90 schools"—schools where more than 90 percent of the students are low-income, more than 90 percent are of color, and more than 90 percent fail to meet set academic standards. He says, "School reformers, state and local education officials, exemplary charter-school operators, and managers of philanthropic foundations make it very clear that they are primarily in the business of educating poor Black and Hispanic children." He added, "Anyone who has spent much time in the company of school reformers in the past decade has seen this practice turn almost comical, as when charter-school operators try to one-up one another over who can claim the most disadvantaged student population." By way of example, it is worth noting that today, according to its website, the KIPP chain serves almost 80,000 students, 96 percent of whom are Black or Latino, and almost 90 percent of whom come from households that exist near the federal poverty level. In almost all major American cities, most Black and Latino students attend public schools where a majority of their classmates qualify as poor or low-income. Such neighborhoods and students are the engines of growth for both charter schools and other educational businesses. Segregation pays.[20]

This is unfortunate, because as Nikole Hannah-Jones has found in her investigative reporting for *This American Life* about our national retreat from racial and economic integration as the solution to unequal achievement levels, "all sorts of people are trying to rethink and reinvent education, to get poor minority kids performing as well as white kids. But there's one thing nobody tries anymore, despite lots of evidence that it works: desegregation."[21]

Indeed, today Black and Latino students are likely to live in neighborhoods that are heavily segregated by race and economics, attend underresourced schools, receive lower grades, score lower on standardized tests, drop out of high school at a higher rate, and face more suspensions. These differences are particularly stark when these students of color are also poor. Because public schools are funded mostly by local property taxes, wealthier communities have the resources to spend more for school buildings, teaching supplies, administration, extracurricular programs, and technology. Such communities can also pay higher salaries and attract the teachers and administrators that they want. As a result, U.S. public schools in economically privileged communities are among the highest-performing schools in the world. Unsurprisingly, poor schools are among the lowest. What that means is that the largest growth potential for those who see education as a business lies in areas with the highest poverty levels and lowest achievement scores.

A report issued in September of 2012 by the Civil Rights Project at UCLA confirms Hannah-Jones's thinking. It shows that school segregation for Blacks, Latinos, and poor students has returned to levels we haven't seen since the 1970s. The report summarizes the consensus of nearly sixty years of social science research on the harms caused by school segregation. Put simply, the research confirms that separate schools remain extremely unequal. This is because schools with concentrated poverty and high levels of racial segregation limit educational opportunities and outcomes as a result of less-experienced and -qualified teachers, high levels of teacher turnover, and inadequate facilities and learning materials. Test scores and college-level success are also far lower for students who attend racially segregated schools. And a recent book called *Taming the River* co-authored by Camille Charles, a sociologist at the University of Pennsylvania, found that when looking at achievement data for Black and Latino students in the top thirty colleges in the country, two-thirds of the difference between their scores and grades could be predicted based on how racially segregated the neighborhoods and high schools were from which they came.[22]

However, Kopp and the other educational reformers with whom she worked chose to focus on teaching, testing, and charter school expansion as the fix for all that was educationally broken. The benefit for poor students of color rarely matched the promises these educational reform organizations made or kept pace with the benefit for the groups of young, elite college students who raised so much money by promising long-term change both in schools and throughout our education system. And the money, as well as organizational growth, is substantial. By 2013, Teach for America could claim over 10,000 corps members and 28,000 alumni. At that point, its members had taught roughly three million students. In terms of funding, by 2015, according to its annual report, the organization had net assets of slightly more than $371 million.[23]

To be clear, the students attracted to working in such communities as teachers or in other roles are often passionate and sincere. They are not bad people. Given their lives and backgrounds, many just believe that their insight, hard work, and will are enough to overcome the poverty, social disorder, financial hurdles, and structured inequality that some argue necessarily doom less-privileged children to a life on the rungs of the second tier. There is not much research to support their beliefs. Nonetheless, such passion and belief, coupled with the need to find employment after graduation, meant that for a time, on some college campuses such as Harvard, Princeton, Yale, Williams, and Swarthmore, public education and the financing, testing, and reform of it became an extremely popular career choice. When my son graduated from Amherst College in 2013, during the commencement the school's president mentioned that equal numbers of graduating students would be pursuing careers in financial services as would be joining some type of business endeavor associated with public education. Schools like Amherst and Princeton were not the only ones sending significant numbers of their students into urban communities with which they might have previously been all but totally unfamiliar. The education pipeline between high-performing schools and early careers in education continues apace.[24]

For example, an article headline from 2013 in the *Yale Daily News*, the student paper, proclaimed that for Yale students, "Leaving the Classroom After Graduation Means Going Back to the Classroom—But as a Teacher." The article chronicles the ways that the school steadily ranked among the highest-contributing colleges for several years. "I think [TFA's] mission resonates with our students at Yale as a way they can have a profound impact on the lives of others, and at the same time expand their personal and professional growth," said the director of undergraduate career services Jeanine Dames in an email to the *Yale Daily News* in 2013. Zak Newman, a political science major interested in education reform, is quoted in the article as saying that he thinks TFA's success in recruiting Ivy League students has largely come from its ability to "insert itself into the mainstream" of postgraduate opportunities along with consulting and investment banking. TFA is now "up there with Citibank" as an option regularly considered by students, he said. While that model was clearly a success for the business conceived by Kopp and others, it has not come close to solving the riddle of educational inequality.[25]

As the next chapter shows, the issue is not white interest in Black education, or that there is something inherently wrong with the wealthy proposing educational strategies for the less fortunate. In our contemporary period, we hear that education is a civil right and unequal education a moral wrong. Between 1880 and 1930, wealthy businessmen, philanthropists, Wall Street traders, and government officials believed the same things and joined together to propose a variety of solutions aimed at ensuring that Black people in the American South had access to publicly funded education. They argued bitterly over the training of teachers qualified to teach in the region, quality, availability of school buildings, taxes versus philanthropic funding, and the relevance of vocational education and job acquisition as the most reliable indicator of whether an education was or was not successful. Even from its earliest days, Black education in the United States was as important to the financial interests of businesses as it is today.

2

WHITE PHILANTHROPY,
BLACK EDUCATION

I have never seen greater human sacrifices made for the cause
of education. Children without shoes on their feet gave from
fifty cents to one dollar and old men and old women, whose
costumes represented several years of wear, gave from one to
five dollars.

—M.H. Griffin, 1925

Between 1921 and 1925, M.H. Griffin traveled the country on behalf of the Julius Rosenwald Building Fund to advise Black communities about how best to qualify for matching funds from the
Rosenwald Foundation to build schools in their rural, southern
communities. By the end of the night referenced in the epigraph
above, when the community had given all they thought they had,
which amounted to some $1,300, they still found themselves short
almost $1,000 of the amount they needed to ensure they would
qualify for matching funds. At that point, Griffin reported seeing
a level of commitment and sacrifice that was emotionally moving
to him. He wrote, "Colored men offered to pawn their cows and
calves for the money and they did do just this thing. They made
notes and gave for security pledges on their future crops . . . and
their other belongings for the money. They raised in this way one
thousand dollars, and we started out for a contractor." This is just
one story among many from the turn of the twentieth century
chronicling the educational partnership between northern white

philanthropists and southern, rural, Black communities to ensure southern educational systems accommodated and included Black children.[1]

From 1877 to 1930, the American South defined the contours of tax-supported public education. By the first decade of the twentieth century, two of the most notable educational philanthropists responsible for conceiving of and implementing public education from elementary school up through college were John D. Rockefeller Sr. and Julius Rosenwald. One founded and funded the General Education Board, an organization chartered by Congress to shape the public education system in the United States, and the other provided seed money to enable the construction of over 5,000 rural schools for children in the South. By the 1930s, these schools had educated almost one-third of the Black students eligible to attend schools in the region. Both men, one who first made his name in oil, the other who did so as the president of Sears and Roebuck, understood how economically and socially necessary an education was for rural and southern Blacks, as well as how important an educated Black population was for the future economic prospects of businesses in that region, if not in the entire country.

This chapter explores the relationship between America's turn-of-the-century business, political, and social elite who had an interest in the education of Black children in the South and their thinking about how to best educate children who were not like their own. It chronicles the earliest moments when white political, corporate, and philanthropic interests in Black education set economic and educational terms for public education that would last for a century. This period birthed both apartheid schools and apartheid education and began a pattern whereby groups that were not themselves poor or of color proposed educational curricula and forms offered only to Blacks and the poor; they were seldom seen in the schools frequented by children who were of means. Skin color and class determined the type of education a student was seen as worthy of acquiring. The legacy of this earlier period is with us today.

For Black communities in the South, a school was not just a building or a means to a particular economic end; it was access to the promises of mobility inherent in the American Dream and contained the potential for equality and citizenship. Accordingly, while the interests of northern white philanthropists and southern Black communities may not have always overlapped in relation to the particular type of education Blacks in the South should have, they did at least agree that education was a worthy goal. In this regard, both groups were aligned against white southerners who, following the end of Reconstruction, sought to deny Blacks as many rights as possible. Particularly in relation to education, southern governments took every opportunity to both reassert Black inferiority and proclaim white supremacy as the cultural and economic law of the land and as the preferred social order. Between 1877 and 1930, apartheid education harmed Blacks to the same degree that it benefited whites.

Public Education and White Supremacy

Though tax funds provided for a functioning public school system in the northern region of the United States from the 1600s onward, it wasn't until Reconstruction, the period following the conclusion of the Civil War in 1865, that taxpayer-supported schools began to expand in the South. Of course, in relation to Black students, this was only possible because federal troops occupied the region in order to ensure that the intentions of the Thirteenth, Fourteenth, and Fifteenth amendments to the Constitution— guaranteeing Blacks freedom from slavery, right to citizenship, and the right to vote—were carried out. During Reconstruction, a relatively short period between 1868 and 1877, in addition to paying for the troops, federal funds made possible schools, teachers, and school buildings for southern children, both white and Black. However, following Reconstruction's end, southern legislatures moved aggressively throughout the South to dismantle the political and educational progress Black communities had made.[2]

All across the former slaveholding South, state and local governments, after wresting control back from Black elected officials, immediately passed laws decreeing that any schools that allowed for an integrated education were in violation of the law. They also used their legislative authority to institute policies forbidding the use of "white tax dollars" to educate Black students. Some states went so far as to require Blacks to pay a double tax if they wanted their children educated—one to educate white schoolchildren, and another for the education of their own. Most southern states allocated less money for instruction and salaries for teachers for Black schoolchildren, and many shortened school terms for Black children from the average of nine months for white students down to as little as three months. The rationale they offered was that Black children were needed in the fields during harvest time and did not need classroom instruction. Schools for Black children were a consistent target of economic and social disinvestment, and white southern legislatures employed a variety of means to ensure that the fewest possible Black children had as little access to schools and education dollars as they could legally manage.

For example, during the post-Reconstruction period, the number of white children attending public schools in Alabama surged from 91,202 to 159,671 between the 1870s and late 1880s. At the same time, before federal Reconstruction funds decreased before drying up completely, the number of Black schoolchildren also increased from 54,595 to 98,919. But, as money for public education was in short supply, the efforts of state and local governments to raise taxes to offset the shortfall proved unpopular, and white elites and politicians came to believe that the only viable source of funding to continue to educate white children in public schools was the money provided by the federal government for the education of Black children. They turned their attention to aggressively diverting these funds from Black to white hands.[3]

As but one example of what was taking place across the South, in 1877 Alabama enacted a post-Reconstruction constitution limiting the funding stream for Black schools to "poll taxes," or the amount Blacks paid for the privilege to vote. A few years later, the state legislature reallocated even that source of funding for the support of white schools. In 1901, Alabama went even further and decreed in its new state constitution that local, not state, officials could at their discretion divert any financial resources they wished from Black schools to those attended by whites. State legislatures across the South joined in to ensure that the expenses for the education of white children would be primarily borne by Black communities. Many changed laws so that school taxes were no longer distributed among all schools based on the number of students enrolled in each class. Instead, the total number of students in the district, white and Black, determined how much funding a county or town received from the state. This was true even if there were no schools in the area for Black students to attend. The author who sponsored the Alabama bill granting local financial control was hailed by one of his peers, who said he "deserved a vote of thanks from the white people of the state." All across the post-Reconstruction South, it quickly became clear that for Blacks, citizenship did not amount to equal treatment. The mandate to educate Black children—a lucrative source of funding for government bodies and white families—did not amount to an equal education for them.[4]

Even in southern states such as Kentucky that instituted "color blind" provisions for financing the education of all children, the state managed to get around legal obligations by simply not providing many actual schools for Black children to attend. Laws mandating equal financing made little difference if there were simply no buildings. Similarly, in Oklahoma the state legislature determined that equal citizenship meant that there would be two districts in the entire state for Black children. Those two districts had relative autonomy, including the ability to elect their own school boards and to determine how funds should be apportioned. If Black children lived outside of these two districts, however, they could not go to school.[5]

This entrenchment and financial hoarding of funds intended for the education of Black children was widespread in the South, and the impact was nothing short of catastrophic. It would disproportionately impact Black communities for decades, if not centuries, to come. In 1891, in one predominantly Black county in Alabama, the total budget for teachers' salaries was $6,545. This was the same basic amount as what was being spent per student at white schools in the same county. However, after the state legislature determined that educational funding was to be decided by white local officials, Black teachers' salaries were immediately slashed. By 1938, in that same county, the past impact of race-based approaches to education funding and availability persisted, and the total amount allocated for salaries for teachers instructing the 8,483 Black children in the county had risen only slightly, to just over $8,000. The budget for white teachers, with fewer than two thousand pupils, had climbed to nearly $60,000 during those same forty-seven years. From one part of the South to another, the story of the expansion of publicly financed education made clear that though they too were American citizens, Blacks could not expect financial fairness from public education officials.[6]

When Black communities rose up to ask questions and demand educational equity, often the response was violence. Whites burned schools to the ground, viciously attacked teachers, and destroyed educational materials. This was true even when schools for Black children were intentionally constructed modestly or even poorly in an effort to ensure that whites did not think the communities that built them were doing so in a manner that could be misunderstood as an attempt to declare Black superiority. No matter the quality of educational materials and buildings, many southern whites simply felt that, as far as they were concerned, Blacks receiving any education at all meant they were rising too far, too fast and needed to be stopped. Terror tactics, including lynching, were widespread as a tool with which white people and communities could assert their racial dominance over the region's political and economic resources. First achieved through slavery, such dominance would be restored and maintained through terror. By the end of the nineteenth century, "southern lynching had become not merely a heinous act of violence, but a tool to control and terrorize Black people."[7]

Lynching in America: Confronting the Legacy of Racial Terror documents the Equal Justice Initiative's multiyear investigation into lynching in twelve southern states during the period between Reconstruction and World War II. Focusing on the former slaveholding southern states of Alabama, Arkansas, Florida, Georgia, Kentucky, Louisiana, Mississippi, North Carolina, South Carolina, Tennessee, Texas, and Virginia, the report confirms that many victims of lynchings in these states were murdered for "demanding basic rights and fair treatment." The states that most aggressively lynched their Black citizens were also those where the education of Blacks was most consistently contested following the Civil War.[8]

The resistance to equal education for Blacks came from all corners of white communities. White politicians in the former slaveholding states argued that educational funds should not be wasted on Black people. Mississippi governor James Vardaman assured his constituents:

> Money spent today for the maintenance of public schools for Negroes is robbery of the white man, and a waste upon the negro. You take it from the toiling white men and women, you rob the white child of the advantages it would afford him, and you spend

it upon the Negro in an effort to make of the Negro what God Almighty never intended should be made, and which men cannot accomplish.

He urged white citizens of his state to simply be patient, as he was sure that Congress would soon repeal the Fourteenth and Fifteenth amendments to the Constitution granting citizenship and voting rights to Blacks. He did not think it made much sense for the white South to continue expending time and energy debating the question of funding schools for Black people. As far as he was concerned, they wouldn't be citizens much longer and, in any case, wouldn't have voting rights to repel the reinstitution of white supremacy.[9]

Despite such clearly race-based economic and political disparities and the rising tide of murderous violence and terror engulfing the region, southern white elites still refused to acknowledge that race or skin color impacted their thinking and decision making relative to Black education. No, they said, it was not racism, or even beliefs in white supremacy that led to such economic funding disparities. Rather, they argued, the decisions around education and its availability and funding were a larger issue of ensuring that Blacks received only the schooling most beneficial to the economic interests of the South. These beliefs were so widespread that even whites who were supportive of the overall idea of education for all, Black and white alike, argued for a narrow focus on industrial or vocational education for Blacks. It is within this context that we might come to better understand the southern educational work embarked upon by white philanthropists of the late nineteenth and early twentieth centuries. They made their money in cotton, steel, railroads, minerals, and financial services. They joined in partnership with each other and with communities of Black Americans who were at the other end of the social spectrum in regard to having access to wealth, power, voting, or citizenship. These philanthropists participated in constructing a particular and peculiar educational system for Black Americans in the southern regions of the United States.

Spoiling a Good Plow Hand

There were no Black people or women on the train that day in 1901 when John D. Rockefeller Jr. traveled south with other members of his social set for a tour of the institutions that were educating "the Negro." They were all white men. Few were southern. Their ages ranged from late twenties to early forties, and, for the most part, they were heirs to great agricultural, marketing, and financial assets. They were men of substance and accomplishment, and if not staggeringly wealthy themselves, they traveled in circles with those who were. Though they often socialized together, this trip was not for pleasure. They came together to discuss a subject of weighty concern, the problem of educating Blacks in the southern United States. They were in accord with the popular thinking of the time that linked Black education to certain forms of work, and Black people to narratives of racial inferiority.

One of the attendees, Charles Dabney, the president of the University of Tennessee, shared his belief that "the only solution [to] the southern problem is free public schools for all the people, Blacks and whites alike and compulsory-attendance laws." While seemingly a statement reflecting openness and a regard for Black humanity, Mr. Dabney quickly made clear that this was not his full meaning. He continued, "The negro is in the South to stay— he is a necessity for southern industries—and the southern people must educate and so elevate him or he will drag them down." However, while Dabney wanted to ensure that his audience understood the danger as he saw it, he added a caveat, "We must use common sense in the education of the negro. We must recognize in all its relations that momentous fact that the negro is a child race, at least two thousand years behind the Anglo-Saxon in its development." [10]

Another college president who was also on the train was George Winston of North Carolina's College of Agriculture and Mechanic Arts. He agreed with Dabney that universal education for Blacks had a role to play in North Carolina and that a submissive and disenfranchised Black presence was crucial to the future of the region. He added, "The Old South was overthrown not by Webster and Greeley and Lincoln, but by the industrial inefficiency of Negro Slavery." In order to forestall further and future harm to the economy of the region, and to make clear how he saw education as related to Jim and Jane Crow, he shared with those gathered that Black people in the South "must be taught to work, to submit to authority, to respect their superiors. The entire system of public education for the negro race from top to bottom should be industrial." There was no dissent from any of the philanthropists gathered together that day. Certainly, there was none from the person who organized the train trip, Robert C. Ogden. [11]

Ogden had long believed that industrial education was the best, and possibly the only, viable choice to educate Black people in the South. Though not nearly as wealthy and well known as some of the others who participated that day, Ogden had shown a consistent interest in Black education. He had helped to establish Hampton Institute in 1868. That school was the one Booker T. Washington attended just a short time after he was freed from slavery, and was one of the two preeminent institutions for university-level Black education from the Reconstruction period through the early twentieth century. The other was the school Booker T. Washington founded, Tuskegee Institute. Ogden was on the board of trustees of both institutions. He not only organized the train trip, but also personally invited all of the participants, spending about $25,000 from his own pocket to do so.

In addition to Ogden, the other heavy hitter in southern Black education was George Foster Peabody, a wealthy Wall Street investment banker who was active in politics. Much like Ogden, Peabody believed that a particular strategy for educating southerners, Black and white, was predicated on vocational education. He too became interested in that region of the country as a result of his respect for the work that institutions like Hampton did to educate Black people. He too believed that vocational educational strategies were the answer to the southern race problem. He did his part to ensure that northern millionaires donated handsomely. According to John Anderson's *The Education of Blacks in the South*, Peabody was able to raise over $8 million for Tuskegee and Hampton, and most of the money he secured came from northern millionaires, such as William Dodge, Collis Huntington, John D. Rockefeller, and George Eastman.[12]

All those present on the train that day would join together a year later to form the General Education Board. Though an organization with a national reach, in the South this group was responsible for proposing workable solutions for ways to best educate Black people and soothe the suspicions of whites in the region who were not inclined to believe that education was what Blacks most needed, but rather thought that low-paid work opportunities would ensure that Blacks did not forget their place. The members of the General Education Board came up with a plan that championed vocational education as the best, most effective, and only form of education to which Blacks should be exposed.

The reasons for this line of thinking relative to race, education, and industry are summarized in a speech given before the Alabama General Assembly by J.L.M. Curry. Curry was an influential lawyer, a soldier, a U.S. congressman, a college professor and administrator, a diplomat, an officer in the Confederate States Army during the American Civil War, and a General Education Board member. He declared simply that too high-minded a type of education "would spoil a good plow hand."[13] His meaning was that education for Blacks in the South should be closely tied to ensuring that what they were taught would raise their economic utility and productivity. "Education," Curry said, "is the fundamental basis of general and permanent prosperity. Poverty is the inevitable result of ignorance. Capital follows the school-house." He concluded by warning the legislature, "If you do not lift them [Blacks] up they will drag you down to industrial bankruptcy, social degradation and political corruption."[14]

Called "enlightened" industrialism, this line of thinking wove education, industry, and subservience tightly together into a cloak of racism that covered much of the South. Another northern philanthropist and General Education Board member, William H. Baldwin, also believed that economics, education, industry, and politics should be linked in order to create an acceptably southern solution to the twin concerns of Black labor and Black education.

> The potential economic value of the Negro population properly educated is infinite and incalculable. In the Negro is the opportunity of the South. Time has proven that he is best fitted to perform the heavy labor in the Southern States. "The Negro and the mule is the only combination, so far, to grow cotton." The South needs him; but the South needs him educated to be a suitable citizen. Properly directed he is the best possible laborer to meet the climatic conditions of the South. He will willingly fill the more menial positions, and do the heavy work, at less wages, than the American white man or any foreign race which has yet come to our shores. This will permit the southern white laborer to perform the more expert labor, and to leave the fields, the mines, and the simpler trades for the Negro.[15]

In his thinking, properly trained Blacks could potentially protect the southern economy from the sort of unionized labor beginning to roil business interests in the North and West, and he believed that Black people could be used to break the rising power of the white labor unions. In a letter to a similar-minded businessman, he wrote, "The union of white labor, well organized, will raise the wages beyond a reasonable point, and then the battle will be fought, and the Negro will be put in at a less wage, and the labor union will either have to come down in wages, or Negro labor will be employed." Another founding member of the General Education Board was the editor of the *Atlantic Monthly,* Walter Hines Page. He chimed in to say, "I have no sentimental stuff in me about the Negro, but I have a lot of economic stuff in me about the necessity of training him." He concluded that Black industrial education is not only "good business especially for the South, but good business for the entire country." [16]

By the 1920s, such sentiments had migrated from isolated addresses given to southern legislatures and future General Education Board members to find a home among the highest branches of the federal government. It became clear that the views about Black utility and inferiority were held not just by philanthropists and politicians. They extended to the executive branch of the federal government as well. The public funding of Black education was not viewed as a right of citizenship, but rather as a way to include Black people in a changing economic order in service to a changing southern economy in a manner mindful of northern industry. Such sentiments were so well understood to be true that President Warren Harding could, as a sitting president, freely opine:

When I speak of education as a part of this race question, I do not want the States or the nation to attempt to educate people, whether Black or white, into something they are not fitted to be. I have no sympathy with the half-baked altruism that would overstock us with doctors and lawyers, of whatever color, and leave us in need of people fit and willing to do the manual work of a workaday world. [17]

The president offered his remarks in support of a continued ban on foreign immigration made possible by his plan to possibly fill northern jobs by conscripting Black southern labor. Given these plans for the region's Black workers, President Harding thought that in order for the South to keep its "labor pool" present in the South, that region of the country should be prepared to offer narrow educational opportunities.

> If the South wishes to keep its fields producing and its industry still expanding it will have to compete for the services of the colored man. If it will realize its need for him and deal quite fairly with him, the South will be able to keep him in such numbers as your activities make desirable.[18]

Given their interest in capitalism, business, industry, and finance, these white education philanthropists shaped one side of a conversation about what Ogden termed "the role of the Black workers in the southern agricultural economy and the relationship of that economy to the emergent urban-industrial nation." He continued, "Our great problem is to attach the Negro to the soil and prevent his exodus from the country to the city." George Peabody agreed with such sentiments, saying that he believed the system of industrial education that they championed could help to build a strong southern economy on the backs of submissive, "non-political, cheap Black laborers." Peabody argued that industrial or vocational education would "help the Negro fit his environment," adding, "I believe that the South needs their labor and would be practically bankrupt without it."[19] The views of the General Education Board philanthropists who founded, funded, and supported the development of what today we would term K–12 public education in the South make clear why they were interested in education for southern Black Americans. They understood that "both schooling for democratic citizenship and schooling for second-class citizenship have been basic traditions in American education." [20]

John D. Rockefeller Jr., then only four years out of college, was relatively new to the conversation swirling around him. It is not fully known how vocal he was in engaging the various viewpoints and conversations. What is known is that he was impressed. He later recalled the 1901 excursion as "one of the outstanding events in my life." Soon after the trip concluded, he and his father, and many of the other philanthropists from the train trip, joined together to found the General Education Board. Tellingly, while initially Rockefeller and his father had envisioned putting together a philanthropic organization that would focus mainly on Blacks and be called the Negro Education Board, once father and son had the opportunity to confer, they determined that their effort could impact so much more than just one region of the country, and one group of inhabitants in that region. They aimed much higher, and no lesser a body than the United States Congress gave the organization its stamp of approval. A particular view of Blacks in relation to education was instituted along with the founding of the new organization. It held that Blacks should not be educated in the same ways as whites. [21]

The Rockefeller Family and the General Education Board

In our dreams, we have limitless resources and the people yield themselves with perfect docility to our molding hands. The present education conventions fade from their minds, and unhampered by tradition, we work our own good will upon a grateful and responsive rural folk. We shall not try to make these people or any of their children into philosophers or men of learning, or men of science. We have not to raise up from

among them authors, editors, poets or men of letters. We shall
not search for embryo great artists, painters, musicians nor
lawyers, doctors, preachers, politicians, statesmen, of whom
we have an ample supply. . . . The task we set before ourselves is
very simple as well as a very beautiful one, to train these people
as we find them to a perfectly ideal life just where they are.
—General Education Board Statement of Purpose

Incorporated by an act of Congress on January 12, 1903, the
General Education Board would, over the ensuing decades, re-
shape education in America in significant ways. Nowhere was this
as true as in the South. Its charter stated that the object of the
new corporation was first and foremost the promotion of education within the United States, without "distinction of race, sex,
or creed." In order to accomplish these goals, it was authorized by
Congress with the power to "build, improve, enlarge, or equip,
or to aid others to build, improve, enlarge, or equip, buildings
for elementary or primary schools, industrial schools, technical
schools, normal schools, training schools for teachers, or schools
for any grade, or for higher institutions of learning." In short, the
new organization had national powers in the realm of education
similar to those invested today in our Department of Education.
It was, however, not responsible to any group or agency other than
itself. Accordingly, in many ways, the mantle for both the development and reform of public education in the United States was
now firmly in Rockefeller hands. This is where the family had
long worked for it to be, especially in relation to the education of
Blacks and poor whites.[22]

Throughout the nineteenth and twentieth centuries, the
Rockefeller family donated millions of dollars to southern educational institutions, from the youngest grades up through college, including my own alma mater, Spelman College. No matter
the age of the student, the more senior Rockefeller and his various philanthropic efforts supported vocational education. The

incorporation of the board subsumed the work of two other great philanthropic entities working in the South: the Peabody Fund, which had previously focused most of its resources on the education of whites in the South, and the Slater Fund, which was focused specifically on the education of Blacks. The founders of both eagerly joined Rockefeller's General Education Board (GEB). Greatly aided by the work of the founders of these two educational foundations, the GEB members decided that a taxpayer-supported, universally available educational system was the only viable long-term solution to the problems of both Black education and southern labor. They believed that such an education system would stimulate and spur greater business interest and hasten modern economic renewal in the region "by the introduction of conveniences and amenities through the telephone, good roads, rapid transit, free delivery, and the parcel post." However, given the lack of readily available funds, and the white supremacist sentiments of those with political power in the South, friend and foe alike, the GEB knew that white southerners were in no hurry to support the education of Black children, vocational or otherwise. It resolved that the only way to have a tax-supported public education system in the region was by couching its significance as a primary benefit to the educational futures of rural white children. The GEB told white politicians that they should not worry about Black children gaining education, because whites would not have to pay for the buildings, land, labor, or materials associated with building "Black" schools.[23]

Much like the Rosenwald Fund had, the GEB resolved to institute a system of awarding matching funds for Black communities that would seed the effort to build Black schools. Furthermore, in order to enjoy the privileges of a public education, Black communities would have to deed the land upon which the school building sat to state authorities in perpetuity, and would have to agree to an additional tax to fund the operation of their separate school system. Of course, Black people would still be expected to pay into the state educational funds used to pay for the expansion of the public education of white children. Black education would be of great economic benefit to whites.

As GEB members began to engage with white community members and political decision makers, they consistently made it clear that, though they were wealthy philanthropists, they were not there to actually give any kind of free ride to Black people. Rather, they were far more interested in helping them help themselves. Toward that end, the GEB determined that "its main purpose required that it cooperate with progressive Southern sentiment in creating publically supported educational systems." It believed that mutually beneficial ends would be not be observed by "founding and supporting schools for him, but rather by helping him [Blacks] found and support schools for himself." The schools would not remain in Black hands, no matter how successful they were, because "fortunately, experience has shown that the Negroes welcome opportunities to turn these schools over to the public-school system when the authorities are ready to support them." As a result, Rockefeller's General Education Board found itself in the business of convincing Black communities that they alone were responsible for paying for educational equality and that no price should be considered too high for them to do so.[24]

After outlining why it believed education would benefit the South, both Black and white, and then laying out the specifics of a plan to expand public education in the region—instituting a series of matching grants for Black communities with which to build rural schools for their use—the GEB turned its attention to making sure that there were teachers in the building who were trained and interested in working with Black children in rural communities. While some of Rockefeller's other philanthropic work provided funds to schools that educated Black teachers, in order to ensure that the development of public school systems in the South continued apace, the GEB partnered with another organization, the Jeanes Fund.

Philanthropist Anna T. Jeanes of Philadelphia founded the Jeanes Foundation—also known as the Negro Rural School Fund—in 1907 with a $1 million donation. An unmarried Quaker, Ms. Jeanes had inherited money from her father and brother's estates. Like other interested, progressive, and curious white northerners of her class, she had attended quite a few lectures describing the poor educational conditions for Blacks in the South. She resolved to help and to focus her philanthropic efforts on recruiting and training Black teachers who could help. In addition, the charity provided funds to employ Black supervisors to oversee the growing Black teaching force. In 1908, Jackson T. Davis, the superintendent of Henrico County public schools in Virginia, named Virginia Randolph as the United States' first "Jeanes Supervising Industrial Teacher." Given the freedom to design her own agenda, she developed the first in-service training program and wrote a reference book for southern schools receiving donations from the Jeanes Foundation called the Henrico Plan. By 1952, there were over 510 Jeanes teachers in the South. As American ideas about race and proper forms of education based on skin color and social order were exported around the globe, Randolph's teaching techniques and philosophy were later adopted in Great Britain's African colonies.[25]

Beside gifts from the Jeanes, Peabody, and Slater funds, among others, following its chartering the GEB also received an initial gift of $1,000,000 from John D. Rockefeller Sr. (almost $28 million in today's terms) to begin the work. Pleased with the progress after the first few years, in 1905 Rockefeller donated an additional gift of $10 million, and in 1907 a further sum of $32 million (almost $850 million today). Even with the tax breaks involved in donating such large amounts of money, the figures are nonetheless astounding. Not surprisingly, with this type of support, the organization was able to expand relatively quickly, and offices were established in Richmond, Virginia, and Baton Rouge, Louisiana, in order to give GEB agents closer contact with southern communities. By 1921, John D. Rockefeller Sr. had personally given $129 million to be used for programs approved by the General Education Board, which continued operating until 1964, when it ran out of money. Long before then, however, part of the work of the foundation had been outshined by another fund that far outstripped the work of the Rockefeller Fund in at least one area: the building of schools. That operation was the aforementioned Rosenwald Fund.[26]

Julius Rosenwald, a clothier who became part owner and president of Sears, Roebuck, and Company, was the founder of the Rosenwald Fund, through which he contributed seed money for schools and other philanthropic causes. The school-building program was one of the largest programs administered by the Fund, as it came to be called. Paul Sachs, the founder of financial services giant Goldman Sachs, first introduced Rosenwald to the issue of Black education. Sachs often stayed with the Rosenwald family when he was in Chicago, and many times their post-dinner conversation would turn toward the social issues of the day. They agreed that the education of southern Blacks was among the most serious of the issues. At some point, Sachs introduced Rosenwald to Booker T. Washington, the founder of Tuskegee University, and Sachs encouraged Rosenwald to do more than just talk or wring his hands. He told him to do something to actually better the poor state of Black education in the United States. The Rosenwald-funded schools were the result.[27]

Using architectural plans designed by professors at the Tuskegee Institute, Rosenwald spent more than $4 million to build 4,977 schools spread over 883 counties in 15 states, from Maryland to Texas. Because the program used a system of matching grants, we know that, all told, between 1906 and 1960 Black communities raised more than $4.7 million to aid in the construction and support of the schools built to educate their children. Across the rural South, the Black community members who contributed their money to such efforts "came from people who represented a poor working class, men who worked at furnaces, women who washed and ironed for white people, and children who chopped cotton in the heat of the day." The schools built with such matching funds had to focus on vocational education for Blacks, whereby they were taught to make bricks or become carpenters or nurses or teachers. Any other form of education was forbidden if Rosenwald funds were to be used. The type of education proscribed mattered little to rural Black communities. It was the opportunity for an education at all that mattered most to these rural, southern residents.[28]

That meant they didn't complain that Rosenwald's matching grants could be accessed by their communities only if they first showed that they believed in "self-help" and proved it by raising a minimum of $500—and potentially more, depending on the size of the school they wanted to build. In 2016 dollars, that would be just over $6,000. Once they had qualified for the program by raising that initial amount, they then had to identify and convince a property owner to donate the land on which the school would be built. Some counties required that the land be formally deeded to county education officials. Next, local Black residents had to identify from where the building materials and labor to build the schools would come and raise the funds to pay for the construction. Once a school was built, they had to provide the money to furnish the buildings and hire teachers. Only once all of these steps were complete would the Rosenwald Fund finally release matching funds.[29]

In Alabama alone, between 1914 and 1927, the Rosenwald Fund supported the construction of 345 schools at a total cost of $905,545. Rural Black communities in the state, comprised primarily of tenant farmers, contributed $349,820 to that total figure. The Rosenwald Fund contributed $194,870 of the amount. Whites in the state contributed $68,391 in tax funds. Taxes paid by Black communities added $292,464 to the total. In short, Black communities, not white philanthropists, contributed more than two-thirds of the total money spent. By far, the largest contributors to Black education in the rural South were Black people themselves. Black communities in the rural South paid a high social, cultural, and personal economic price to acquire an education supposedly at public expense. White communities did not have to resort to such measures to raise funds to send their own children to public schools.[30]

States and county school districts benefited financially from the building program because they received a deed to what was often valuable land. They also received extra tax fees from Black people. The foundation benefited because it received widespread positive publicity. Black communities benefited as well, but they paid a dearly high price for those benefits. Despite the popularity of the rural school-building programs, educational achievement remained in short supply. In Alabama, Georgia, Louisiana, South Carolina, and Mississippi, states with a combined population of 4.7 million Black people, by the mid-1940s less than half could claim five years of formal education. In South Carolina and Louisiana, 60 percent of Black adults had no more than a fourth- or fifth-grade education. Though significant and important, the building program was not a silver bullet aimed at the heart of educational inequality.[31]

Nonetheless, Rosenwald schools did more to further the cause of Black education than did any other educational entity of the time. By 1932, so many schools were built that they could have accommodated one-third of all Black children in southern schools. They also accounted for a sizable educational gain on the part of rural southern Blacks, with significant effects on school attendance, literacy, years of schooling, cognitive test scores, and northern migration. The highest gains were in the most disadvantaged counties. At the same time, in order to ensure the continued cooperation of white southern authorities, the philanthropists and often the communities were forced to downplay their contributions toward these successes.[32]

Giving Their All

While the newly built schools and the financial support of philanthropists were clearly important, we would do well to give a
thought to the partnership that these early-twentieth-century
philanthropists developed with local Black communities who,
though poor, were deeply invested in the education of their children. M.H. Griffin, the rural agent who worked with the Rosenwald Foundation from 1921 to 1925, was one of the first Black
agents to work as a liaison between Black communities and the
wealthy white financiers. He reported that in 1925 in the small
rural enclave of Boligee in Greene County, Alabama, he met with
rural Blacks in a "little old rickety building without any heat" to
plan the construction of a school. He said that the majority of
Black people who attended were tenant farmers or sharecroppers.
Under the sharecropping system, landowners were supposed to
split the profits from the cotton crop with sharecroppers at harvest time. However, bales would often mysteriously vanish during
the count, or the agreed upon financial arrangements might on a
whim be altered to benefit the landowner. It was almost impossible for such families to get ahead. That was, after all, the point of
the economic system. Sharecroppers such as those who met with
Griffin in 1925 knew it was often very difficult for them to get out
of debt and that public protest could mean arrest, forced labor, or
even lynching.

The year that Griffin attended the Alabama gathering, the
farmers had been hard hit because the boll weevil had wreaked
havoc on the cotton plants. They knew it would be a rough economic season for them when it came time to settle up. As the gathering got started, the master of ceremonies for the event said to
those who were attending the fund-raiser, "We have never had a
school in this vicinity, most of our children have grown into man-
hood and womanhood without the semblance of an opportunity

to get an insight on life." Griffin, in writing a letter to his supervisors, recounted to them that as the speaker continued, tears began to trickle down his face. Just then, "one old man, who had seen slavery days, with all of his life's earnings in an old greasy sack, slowly drew it from his pocket, and emptied it on the table." He then turned to address the crowd and said, "I want to see the children of my grandchildren have a chance, and so I am giving my all." What he had to offer was $10. The sum total he had been able to save throughout the totality of his life. His sacrifice spurred further giving by the group, and they finished the night raising over $1,300. Griffin reports that when all was said and done, after calculating the amount of money they raised, along with their additional donations in labor and materials, the full total the impoverished community contributed toward the five-room country training school (a euphemism for high school) was almost $6,500.[33]

In another instance that exemplifies the important contributions of Black southern communities in the growth of southern Black public education, in 1915 Mary Johnson of Notasulga, Alabama, wrote to Booker T. Washington, whose Tuskegee Institute was then primarily responsible for administering the Rosenwald building campaign, to ask how she could make sure her community participated. Those in charge of the funds responded with the specific instructions, including the information about the necessity of collecting funds in the amount of at least $500 for a one-room schoolhouse before applying for Rosenwald matching funds. As recounted by a Boston newspaper, Johnson organized the women of the community, who raised the funds by organizing a community bake sale. Unfortunately, a dishonest treasurer absconded with the money, and Johnson was forced to start over again from scratch. She and her compatriots again raised the funds through selling various food items and went so far as to purchase the required lumber. This time, "not having enough to pay for the building of the structure, the men of the community let the lumber rot on the ground."[34] Determined, Johnson began the project for a third time. This time around, two local teachers joined in with organizing and planning, and a few months later they began a spate of fund-raising activities, including "a Thanksgiving rally, an entertainment at a private home, a school concert, and a birthday party to which the invited guests brought bags of pennies." Patrons and "friends" made private donations, as did three local churches. Community members donated over $100 in labor, and a local church donated the land for the building site. Once again, they purchased lumber, and the community showed up over the space of a few weeks to help with the building project. The entire journey took a total of nine years, but in May of 1923 the school opened for the use of Black children.[35]

These stories of sacrifice were repeated so often so as to become common during the years when the building fund was operative. While the period between the end of Reconstruction and the 1930s offers us a lens through which to understand the involvement and relationships between philanthropies, wealthy businessmen, and an overwhelming interest in alternative, or specialized, forms of education designed for the education of schoolchildren who are poor and not white, it also provided at least one example of what could happen in the Jim Crow South when Black children were educated in schools in the same way as were white children: they thrived. Paradoxically, the following example of how this works relates to a work community owned and operated by a U.S. Steel subsidiary central to the development of the convict lease system.

The Company School

Up until the first decade of the twentieth century, most Blacks in the South only found employment options as unskilled laborers. Jim Crow ideologies ensured skilled occupations were regarded as the natural province of white workers. As industrialization made its way from south to north, Alabama coal and iron mines were the first industries to open their doors, if only just a bit, to Blacks. Previously, in Alabama, Black convicts, farmed out to private companies by the state of Alabama, were the answer to the area's dwindling labor supply. Given the racial animosity still pervasive in the South, many Blacks preferred to just leave the state as opposed to staying and trying to find gainful employment. Faced with losing their workforce, some companies based in the South began at least trying to improve conditions to some extent. They began to recruit Blacks as workers and, in order to entice them, offered them the opportunity to reside in company towns where education and housing were provided. Tennessee Coal and Iron, for one, opened and operated at least ten towns that were highly segregated yet provided schools in which Black children thrived.

Tennessee Coal and Iron did not build separate towns for Blacks but instead provided complete neighborhoods within already established white towns; these towns included hospitals, social service centers, and schools. The company made a point of explaining that their actions should not be seen as philanthropy: "The Steel Corporation is not an eleemosynary institution," and its first object is "to make money for its stockholders." In regard to schools, the company made it clear that the low educational achievement on the part of a majority of its Black workers—as well as the fact that the "inadequate pay offered teachers failed to attract men and women competent to train the youthful mind"— would have to be addressed. As a first step, Tennessee Coal and Iron made an agreement with county officials whereby the company agreed to build a sufficient number of schoolhouses in its company towns to educate Black children. For their part, county authorities agreed to turn over to the company the state education funds they received to pay teachers.[36]

The result was that the Tennessee Coal and Iron Company (T.C.I.) was able to operate an educational system for its workers, both Black and white, using state educational funds but free of any regulation from local school officials. Independent reviews of the educational outcomes found that "the instructors in charge are of a high average type and the schools are recognized as having no equals in the South." A 1919 survey of Alabama schools described the T.C.I. system as "one of the most interesting educational experiments in the bituminous coal region of the Appalachian system." The report continued:

> the work is done in complete cooperation with the county school board, which apportions funds to the mining town school on the same basis as to other schools. . . . The classroom work is of splendid quality. The teaching staff shows good organization, enthusiasm, loyalty, and a high degree of professional spirit. . . . It shows conclusively what can be done by the expenditure of reasonable funds, business encouragement, and professional service . . . [and that] what can be accomplished here can be accomplished elsewhere, with similar management and expenditure.[37]

One of the "model" examples of such company-owned communities was Westfield, Alabama, which, in addition to new schools, had modern houses, a community house, and athletic fields. The company freely admitted that all this was "a deliberate policy of flattering the Negro workers," by building schools from the same plans as the white schools. By all reports, the company achieved its economic aims, as it was able cut down on turnover, and "wages of laborers in the Alabama steel industry remained at a level of about 60 per cent of that of the steel industry in Chicago, and Pittsburgh."[38]

T.C.I. schools were among the best in the state when it came to educating Black students. In 1930, state officials administered tests to all of the children enrolled in the third and sixth grades. Comparative scores indicated a considerable superiority for the Black children who attended T.C.I. schools when compared with the Black children enrolled in other county and city schools and in the South at large. The average scores were the same as those achieved by white students. Equal resources, curriculum, expectations, and infrastructure—even in a segregated environment—produced equal outcomes. It was as close as a Jim Crow–era school system would come to racial equality.

Though an experiment that came about as a means to benefit the bottom line of a corporate entity—in this instance, T.C.I.'s bottom line—the educational futures of Black children equally benefited. However, the schooling on offer was equal to what was on offer to wealthy whites. It wasn't vocational in nature, and though the system benefited the corporation providing it, the Black children educated within the system consistently benefited as well. It is not clear that today we are any closer to understanding the nuanced difference. Today, corporations are finding new ways to augment their workforce by providing even more highly specialized forms of vocational education, primarily to students who are poor and of color.

The Rise of Contemporary Company Schools

In the spring of 2011, the business giant IBM, in partnership with the New York City Department of Education, the City University of New York, and CUNY's New York City College of Technology, announced that it was set to pilot a new six-year organizational structure for high schools whereby corporate employers would help to shape the curriculum, and students would leave with a traditional high school diploma, a community college degree, and possibly a job by the time they graduated. Of the 520 students enrolled, 96 percent were Black or Latino and 74 percent were young men. For many of the students, their community college degree would be the first college degree ever earned in their family. For the economically vulnerable Black and Latino students who have long been beset by high unemployment rates, skyrocketing college costs, and a job market that offers only unskilled low-wage jobs, the new school, some argued, could be a lifeline. IBM promised to provide mentors and even internships to students who were qualified. As a result, many believed this new educational form would address at least a couple of stubborn social issues, namely high unemployment rates for students of color and their low completion rates at community colleges. They might also provide companies with a stable workforce. Though they were not identified as such, these high schools were a contemporary form of company schools, absent the towns, health care, family jobs, and guaranteed housing that were a feature of the twentieth-century form.

The idea went over well. By 2014, IBM announced that its model was spreading and that the corporation was on track to open sixty such schools in the next few years. In addition, a wide variety of companies, including Microsoft and Con Edison, agreed that the plan was a good one and began to consider the possibility of opening their own company schools. New York governor Andrew Cuomo announced that sixteen new schools would open their doors across the state of New York by 2017 and that they would focus on areas including manufacturing, clean technology, and health care. President Obama announced a $100 million competitive grant encouraging similar partnerships between high schools, private industry, and U.S. universities. Though not exclusively educating low-income students of color, that group is a consistent focus. Arguably, it is vocational education by any other name, as well as an example of a more utilitarian form of segregated education of the sort that has long been overprescribed for young people in struggling circumstances. We will have to wait and see if the results actually benefit the students for whom such an idiosyncratic form of education was designed.[39]

3

BROWN CHILDREN,
WHITE RETRIBUTION

I had never thought of myself as integrating anything until my husband found my fifth grade class picture one day and, I believe mostly because he found my large though slightly askew afro humorous, framed it and hung it on our living room wall. There I was, the only Black or even brown child in a room with twenty-five white students. As I looked at the photograph, I remembered that I was among the first group of Black students bused from our all-Black Clearwater, Florida, neighborhood called "The Heights" out to Pinellas County to attend school with white children. I could feel the "see your breath" cold winter mornings while I waited for the bus in front of an auto repair shop; the absolute fear of missing the bus back home after school, since it left before any of the others and didn't wait for anyone; and the absence of any memories of birthday parties or afternoons spent chatting with white friends. I didn't have any. I remember learning to square dance and to recite from memory all fifty-two prepositions. Other than that, I have nothing particularly traumatizing or momentous to report about the experience. I was perfectly tolerated.

Perhaps the most notable thing about my integration experience is that it took place almost twenty years after *Brown v. Board of Education* decreed that integrated schools were the law of the land. My school was not the only one that dragged its feet. As historian Michael Klarman has pointed out in *Brown v. Board of Education and the Civil Rights Movement*, in 1959, five years after the Supreme Court's decision, a grand total of forty of North Carolina's nearly 300,000 Black students attended an integrated school. By 1960, only forty-two of Nashville's more than 12,000 Black students were in classrooms with whites. These numbers are not percentages; they are the literal numbers of Black children who integrated predominately white schools across the South. By 1964, a decade after the Supreme Court decision, only one out of every eighty-five southern Black children attended an integrated school.[1]

While *Brown v. Board* is an oft-celebrated and triumphantly emphasized feature of the promise and progress of American democracy, it's incumbent on us all to remember the frenzy of violence unleashed by whites on Black citizens at the very idea that they and their white children would have to sit next to children of African descent in classrooms, and that Black children would have access to the same level of instruction as did their own. White southerners found new ways to keep from providing Black children with educations that were the same as those their own children received. This resistance was massive and, at the extremes, included decisions to close entire school systems for periods ranging from one to five years. This chapter tells the story of how southern whites resisted school integration after the *Brown v. Board* decision, as well as the economic and psychological costs Blacks suffered as a result. It also explores how it is that those who were staunchly opposed to integration plundered public funds to start what were termed segregation academies while at the same time starving Black schools in order to keep Black children from integrating into white public schools.

All across the South, groups of whites undertook a campaign of "massive resistance" against the Supreme Court decision. This resistance was called forth by a document termed a Southern Manifesto and authored by members of the United States Congress in March of 1956. South Carolina senator Strom Thurmond first conceived of the idea and wrote the first draft before enlisting the aid of Virginia's senator Harry Byrd. At the time, Byrd was one of the most powerful men in the state, if not in the South as a whole. He was joined by nineteen senators and eighty-two representatives in signing the document, "including the entire congressional delegations from Alabama, Arkansas, Georgia, Louisiana, Mississippi, South Carolina and Virginia. With the exception of two Republicans from Virginia who signed on, all of the signatories were Southern Democrats." Only three southern Democrats refused to sign: Albert Gore Sr., Estes Kefauver, and the future president Lyndon B. Johnson. The resolution condemned the 1954 Supreme Court decision in *Brown v. Board of Education*, calling it "a clear abuse of judicial power" and pointing out that the "original Constitution does not mention education." [2]

Building on those sentiments, following the *Brown* decision, white elected officials across the South passed laws to impede the possibility of racially integrated schools' ever becoming a reality. One such law in Virginia forbade any integrated schools from receiving state funds and authorized the governor to close schools that allowed even one Black child to register. Another in Mississippi established a three-member Pupil Placement Board to determine which school a student would attend. In almost every instance, they decided that white children should attend school with students of their own race and that Black students should do the same. In a number of states, legislatures passed laws creating tuition-grant schemes that channeled funds to the coffers of schools serving white students, funds that were formerly allocated to public schools that had been closed in order to prevent the possibility of racial integration.

What that meant was that, though generally states paid tuition dollars directly to private schools, in some extreme iterations of the segrenomic scheme, once a month white parents would line up to receive a check from the Board of Education that had been drawn from the funds contributed by both Black and white taxpayers. They would take their checks to the bank, cash them, and then use those funds to pay for their child's education for that month at a whites-only "private school" financed almost entirely with public tax funds. Called "segregation academies," these schools were legal because the *Brown* decision did not apply to private schools. As a result, throughout the 1950s, 1960s, and 1970s, such schools flourished. Though privately owned and run, they were primarily dependent on tax dollars to operate. Even after the Virginia Supreme Court of Appeals struck down the law that allowed communities to close entire districts in an effort to avoid integration, individual state tuition grants to parents continued, which allowed the all-white schools to carry on. It was not until 1964 that the U.S. Supreme Court outlawed Virginia's tuition grants to private schools, and it wasn't until 1978 that the last school district to have used public money to support private white schools ceased to do so. The toll exacted on Black children and families by this theft of both the funds for their education as well as the education itself would negatively impact the educational futures of Black children for decades. In some ways, since thousands of children were denied access to any sort of public education, the situation was even more devastating than the system of separate but equal education that had preceded it.[3]

Building Up to *Brown*

In regard to education, for Black Americans the period between Reconstruction and the 1940s was most specifically about the building of schools, determinations as to acceptable content and curriculum for the Black children, and the racially specific growth of a taxpayer-supported school system in the South. From the 1950s on, the story evolved into a tale about how to reconcile the accepted forms of Black education, shot through as they were with white supremacy and purported Black inferiority, with Black citizenship, which bestowed the promises of the Thirteenth, Fourteenth, and Fifteenth amendments to the Constitution—Black freedom, citizenship, and voting rights. In the infamous 1896 case *Plessy v. Ferguson*, the Supreme Court grappled with the argument that racially separate public facilities always advantaged whites and disadvantaged Blacks. In response, the Court declared, "We consider the underlying fallacy of the plaintiff's argument to consist in the assumption that the enforced separation of the two races stamps the colored race with a badge of inferiority. If this be so, it is not by reason of anything found in the act, but solely because the colored race chooses to put that construction upon it." The Court further decreed that it did not see racial segregation in and of itself as problematic if facilities were indeed "separate but equal." In relation to southern school funding measures, separate—while preferable and lucrative for whites—never came close to ensuring Black equality.[4]

Beginning in the 1950s, as courts at the state and federal levels along with the Supreme Court struggled with the mechanics of how to have enforced racial separation exist alongside educational equality, it became clear that the law would have to change. *Brown v. Board* brought all of this to a head. The case was as much about control of and access to educational funds as it was about states agreeing to educate Black and white children in the same room. White southern community members were comfortable with Black communities alone paying the total cost of both the education and transportation of Black children. It lessened the burden on their own pocketbooks.

Transportation came to be as divisive an educational issue as were classrooms. In the rural South, Black children could walk miles each day to get to school while white children often rode on taxpayer-supported buses. Sometimes, Black children were splattered in mud as the buses rolled past on rainy days. Other times, the white children taunted them or threw things out of the windows at them. All across the South, in an educational logic reminiscent of the growth of Rosenwald-funded schools, Black parents were repeatedly told by education officials that if they wanted their children to ride on buses then they should feel free to purchase them, fill them with gasoline, hire a driver, and repair them—all at their own expense. However, there would be no tax dollars spent on the transportation needs of Black children. After all, white supremacy, education, Black inferiority, and economics were a sanctioned part of the law and certainly were part and parcel of the southern way of life. Accordingly, between the 1930s and the 1950s, for Black children and parents interested in attaining some semblance of a quality education, two key educational issues consistently arose that led them to beat a path to the courts: the unsafe and unsanitary nature of the schools in which Black children were expected to learn and the funding for buses to get them to and from schools located far away from their homes. Those two issues were central to the Supreme Court's decision in *Brown v. Board* decreeing that separate but equal schools were unconstitutional.

There were actually five cases—from four states and Washington, D.C.—that the Supreme Court joined together to make up the case that ultimately led to the decree that public schools would have to racially integrate. In Delaware, there were two separate cases, one having to do with the lack of buses to transport Black children and the other with the decrepit nature of the school buildings to which Black children were assigned. In Virginia, the case was brought on behalf of four hundred high school students who staged a walkout and strike to protest the fact that their education was supposed to take place in tar paper shacks or outside on disabled school buses. In Kansas, the concern was the lack of bus transportation to a nearby Black school and the legal exclusion of Black students from the white school. In South Carolina, transportation and school quality ignited the fires. It was only in D.C. that racial segregation itself was targeted.

Delaware

First petitioned in 1951, the Delaware case that became one of the *Brown* cases was actually two cases. One involved a woman named Ethel Belton and six other parents from Claymont, Delaware; in the other case, Sarah Bulah, a lone parent from Hockessin, Delaware, was at the center. The Claymont parents were concerned about the refusal of state education officials to allow their children to attend the local white school, which sat on fourteen acres and accommodated four hundred students from grade school through to high school. It had large playing fields and pristine landscaping. Black children were bused into downtown Wilmington to attend Howard High. There were thirteen hundred students there, and the building was run-down and overcrowded, and instead of decorative landscaping the students looked out on warehouses and tenement buildings. In addition to having nice grounds and surroundings, Claymont, the white school, also offered courses and extracurricular activities such as economics, trigonometry, art club, driver's education, and a student-run newspaper. The only special classes or activities offered to the Black students took place at a vocational-training annex located nine blocks away from the school in Wilmington. The group of Black parents who eventually filed suit simply wanted their children to have the opportunity to be educated in the better school. They took their concerns to a Black lawyer named Louis Redding, who advised them to petition the State Board of Education to admit their children to the local school. Their request was denied.[5]

During the same period, in Hockessin, another Black parent, Sarah Bulah, decided to seek legal advice from the same lawyer, Mr. Redding. She did not go to see him because she wanted to send her child to a white school, however. She had made peace with the fact that her daughter attended a one-room, segregated schoolhouse. She just didn't want to have to drive her there every day. Instead, she wanted her daughter to ride to school on a district-provided school bus. Like the parents in Claymont, she too petitioned the State Board of Education. Her request was likewise denied. When she went to seek advice from Redding, he told her he was unwilling to sue the district for a "Jim Crow school bus" to take Black children to a "Jim Crow school." Instead, he wanted to challenge the legality of separate but equal itself. In order to make clear that education, not transportation, was the key issue, Redding urged Sarah to try and enroll her daughter at the white school near her house. Once her request was refused, Jack Greenberg from the NAACP Legal Defense and Educational Fund joined Redding, and together the two lawyers filed suit on behalf of the two sets of parents to challenge the constitutionality of the separate but equal doctrine itself.[6]

At trial, Judge Collins Seitz agreed with the lawyers that the state was not living up to its responsibility to provide an equal education for Black people. However, instead of declaring the doctrine of separate but equal unconstitutional, he ruled that the state of Delaware should be made to actually fund racially segregated schools equally. He noted, "It seems to me that when a plaintiff shows to the satisfaction of the court that there is an existing and continuing violation of the 'separate but equal doctrine' he is entitled to have made available to him the state facilities which have been shown to be superior." The judge did not agree that racial segregation was itself unconstitutional; he simply thought that the state needed to equally fund separate education for Blacks. Even so, the State Board of Education, which did not think that it should be forced to spend additional state funds to provide Black children with equal facilities, appealed the decision to the Supreme Court. This led to its becoming one of the five cases bundled under the name *Brown v. Board of Education*.[7]

Washington, D.C.

The education case from D.C. that the Supreme Court chose to include with the other *Brown* cases began in 1947. Gardner Bishop, a local Black barber, raised funds from members of the Black working class in the nation's capital, including hairdressers, prostitutes, janitors, and domestic servants, to protest unequal education. In one instance, the group funded a months-long boycott of Washington schools. Due to an influx of Blacks relocating from the South to the North, the enrollment in many D.C. schools was twice what the buildings were built to handle. Instead of allowing Black children to attend white schools, many of which were underenrolled, the school board instead decided to double the school sessions at Black schools. What that meant was one group of Black students would attend school from 8 a.m. to 12:30 p.m., and the second group began their day at noon and ended at 4:30 p.m. Both groups lost ninety minutes of school each day when compared to the school days in white schools. What made the situation particularly galling to Bishop and other community members was that "nearby Eliot Junior High, a school for whites, had several hundred unoccupied places," as more white families were putting their children in private schools or even moving out of the city to the Maryland and Virginia suburbs.[8]

As tensions continued to simmer, in September 1950 Bishop organized a direct protest action designed to lead to a lawsuit challenging segregated schools that would be filed by the NAACP. He took a group of eleven Black schoolchildren to John Philip Sousa Junior High School. It had a six-hundred-seat auditorium, a double gymnasium, a playground with seven basketball courts, and a softball field. Bishop asked that the Black students he brought with him be allowed to immediately enroll. They were refused. One of the children was twelve-year-old Thomas Bolling Jr. He attended Shaw Junior High. It was old and located in a run-down neighborhood, and its science laboratory consisted of "one

Bunsen burner and a fishbowl with goldfish." Bolling's name led the list of plaintiffs when the NAACP lawyer filed suit against the Board of Education in D.C. The suit argued that segregation was wrong and that the burden of proof was not upon the Black plaintiffs, but rather upon the District government to prove that there was a reasonable basis for or public purpose in racial restrictions on school admission. The schoolchildren lost. However, while the lawyer was waiting on the appeal, the clerk of the Supreme Court telephoned him. The case of *Bolling v. Sharpe* was now to be one of the *Brown* cases.[9]

Virginia

In April 1951, Barbara Rose Johns, a high school student in Farmville, Virginia, helped organize a student strike to protest poor school conditions at her school, Robert Moton High School. It was the only student-initiated case consolidated into the *Brown* cases. By 1950, the school, originally constructed for 180 students, had 477 children attempting to learn there. The Black community in Farmville was well aware of the overcrowding. It was longstanding. They had formed a parent-teacher association in the early 1940s to address it, but their requests and proposals were repeatedly denied. Finally, in 1948, the board agreed to pay for three additional substandard classrooms. According to a first-person account from Barbara's sister, Joan:

> The school we went to was overcrowded. Consequently, the county decided to build three tarpaper shacks for us to hold classes in. A tarpaper shack looks like a dilapidated black building, which is similar to a chicken coop on a farm. It's very unsightly. In winter the school was very cold. And a lot of times we had to put on our jackets. Now, the students that sat closest to the wood stove were very warm and the ones who sat farthest away were very cold. And I remember being cold a lot of times

and sitting in the classroom with my jacket on. When it rained, we would get water through the ceiling. So there were lots of pails sitting around the classroom. And sometimes we had to raise our umbrellas to keep the water off our heads. It was a very difficult setting for trying to learn.

And I remember we were always talking about how bad the conditions were but we didn't know what to do about it. So one day my sister and a group of students that she chose decided to do something about it.[10]

Over several weeks, Barbara approached a number of similarly motivated students at the school. There was John Stokes, the president of the senior class who often said that the tar paper shacks weren't even fit for animals, let alone students. She also reached out to John Watson, the editor of the school newspaper. Barbara told them that she thought a student-led strike would draw more attention to the conditions at the school. At John Stokes's suggestion, the students named their secret plan the Manhattan Project, after the code name for the effort by the Allied forces to develop nuclear weapons during World War II. In late April of 1951, after taking almost six months to plan, the group concluded they were ready to proceed. The first step involved John Watson's leaving school to make a phone call to the principal. Pretending to be a white business owner, he told the principal that students had left school grounds and were causing trouble downtown. Then, the students sent notes to all the classrooms announcing an emergency meeting. Barbara had signed the notes with her initials, "BJ," which were the same as those of principal Jones.[11]

As students sat packed into the auditorium, Barbara told them that in spite of their parents' urging, the school board had not acted to improve the intolerable conditions. Nothing would change, she told her classmates, unless they banded together and demanded a new school. She called on the group to stay out of school and told them that the Farmville jail wasn't big enough to hold all of them. As she marched out of the school, 450 of the students followed her. Some held signs that read "We Want a New School or None at All" and "Down with the Tar Paper Shacks." In May of 1951, lawyers from the local NAACP filed suit on behalf of 117 of the students who attended the school. They asked that the state law requiring segregated schools in Virginia be struck down. A three-judge panel at the U.S. District Court unanimously rejected the request. They didn't agree that racial segregation was wrong. The court did, however, think that Black schools should be equally funded. They explained, "We have found no hurt or harm to either race." The school board was ordered to proceed with plans to equalize the facilities. On appeal, the Supreme Court asked that the case be bundled with the other school desegregation cases that would become *Brown v. Board of Education*.[12]

South Carolina

In South Carolina, transportation was a key issue leading to the suit, as was true in a few other of the *Brown* cases. State education officials refused to allocate funds for buses for Black children. The Board of Education said that since the Black community did not pay much in taxes, it would be unfair to expect white citizens to provide transportation for Black children. Initially accepting this reasoning, Black parents collected donations to purchase a secondhand school bus. Soon, the continual repairs on the bus proved to be too costly. The NAACP wanted to file suit but, fearing reprisals, there were few families willing to step forward to become a plaintiff. Finally, a local community member, Reverend Joseph DeLaine, agreed to help find residents willing to sign on to a court case challenging such unequal treatment.[13]

In March of 1948, local attorney Harold Boulware, together with future Supreme Court justice Thurgood Marshall, filed a first case to attempt to get the state to provide busing to Black children. However, that case was dismissed because the court ruled the petitioner had no legal standing because he paid taxes in another district. This did not stop Rev. DeLaine, and by 1949 he had obtained over twenty signatures, enough to file a second case. The first name on the list, which was organized alphabetically, was Harry Briggs, a veteran of the navy and father of five, and with support from the national office of the NAACP, in May of 1950 the case of *Briggs v. Elliott* was filed. The complaint claimed unequal treatment and said that during the 1949–1950 school year, for every dollar spent on a white child, state officials allotted only 24¢ for Black students and that Black adults in the county only averaged just over four years of education. At the beginning of the hearings in U.S. District Court, the school district admitted that "the educational facilities, equipment, curricula and opportunities afforded in School District No. 22 for colored pupils are not substantially equal to those afforded for white pupils." Nonetheless, the court ruled against the students' request that the court find legally sanctioned racial segregation unconstitutional. However, the court did order that funding and facilities in the district should at least be equalized. The NAACP appealed to the U.S. Supreme Court, and the *Briggs* case became part of the *Brown* litigation.[14]

Once news of the second lawsuit became public, the economic retribution was swift, comprehensive, and brutal. Reverend DeLaine was fired from his job at a local school. His wife, Mattie, was also fired from her job as a school principal, as were all the other twenty-two Black parents who had signed on to the lawsuit. DeLaine's home and church were both burned, and he was forced to flee to New York City in 1955 after surviving an attempted drive-by shooting. Harry Briggs, the lead plaintiff, and his wife, Eliza, both lost their jobs. Harry had worked as a gas station attendant for sixteen years before his boss fired him. He reflected that,

There didn't seem to be much danger to it. But after the petition was signed, I knew it was different. The white folks got kind of sour. They asked me to take my name off the petition. My boss, he said did I know what I was doin' and I said, "I'm doin' it for the benefit of my children." He didn't say nothin' back. But then later—it was the day before Christmas—he gave me a carton of cigarettes and then he let me go. He said, "Harry, I want me a boy—and I can pay him less than you."[15]

Briggs's wife, Eliza, cleaned rooms at the local hotel. When questioned about her involvement in the case, she recalled, "They told me that they were under a lot of pressure to get me and one of the other women working there to take our names off the petition," she said, "or the motel wasn't going to get its supplies delivered anymore." Eliza Briggs told her questioners that her name was not even on the petition. They told her she'd better tell her husband to take his off. She said he was old enough to have a mind of his own and that she wouldn't do that. They told her she no longer had a job. Following their being fired, Harry and Eliza tried farming for a living. But that failed once whites cut off Harry's credit at the local bank. Without credit, he wasn't able to buy the seed or equipment he needed to survive. In order to fight for his family's survival, he drove up to Sumter, a town about twenty miles away, and got a bank loan in that town. When the bank officers found out Harry Briggs was the lead plaintiff in the lawsuit, they immediately called in the loan. The last straw was when, in addition to the fact that he and his wife had lost their jobs and no banks would lend to them despite pristine credit, the family's cow broke loose and damaged a gravestone in a local cemetery. Policemen came and arrested the cow.[16]

The Briggses were not the only petitioners targeted for retribution. The white community response to Blacks in the town petitioning the court for equal educational treatment was an economic wrecking ball aimed at the heart of the Black community. One of the signers of the petition, Bo Stokes, was fired from his position at a local garage. Teachers were let go, farmers were denied access to the local cotton gin, and

Mrs. Maisie Solomon not only lost her job at the motel, but was also tossed off the land her family rented. John Edward Mc-Donald, a veteran of Iwo Jima and Okinawa, couldn't get financing for a tractor to farm his hundred acres, and Lee Richardson, who had a hefty debt outstanding at McClary's feed store, was told to pay up at once . . . McClary's people were about to seize Richardson's two mules as payment when Black community members passed the hat for him.[17]

In addition, the owners of the Fleming-DeLaine funeral home, one of whom was a family member of Reverend DeLaine, who initially organized community members to participate in the lawsuit, soon learned that Black sharecroppers on some farms were no longer allowed to bring their dead to him for burial because he was Reverend DeLaine's nephew. They got the message when a family brought in their infant for burial soon after the lawsuit was filed but had to come collect the child because their white boss, who had previously agreed to pay the bill, refused to pay anyone with the last name of DeLaine. Despite their travails, the community stood strong: "We ain't asking for anything that belongs to these white folks," said Reverend J.W. Seals of St. Mark's. "I just mean to get for that little Black boy of mine everything that any other South Carolina boy gets—I don't care if he's as white as the drippings of snow." As with the other *Brown* cases, it was initially for naught as the court ruled against them. Upon appeal, it was tapped to be one of the *Brown* cases.[18]

Kansas

In many ways, this case, though the namesake and best known of the group bundled together in *Brown*, was the least eventful in terms of organic grassroots activism. Initiated by members of the local NAACP chapter in Topeka, Kansas, it involved thirteen

parents who volunteered to test the legality of racial segregation in schools by attempting to enroll their twenty children in
white schools in their neighborhoods. They were all turned away.
In 1950, the Topeka Board of Education operated separate elementary schools under a post–Reconstruction era, 1879 Kansas
law that allowed districts that chose to do so to maintain separate elementary school facilities for Black and white students in
communities with populations over fifteen thousand. The case,
Oliver Brown et al. v. The Board of Education of Topeka, Kansas,
was named after Oliver Brown as a legal strategy. The NAACP
thought a man would be better received by the judges.[19]

In 1950, his daughter Linda, a third grader, had to walk six
blocks to her school bus stop to ride to Monroe Elementary, her
segregated Black school one mile away, despite the fact that Sum-
ner Elementary, a white school, was seven blocks from her house.
Linda Brown Thompson later recalled the experience during a
2004 interview for the PBS program *Newshour*:

> Well, like I say, we lived in an integrated neighborhood, and I had
> all of these playmates of different nationalities. And so when I
> found out that day that I might be able to go to their school, I was
> just thrilled, you know. And I remember walking over to Sumner
> school with my dad that day and going up the steps of the school,
> and the school looked so big to a smaller child. And I remember
> going inside and my dad spoke with someone and then he went
> into the inner office with the principal and they left me out . . . to
> sit outside with the secretary. And while he was in the inner of-
> fice, I could hear voices and hear his voice raised, you know, as the
> conversation went on. And then he immediately came out of the
> office, took me by the hand, and we walked home from the school.
> I just couldn't understand what was happening because I was
> so sure that I was going to go to school with Mona, Guinevere,
> Wanda, and all of my playmates.[20]

Strategy notwithstanding, the district court still ruled against the parents and in favor of the Board of Education, once again, as in a number of the other cases, relying on the Supreme Court precedent set in *Plessy v. Ferguson*, which had upheld a state law requiring "separate but equal" segregated facilities in railway cars. They noted that, in Topeka, "the physical facilities, the curricula, courses of study, qualification and quality of teachers, as well as other educational facilities in the two sets of schools [were] comparable." They further found that "colored children in many instances are required to travel much greater distances than they would be required to travel could they attend a white school," but also noted that the school district "transports colored children to and from school free of charge" and that "[n]o such service [was] provided to white children." They did note that segregation in public education had a detrimental effect on Black children. Because this was the one case not located in the South, it became the lead case of the five bundled together that would ultimately result in the Supreme Court declaring racial segregation in schools unconstitutional.[21]

After *Brown*

Given how hard white school boards, courts, and communities worked to keep it from happening, it should not surprise anyone that the white backlash to the case was massive. In Little Rock, Arkansas, Melba Patillo-Beals recalls that she was twelve the day the Supreme Court decided the *Brown v. Board of Education* case. She knows because that was the same day a white man attempted to rape her. That day, school officials at her segregated Dunbar Junior High School were so sure about the potential for the ruling inciting white anger against Blacks, they chose to release the students early. As Patillo-Beals made her way home, enjoying the unexpected freedom and walking along daydreaming, she was startled from her thoughts by a male voice she didn't recognize asking if she would like a ride home. Wary, she told him no and continued on her way, only to hear the sound of running feet coming closer to her. As she recounts:

> I couldn't hear anything except for the sound of my saddle shoes pounding the ground and the thud of his feet close behind me. That's when he started talking about "niggers" wanting to go to school with his children and how he wasn't going to stand for it. My cries for help drowned out the sound of his words, but he laughed and said it was no use because nobody would hear me.

Though Melba ran as fast as she could, when her feet became tangled up she fell to the ground, giving her attacker time to catch up. He pulled her down, turned her on her back, slapped her across the face, and began taking his pants down. As Melba continued to fight him, he landed a closed-fist blow across her face. Chillingly, as he ripped at her underpants he said, "I'll show you niggers the Supreme Court can't run my life." Luckily for Melba, just then a friend happened by, hit the man in the head with a rock, and saved her from what was sure to have been a brutally life-altering act of rape. Once we remember that rape is a crime of power, humiliation, and degradation, not passion, or even sex, we realize this scene exemplifies the deep feelings stirred up in whites at the very thought of Black children receiving an education in an integrated classroom.[22]

While some were moved to attempt rape as a means to reassert a culture of white supremacy and domination of Black southerners, others sought to warn white community members that the request for educational autonomy was much more ominous than perhaps they knew. Joseph Kamp's thirty-six-page pamphlet *Behind the Plot to Sovietize the South*, first published in 1956, says, "The issue is not simply a question of whether white and Negro children are to play and study together in the schools." What Kamp wants to warn American citizens about is the creeping reality of what he terms "Sovietism." He warns that communism's first goal is to bring about "Black Supremacy," then use that supremacy to bring into being a "Soviet South" with the ultimate goal of a "Soviet America." Integrating southern schools was then merely a steep slide down a much more treacherous slope that would lead directly to the takeover of the entire nation.[23]

Given the depth and nature of resistance to racially integrated educational spaces, it is no wonder that segregated schools were not immediately abolished in the South. Many segregationists actually viewed the ruling as somewhat vague, if not timid. There were not, after all, either specific timelines for implementation or any real consequences for disobeying, and, as such, it wasn't clear that they needed to pay the new law much mind. Others, however, went to great lengths to openly and spectacularly resist. In 1957, Arkansas governor Orval Faubus called out the National Guard to block nine Black children in Little Rock from entering the previously all white Central High School. The integration of the high school in Little Rock is one of the most recognizable acts of southern resistance to the integration of public schools. Little Rock became ingrained in public memory because it was covered extensively by the press and on television, where the images of the white violence accompanying educational integration created nothing less than a spectacle. What news reporters termed The "Crisis at Little Rock" escalated to such an extent that President Dwight Eisenhower had to call out the 101st Airborne army regiment to ensure the Black students could even enter the building.

In addition to numerous threats against the children themselves, the entrance to the school was blocked by screaming and cursing white parents and young people howling racial epithets and threatening beatings, lynchings, and sexual violation. Even once the presence of soldiers and combat-ready weaponry ensured that the children could at least enter the school and attempt to learn, the integration experiment did not proceed smoothly. As described in her memoir about her year spent integrating the school, Melba Patillo-Beals recalled that each child had a soldier assigned to help them evade the attacks that rained down upon them. Evasion was the only option because the soldiers' orders precluded them from physically restraining or in any way physically confronting any of the whites inside the building. Even with soldiers following them around, the children had dynamite thrown at them while in the school stairway, a white classmate hurled acid in one young woman's face, and teachers and students alike physically and verbally harassed and bullied them. Only one of the children graduated from the school that year, and at the end of the school year, rather than accept integration, politicians and community members chose to close all of the high schools in Little Rock. What followed is known as the Lost Year, which refers to the 1958–1959 school year when, instead of complying with desegregation, Governor Faubus closed Little Rock's four high schools. The decision denied a total of 3,665 students, both Black and white, access to public education by locking them all out of the schools.

There were a few events that set the the Lost Year in motion. First, the Little Rock School Board requested a delay in implementing desegregation at Central High and, in response, a federal judge granted a three-year reprieve from federally mandated integration efforts. The NAACP, of course understanding that this was a delay tactic, immediately petitioned the U.S. Supreme Court to overturn the decision. Before the Supreme Court could rule, however, the Eighth Circuit Court of Appeals agreed with the NAACP that the delay was a slap in the face of the rule of law in the United States. It said, "We say the time has not yet come in these United States when an order of a federal court must be whittled away, altered down or shamefully withdrawn in the face of violent and unlawful acts of individual citizens in opposition thereto." The ruling meant that desegregation was still to take place immediately in Little Rock.[24]

In response, Governor Faubus called for an emergency session of the Arkansas General Assembly, which quickly passed sixteen separate bills, all designed to make implementation of the federal law difficult if not impossible. Act 4 gave lawmakers the right to simply close any school in the state that was "threatened" with court-ordered racial integration. Another, Act 5, allowed state monies to follow any white student faced with racial integration to either public or private schools. The act did not allow for the same considerations for Black students. Despite the fact that the federal government had ruled that states had to racially integrate, Arkansas had now legislated new segregationist legal ground on which it could stand as the state fought back against the ruling. Whites could both close public schools and have access to local, state, and federal school funds that allowed them to send their children to all white schools—public or private. Legislators also sought to exact retribution on the NAACP and on teachers who were thought to support integration efforts. Act 10 required all teachers and public employees to "sign affidavits listing all organizations to which they belonged and/or paid dues," while Act 115 made it possible to immediately fire any teacher or state employee who was a member of the NAACP. Interestingly, though no academic work was conducted in public high schools in 1958–1959, by order of Governor Faubus, high school football games continued for the season.[25]

In response to the continued defiance on the part of Arkansas state legislators, the U.S. Supreme Court met in special session in September 1958 and ordered that its desegregation order be immediately implemented at Central High School. Not the least bit deterred, the same day as the Supreme Court ruling Governor Faubus signed all sixteen bills previously passed by the Arkansas General Assembly. They required voter approval to become law.

On election day, the ballots read simply: "For racial integration of all schools within the Little Rock School District" and "yes" or "no" were the only available options offered. By a three-to-one margin, voters overwhelmingly voted in support of Governor Faubus and racial segregation. The costs were staggering. White leaders attempted to form a private school corporation empowered to lease closed public school buildings and hire public school teachers in order to continue to teach white children, but federal courts prevented this. Soon, new private schools opened to accommodate displaced white students and taxpayer funds could be used to fund their educations.[26]

Of course, the biggest impact was on Black students and their families. Nearby school districts absorbed as many students as they could. Other students attended out-of-state public and private schools, took correspondence courses, or applied for early entrance into college. Some students moved in with relatives in other parts of Arkansas or out of state. All told, 93 percent of white students found some form of schooling either in Little Rock or in nearby towns. This was not the case for displaced Black students. Among the 750 Black students who were denied access to public schools that year, only 200 or so found a place in public schools to attend in Little Rock; 50 percent never found another school. Whatever the choices the students made, the impact of the closure surely lasted a lifetime.[27]

The Lost Year ended when voters went to the polls and voted to recall the segregationist members of the Little Rock School Board who were most intent about keeping Little Rock schools closed if it meant even one school had to be integrated. The schools had by then been closed for a year. While the vote allowed schools to reopen and affirmed that the city was ready for racial integration, in practice the numbers of Black children placed in white schools was tiny, a maximum of three in any one school. It was racial integration in name only. Though Little Rock's drama was coming to an end, the efforts on the part of the South's white citizenry to keep their schools racially segregated and federal and state education funds firmly in the hands of whites would continue apace, and indeed grow. Such efforts were so popular and successful that when asked by the press about his congressional leadership of anti-integration efforts, Senator Byrd of Virginia, one of the leaders of southern resistance, declared, "If we can organize the Southern States for massive resistance to this order I think that in time the rest of the country will also realize that racial integration will not work."[28]

Though Little Rock's history might have been more extensive and extreme than some other states, all across the South, states learned various lessons about how they too might slow their own schools from integrating. However, even without such efforts, fear, lack of transportation, and other practical considerations kept most public school students, both Black and white, in largely (or completely) segregated schools. By 1958, the so-called massive resistance to desegregation was fully in place and took the form of laws passed to prevent the integration of public schools in a variety of ways. Across the South, a spate of legislation made its way into law that cut off state funds for schools with integrated student bodies or automatically closed any public school that agreed to integrate. Others authorized tuition grants, using state funds for white students who opposed attending integrated schools. In addition, southern officials throughout the states of the former Confederacy created new agencies, like Mississippi's Pupil Placement Boards. These all-white governing bodies were given the sole power to assign specific students to particular schools and, not surprisingly, used their authority to assign white students to schools that were white and Black students to those where the student body was likewise Black. Other states instituted so-called Freedom of Choice plans under which families and students could opt to attend the public school of their choice. White parents always chose white schools for their children and Black parents who might also choose a white school for their children were threatened until they rethought their "choice." Some states even created tuition-grant structures that could channel funds formerly allocated to now-closed schools to students so they could attend private, segregated schools of their choice. In practice, this caused the creation of what came to be known as segregation academies. These were private white schools funded totally by private donations and tax dollars, some of which were contributed by Black families. Within a decade, these segregation academies would be an accepted part of the southern educational landscape.[29]

In 1959, after Arkansas "integrated," Virginia was one of only seven states that still maintained completely segregated public schools; the others were South Carolina, Georgia, Alabama, Florida, Mississippi, and Louisiana. Those were the states where taxpayer-supported segregation academies proliferated. It would not be until 1964 that South Carolina would open its first segregation academy. That same year, the White Citizens' Council, based in Mississippi, opened the first of a chain of thirteen segregation academy schools across the South. They too were funded by taxpayer dollars. Black children were forbidden to attend. Though today perhaps a dubious distinction, in 1959 Virginia's Prince Edward Academy was the first such school. It wouldn't be the last.[30]

By the late spring of 1959, all of Prince Edward County's public schools were officially closed because of the "integration threat." White community leaders had only three months to complete the work of opening a new private school for white students. There were 1,500 white children in the county, and in addition to their needing a building within which to be educated, the county needed money to fund the undertaking. The first step, according to an interview conducted by Kristen Green for her book on the history of Prince Edward Academy with Robert T. Redd, the longtime headmaster, was to raise money. He recalled that the white academy had already raised about $11,000 before the board of supervisors' historic vote to end public education in 1959, and its directors wanted to secure an additional $200,000 that had been pledged years earlier. The private school foundation would also be supported by tuition grants from the state and tax credits from the county. The board of supervisors in 1960 would adopt a tuition grant law that provided one hundred dollars for each child from county funds and allowed taxpayers to donate up to 25 percent of their real and personal property taxes to a private school.[31]

After one year, a federal judge found taxpayer-funded aid for segregated schools to be illegal. No matter. Upon hearing the news, whites from all over the country donated money to support the school. In addition, in order to help get the school off the ground, officials helped themselves to public school resources, simply taking whatever they needed from the closed, locked, and abandoned public schools. They took books, desks, and even goalposts for a new football field at the private, whites-only school. A local businessman, Robert Taylor, recalled that officials took "everything but the clocks."[32]

According to Green, "by 1969, three hundred thousand students were enrolled in all-white schools across eleven southern states. And twenty years after *Brown*, in 1974, 10 percent of the South's white school-age children were attending private schools," most of which had opened in response to white distress over the *Brown* case. Across the South, "3,500 academies enrolled 750,000 white children. In Jackson, Mississippi, white enrollment in the public schools fell by twelve thousand students, from more than half of the student body in 1969 to less than a third eight years later." Their effect was to help create underfunded, all-Black public school systems in the rural South. In 1961, only 6 percent of Black children across the South were attending integrated schools. This was true in part because various terror campaigns, both economic and physical, launched against Black people by white segregationists ensured that Blacks "chose" to stay in under-funded, segregated schools. Those who attempted to do otherwise were subjected to numerous forms of both physical and economic intimidation such as job loss, eviction, threatening phone calls, and physical attack.[33]

As a result of the ultimate failure of the court ruling in the *Brown* decision to achieve real change, it fell to Congress to step in and attempt to ensure that school integration would actually be followed by recalcitrant southerners. The unlikely vehicle was the Civil Rights Act of 1964, which, while primarily targeting private discrimination, also contained two provisions that greatly aided the federal government in desegregating public schools. The act allowed the Justice Department to step in and file suits in the name of the federal government against schools that refused to integrate and also enabled federal officials to withhold funding from segregated schools. These two provisions proved successful and, at the end of 1966, the Johnson administration had termi-nated federal funds for thirty-two southern school districts based on their refusal to end racial segregation in schools. In addition, as journalist Ian Millhiser has noted, when President Johnson left office, the Justice Department was investigating over 600 school districts and had terminated funding for more than 120 of them. Turning the economic power of the federal government loose on segregationist southern governments was what finally broke the back of state-sanctioned segregation in the South. By 1973, al-most 90 percent of southern schoolchildren attended integrated schools. However, integration is hardly the same thing as ensuring educational equality. As W.E.B. DuBois contended in 1935, "the-oretically the Negro needs neither segregated schools nor mixed schools. What he needs is education." The truth of that sentiment cannot be overstated.[34]

Today, school segregation for Blacks, Latinos, and poor stu-dents has now returned to levels we haven't seen since the 1960s. In our present moment, 60 percent to 80 percent of districts in major metropolitan areas such as Chicago, New York, Philadelphia, Los Angeles, and Dallas have schools that are overwhelmingly segregated by race and economic level. It didn't have to be this way. On the one hundredth anniversary of the original Emancipation Proclamation ending enslavement in the United States, Martin Luther King Jr. asked President John F. Kennedy to take the bold step of signing a second proclamation, this one aimed at eliminating all forms of segregation, both racial and economic. He asked that the president make discrimination based on those factors illegal. As King said at a June 1961 press conference about his proposal, "Just as Abraham Lincoln had the vision to see almost 100 years ago that this nation could not exist half-free, the present administration must have the insight to see that today the nation cannot exist half segregated and half-free." President Kennedy considered it but ultimately declined to sign such an executive order. But King's sentiment is no less true for us today. Ultimately, that is the lesson of educational segregation in our present. It has a past, is with us today, but doesn't have to have a future.[35]

The Past in the Present

On August 9, 2014, officer Darren Wilson fatally shot Mike Brown, an eighteen-year-old unarmed Black teenager, in Ferguson, Missouri. The disputed circumstances of the shooting ignited long-standing tensions in the predominantly Black St. Louis suburb, led to sustained protests, and, along with other such shootings that took place within a few months of each other, became a catalyst for an international movement against police brutality. Participants in the movement organized themselves both locally and internationally under the slogan Black Lives Matter. Four months later, *Pro Publica* reporter Nikole Hannah-Jones published a story about the racial and economic struggles of the area's school system and the difficulties its Black residents had long endured while trying to secure quality public education. Focusing on a school system that was bankrupt, unaccredited, and full of students who were overwhelmingly poor and non-white, the exposé made clear that abuse at the hands of the police was but one of the systemic and societal ills that Black children had to navigate as they progressed toward adulthood. In Mike Brown's Ferguson, where *urban* meant non-white and poor and *suburban* meant white and affluent, segregation became both a catalyst and a proxy for educational achievement itself.

Racial and economic segregation, racially specific forms of educational instruction and testing, subpar facilities, undertrained teachers, and white parents determined to keep Blacks out of their more stable and functional school systems were all as much a part of Michael Brown's life as they were for the students involved in the cases that formed the plaintiff group in *Brown v. Board*. Indeed, the school system from which Mike Brown had graduated, Normandy, had lost its accreditation the year preceding his death. As a result, in the fall of 2013 nearly one thousand Normandy students, representing almost a quarter of the district's enrollment, left the schools in that district and attempted to move to schools in nearby accredited, suburban districts. All of the districts in which the Black students attempted to enroll were affluent and overwhelmingly white. Offering rationales uncomfortably reminiscent of those offered by white parents in the pre–*Brown v. Board* South, the parents in the suburban Missouri districts objected to the influx of Black children, saying that they were concerned the students would lower the schools' test scores and negatively impact the value of the education their own children received. They were also worried that an increase in Black students would lead to more violence and disorder and necessitate new and unfamiliar security measures, such as metal detectors and private police officers. However, once the courts made clear that they had no choice, the white districts relented, though the complaints never ceased.[36]

According to Hannah-Jones, the temporary desegregation of the school districts surrounding Ferguson, Missouri, was as lucrative for the more affluent white school districts as it was financially unsustainable for the districts that were poor and nonwhite. This was true because the state of Missouri required failing and unaccredited districts whose students were allowed to transfer to neighboring areas to pay the complete cost of the children's education in the adjoining districts. For the whiter, more affluent districts, it was a replay of what had happened during the long-abandoned court-ordered desegregation plan designed to bring the state schools into compliance with the *Brown* decision. At that time, during the 1980s, transfer students were referred to as "Black gold" because of the high level of profit the all-white systems were able to make for themselves by educating Black children. By 2014, the millions of dollars in payments to other districts had drained Normandy's finances, and in only a few months, the district shuttered an elementary school and laid off 40 percent of its staff. Already deeply troubled, the Normandy schools were headed toward a complete financial collapse.

In a statement that harkens back to the late 1960s, when state and federal officials struggled to both comply with desegregation orders and appease white residents concerned about forced integration, in 2014 one of Missouri's top education officials admitted that anytime white school districts are forced to take in poor students from majority Black school districts, the resulting firestorm can lay bare the ways that racial divisions shape education, among other issues. Indeed, what these tensions are all about—race, money, housing, and economic inequality—have long defined Black education. Today, as the contemporary battle to educate the schoolchildren of Ferguson, Missouri, illustrates, such unresolved tensions loom large. Unfortunately, failed free-market solutions, such as vouchers promising poor parents of color freedom of choice, do so as well.[37]

4

HOW THE NORTH WASN'T ONE

If the period between 1915 and 1968 makes clear how, in regard to education, continued segregation and the economic rewards of white supremacy combined to become a lucrative norm in the South, the story of northern desegregation is the other side of this two-headed coin. There, public school integration efforts stalled because of an equally racially segregated metropolitan landscape and comparably persistent concerns about the financial and electoral costs of forcing white communities to participate in the schooling of Black children. These issues came to a frothy head in the 1970s when President Richard Nixon lobbied fiercely against including the white suburbs in the busing and other desegregation orders covering public schools. The result was that by the 1970s, decades after the 1954 *Brown v. Board* decision made such practices illegal, America's northern urban school system remained overwhelmingly separate and unequal, though now the intractable problem was one of geography as much as racism. In many cities, whites had overwhelmingly picked up and moved to the suburbs out of the reach of municipal desegregation orders. Blacks were left behind in urban cities with chronically underfunded schools, and the federal government was increasingly unwilling to fund the buses that would make meaningful efforts at racial integration possible. It didn't take long for business interests backed by the federal government to find a way to profit from educational segregation and poverty.

This chapter looks at both the educational context and historical backdrop of how urban education became synonymous with
race, poverty, and violence and suburban districts with wealth and
prosperity. It explores the role of the federal government in bringing about these conflicts between place and educational quality
once it was decided to abandon, or at least avoid, educational integration as a national priority. In response, from the late 1960s
through the early 1980s, Black parents and community members
started and maintained innovative, high-quality private schools
specifically geared toward the education of Black children. They
did so in order to address the undereducation of their children in
the apartheid schools in which they had lost all faith. They opened
private schools because it became clear to them that if they did
not, no one else would. This chapter ends with a look at the rise
of privatized segrenomic educational schemes, such as vouchers,
designed specifically for inner-city schools.

When in 1954 the Supreme Court ruled in the *Brown v. Board
of Education* case that *de jure*, or legally, segregated school systems
were unconstitutional, most northern school districts, courts,
and politicians claimed the decision did not apply to them because they did not have racial segregation written into law. In the
North, lawyers and politicians argued that racial segregation was
based on racist discrimination in housing, not schools. Schools
just so happened to be segregated, they said, because neighborhoods were. This de facto segregation, though damaging to the
prospects of societal advancement for American citizens who were
poor and of color, was legal, they said. Of course, the NAACP argued that the *Brown* decision should apply to de facto segregation
as well, and civil rights groups sued school boards in cities such as
Cincinnati, Ohio; Detroit, Michigan; Richmond, California; and
Boston, Massachusetts, among others, urging school districts to
integrate. But in the 1960s North, rising levels of anti-integration
activism, not courtroom battles, most forcefully brought the issues of race, segregation, and education to a head. Busing was key.[1]

By the early 1960s, southern courts and school districts were struggling to make the case that they could legally educate Blacks with racially separate but equally funded schools. White nationalist citizens' councils had opened chains of whites-only charter school–like segregation academies across the urban South, and in cities like New York there was also great concern among citizens and elected officials alike about the *Brown* decision. Some wanted New York to get a jump on desegregating schools, while others were worried that they should get an equally early jump on repelling any legislative efforts to force racial integration upon them. Black parents and civil rights advocates, like seasoned activist Ella Baker and sociologist Kenneth Clark—whose research with his wife Mamie was central to the *Brown* decision—urged city officials to institute desegregation plans. Whites who opposed mandatory-integration decrees protested as well, with white parents and politicians expressing their opposition to plans to bus Black and Latino students between Harlem and the predominantly white Staten Island. There were also rallies to oppose plans to "transfer students between predominantly Black and Puerto Rican schools and white schools."[2]

In the spring of 1963, the Massachusetts Freedom Movement, a coalition of civil rights groups, organized a school boycott that kept a quarter of Boston's Black students at home. Then, in one of the largest civil rights demonstrations on record, in New York, in February 1964 "more than 460,000 students and teachers stayed out of school to protest the lack of a comprehensive plan for desegregation." These protests attracted national attention from the news media, and United States congressmen who were debating the Civil Rights Act in the spring of 1964 could not have helped but notice. Historian Matthew Delmont believes that this is how it came to be that the Civil Rights Act of 1964, credited with breaking the back of organized southern white resistance to educational integration by tying federal funding to school desegregation efforts, at the same time included an antibusing provision.

Designed to calm the fears of the protesting white parents and politicians in New York and other northern cities, the legislation promised that white communities would not be forced to integrate their suburban or all-white urban schools. The government would not pay for the buses that would make it possible for racial integration in schools to take place. That decision was a blow to civil rights activists, many of whom had been confident that the Johnson administration would keep its promise to confront the issue of de facto segregation in the North. While the Johnson administration urged racially imbalanced northern school districts to take steps to correct the imbalance, it forbade the use of either busing or federal funds to do so.[3]

The northern story of education, economics, and politics is well illustrated by a popular saying among southern civil rights leaders: "In the South, the white man doesn't care how close you get, as long as you don't get too high. In the North, he doesn't care how high you get, as long as you don't get too close." That was surely one of the "northern" lessons Dr. Martin Luther King Jr. learned in 1966 when he attempted to take his primarily southern civil rights campaign north. When he arrived in Chicago in 1966, unlike his political activities in the South, he didn't go to march for Black voting rights. Blacks in Illinois had been voting in the state since the nineteenth century. They even had their own political structure, complete with Black aldermen, legislators, and congressmen. Rather than the right to vote, King went to Chicago to press for an end to racial segregation. He saw this as a first step toward increased racial and economic integration and specifically chose Chicago because it was known as the most segregated city in America. Earlier that year, King had urged those of a like mind to "march on segregated schools until every vestige of segregated and inferior education becomes a thing of the past, and Negroes and whites study side-by-side in the socially-healing context of the classroom." Many northern whites were opposed to such "side-by-side" healing in both housing and education. As far as they were concerned, Blacks could reach social heights in terms of politics and career, but they were not at all allowed to live near or go to school with whites. That is where the line was drawn. These sentiments breathed life into a hardening body of thought and called forth public policy solutions centered around educational segregation in the urban North.[4]

Mayor Richard Daley of Chicago had few peers when it came to resisting integration. He worked hard to keep the city segregated because he feared that if he did otherwise it would almost guarantee that middle-class whites would flee to the suburbs and take their tax dollars with them. In addition, racial integration could weaken the economic and political prospects for the powerful— Black and white both. An all-Black "ghetto" guaranteed Black politicians a political base in ways that were not guaranteed by racially integrated neighborhoods. In all, racial segregation was both financially and politically beneficial to the powerful and well connected across the northern color line. Many white northerners had as little interest in educational integration as did their southern kinfolks. Instead of closing whole school districts, they simply voted with their feet, left the cities, and to a large extent set up their own school systems in the suburbs that did not bar Blacks from attending but did little or nothing to encourage their presence.[5]

In some cities, like Boston, Chicago, and Philadelphia, elected officials were able to promise and deliver to white parents a level of racial segregation in city schools that kept them from decamping to the suburbs. In other cities, like Detroit, Baltimore, Newark, and St. Louis, whites were moving in increasingly large numbers to predominantly white suburbs by the middle of the 1960s. Termed "white flight," white migration from city to suburb was as significant in terms of Black education as had been the movement of Blacks from rural areas to cities. For example, in 1957 in Baltimore, Maryland, the Clifton Park Junior High School had 2,023 white students and 34 Black students; ten years later, it had 12 white students and 2,037 Black students. In northwest Baltimore, Garrison Junior High School's student body shifted from 2,504 whites and 12 Blacks to 297 whites and 1,263 Blacks in that same period. There may have been, with creativity and commitment, a way to stem the white urban–suburban tide. But then the riots came to urban America.[6]

Race, Riots, and Education

In May of 1968, the National Advisory Commission on Civil Disorders, known as the Kerner Commission, released a report announcing that racism was to blame for the surge of violent uprisings that had engulfed American cities over the previous few years. President Lyndon Johnson had formed the eleven-member bipartisan commission, headed by Illinois governor Otto Kerner. In his charge to them, the president told the commission that he wanted to know the following: "What happened? Why did it happen? What can be done to prevent it from happening again and again?" They were nothing if not thorough given that the report clocked in at over seven hundred pages. After identifying more than 150 incidents of unrest between 1965 and 1968, they said that though many, such as the powerful FBI director J. Edgar Hoover, believed the rising tide of Black militancy, including individual Black militants, was the cause of the violence, their findings made clear that "white racism" was in fact to blame. After asserting in what would become the most memorable single line from the report that "our nation is moving toward two societies, one Black, one white—separate and unequal," the report called for expanded aid in order to foster greater educational, economic, and employment options and outcomes for urban Black communities as a means of preventing further violence.[7]

In regard to education, the commission affirmed that a

democratic society "must equip children to develop their potential to participate fully in American life." As commission members traveled across the country conducting interviews, they found that for white and wealthy students, the schools "discharged their responsibilities well." However, unsurprisingly, the commission found that children attending schools in urban ghettos across the whole of the country were not as well served. Their schools "have failed to provide the educational experiences which could overcome the effects of discrimination and deprivation." In terms of how the urban uprisings were fueled by the poor educational system, they said that failing schools were one of the most persistent sources of grievance and resentment in urban Black communities and that "the hostility of Negro parents and students toward the school system is generating increasing conflict and causing disruption" in many cities. Additionally, the report noted a high incidence of riot participation "by ghetto youth who have not completed high school."

Before turning to solutions, they offered a sobering assessment: the "bleak record of public education for ghetto children is growing worse. . . . Negro students are falling further behind whites with each year of school completed . . . and the underemployment rate for Negro youth is evidence, in part, of the growing educational crisis." In cities in the North and South alike, the commission found education for poor Blacks to still be separate and unequal. Having diagnosed the extent of the problem confronting the nation, the members of the Kerner Commission offered a tentative treatment plan, if not a promising cure. They began by saying that they thought racial integration was the priority and was indeed essential to the future of American society as a whole, noting that the riots themselves offered an example of "the consequences of racial isolation at all levels, and of attitudes toward race, on both sides, produced by three centuries of myth, ignorance and bias. It is indispensable that opportunities for interaction between the races be expanded." However, at the same time, they acknowledged that the migration of whites out of urban areas had left a racial imbalance in city schools that would not be easily reversed. They added, "No matter how great the effort toward desegregation, many children of the ghetto will not, within their school careers, attend integrated schools."

Accordingly, the committee proposed finding ways to take seriously any creative solutions to improving poor urban schools to such a level where they could be considered equal to all white schools. In order to give Black children the educational chance they were currently denied, the commission recommended a sharp increase in "efforts to eliminate de facto segregation in our schools through substantial federal aid to school systems seeking to desegregate either within the system or in cooperation with neighboring school systems." It also called on the government to enforce federal laws governing racial discrimination in both the North and the South and called for intensive year-round "compensatory education programs, improved teaching, and expanded experimentation and research . . . and the creation of greater opportunities for parents and community members to participate in public schools," among other recommendations. President Johnson rejected all of the recommendations the committee proposed. In response to recommendations found in other areas of the report, he did authorize hiring more urban police and giving them more weapons.

While the South often receives a lion's share of the focus on the difficulty in racially integrating our nation's schools, the North was far from enlightened. The schools there were certainly not integrated, and there didn't seem to be much urgency to make them so. One of the educational questions continuously confronting parents, educators, and communities was whether an integrated education with whites was actually the only path to equal education for Black children. The second, equally persistent query was about how integration could possibly be accomplished if large swaths of white communities simply refused to participate. In the process, northern communities began to re-litigate the supposedly resolved matter of schools' continuing to be separate—but more equally funded—spaces. Those who were not eager to force whites to integrate found an advocate in the new president, Richard Nixon.

Soon after taking office in 1969, Nixon dropped the government's plans to withhold funds from southern school districts that remained segregated, and he backed southern attempts to postpone the 1970 deadline for the abolition of segregated schools. Nixon and his attorney general John Mitchell used the rhetoric of "community control" to explain the administration's opposition to busing. This was not quite the same thing as the "states' rights" arguments that southerners had historically made to justify their practices in opposition to federal policy, but it was close. As one observer noted, for the first time since the 1954 *Brown* decision an administration "openly sided with segregationists." Nixon's reluctance to force northern compliance with desegregation orders emboldened whites all over the country who themselves saw nothing particularly wrong with racially segregated schools. As the debate intensified, the mood turned uglier.

In 1970, a mob of two hundred whites attacked buses carrying thirty-five Black school children in Lamar, South Carolina. The next year, in Pontiac, Michigan, whites bombed ten empty school buses. Six members of the Ku Klux Klan were indicted for the crime. Even these violent acts were not enough to convince President Nixon or other political elites to throw their legal and ethical weight and authority behind efforts to desegregate public schools.[8] Instead of acknowledging these acts of domestic terrorism by white racists against Black children and communities, when speaking of the mood of the country Nixon said to his domestic adviser H.R. Haldeman that "you have to face the fact that the whole problem is really the Blacks. The key is to devise a system that recognizes this while not appearing to." Among other things, Black families and children were to be blamed for wanting

a quality education, as opposed to blaming those whites who vehe-
mently opposed racial integration.[9]

As the 1972 presidential elections approached, Nixon decided
that he needed to find a way to win the votes of the whites who
were opposed to racial integration if he was going to win reelection. The problem for him was that a former governor of Alabama,
George Wallace, was already very popular with voters who believed deeply in racial separation, and he had a history that made
it very clear where he stood in relation to the topic. In 1963, as
governor of Alabama, Wallace stood in front of a door to the University of Alabama, saying that he would never support enrolling
Black students at the school and declaring his support for "segregation now, segregation tomorrow, segregation forever." Almost
ten years later, during the 1972 presidential campaign, he told voters that his earlier views remained intact and promised that if he
were elected, he would propose a national moratorium on all busing aimed at bringing about racial integration in public schools.
In terms of campaign strategy, the problem for Nixon was that
if he were going to prove himself a suitable candidate to racists
who supported racial segregation, he needed to get himself firmly
on the antibusing side of the public-school integration debate. In
order to do so, he made it clear that he opposed busing and that
without federal support for busing Black schoolchildren could not
integrate into suburban schools and white children could, instead
of being bused, remain in their neighborhood schools.

While the beliefs of those at the top of the political ticket were
important, it is equally important to note that, across a variety of
political beliefs, in 1970s America there was little to no political
will to fund measures that would allow for racial integration in
public schools. It is an understatement to say that busing was unpopular among many northern whites. In Congress, antibusing
legislation was just as likely to come from politicians considered
northern moderates or "liberals" as it was from those considered
southern racists or "conservatives." That may explain the fact that

the proposal for the federal government to refuse to fund the purchase of gasoline for school buses if they were going to be used to transport Black children to white schools came from John Dingell, a Democrat from the Detroit suburbs. White voters in his district had made their resistance to accepting Black students loudly clear. Similarly, Democrats Joseph Biden from Delaware and Birch Bayh from Indiana each introduced legislation to either severely limit or prohibit outright busing across district lines if it was for the purpose of school desegregation. Of course, they undertook these actions in response to political pressure from their suburban constituents, but the point remains that in this matter they chose to follow racially tinged thinking instead of leading by example.[10]

In recalling the period, Nixon aide Bryce Harlow said that many of the Nixon administration's statements on busing were designed to send different messages to different audiences "who could interpret his intentions as they so choose." According to John Ehrlichman, Nixon's domestic affairs adviser, Nixon's "political compass told him to stay away from the whole subject of race." He added though that Nixon and his advisers believed that if he could not completely avoid talking about race, the best political course for him would be to make clear that he was "on the side of the white parents whose children were about to get on those hated buses." Given that most saw him as their ally in the construction of a hypothetical white wall keeping Black children out of their white schools, it meant that Nixon won reelection handily.[11]

With such a political wind at his back, following the election Nixon believed he had a mandate to put the brakes on busing, even if he couldn't officially recommit the nation to legally segregated schools. He seized that moment and proposed the Equal Educational Opportunities Act in 1972. It directed more federal funding to inner-city urban schools. He didn't use the words, but in effect Nixon retreated to the failed logic of separate but equal that the *Brown v. Board* decision had overturned in 1954.

Historian Matthew Delmont summarizes Nixon's actions by stating that "the compromise Nixon offered was quite explicit: students in the city would remain in the city and not be permitted to attend suburban schools; in exchange for staying put, they would get more resources." It was a compromise that responded to white fears about public policies that supported racial integration at the educational expense of urban communities.

The impact of all of this resistance and rhetoric about racial integration in public schools was monstrously impactful on Black people and in Black communities. As the noted activist, intellectual, and playwright of *A Raisin in the Sun*, Lorraine Hansberry, explained in a 1965 speech to writers in the *Monthly Review*,

> Black folk in America have historically regarded education with reverence. All the more poignant and ugly, then, that the withholding of education has been one of the prime instruments of the oppressors of American Negroes—oppressors who have seen to it that even when education could not be entirely withheld it could certainly be made substandard.[12]

A product of Chicago's system herself, Hansberry shared with the crowd that because of her personal experience with America's racially segregated, overcrowded schools in the 1960s, she knew what it felt like to be taught by disinterested teachers and to have school days shortened to accommodate two separate groups of students. Despite tests showing she was considered gifted and was reading at a college level, "To this day, I do not add, subtract, or multiply with ease. . . . This is what we mean when we speak of the scars, the marks that the ghettoized child carries through life. . . . To be imprisoned in the ghetto is at best to be forgotten, or at most to be deliberately cheated out of one's birthright."[13]

While Hansberry's observations were arguably true at the level of the public schools ubiquitously available in poor, urban areas of color and created by the public policies of successive federal, state, and local political administrations, it is worth noting that there were those in urban communities during the 1970s who envisioned very different educational futures for their children. Much like the way rural southern community members had taken responsibility for building schools and hiring teachers to ensure the education of their children, Black parents and community members in Nixon-era America also worked to fill the educational void. They wanted to save the futures of Black children by crafting a very different meaning of and future for the possibility of quality education in America's urban schools.

Black Communities, Black Schools

Ericka Huggins was a young mother and founding member of the Black Panther Party chapters in Los Angeles, California, and New Haven, Connecticut, when she became the director of the Oakland Community School in 1973. From that time until 1982, when the school closed as a result of the disintegration of the Black Panther Party, it was a model for how to educate poor children from struggling urban areas and an award-winning example of how innovative teaching could turn students who were often undereducated in urban public schools into eager students. The school grew out of point No. 5 in the Black Panther Party's Ten Point Program, which called for educating Black and poor people about their "true history" in the United States. Though Huggins often described the school as "a model for education that was replicable anywhere," such high levels of educational replication were rarely evident in poor urban public schools that educated poor children of color. Tuition was basically free for the children who were as young as two and a half and as old as eleven. Most of the costs were covered by donations, and parents didn't have to pay much, if anything. It all worked beautifully. Not only did students attending the school perform, on average, better than students enrolled in surrounding schools, but also in 1976 the Alameda County Board of Supervisors gave the school a special commendation for educational excellence, and in 1977 county lawmakers held a ceremony to recognize the Oakland Community School for its "highly effective service in educating children in the community of Oakland."[14]

Like other schools opened by Black parents and community members during the era, this one had a very particular educational philosophy, the guiding principle of which was that children would be taught "how" more than "what" to think. Huggins was ahead of her time in regard to educational innovations, many of which are just now beginning to gain traction in our contemporary moment. Children attending the school learned meditation and yoga and were assigned to small classes of ten or less based on ability, not age. There were full periods of poetry writing, math, science, foreign languages, history, and current events. In addition, in terms of discipline, a child who misbehaved might be sent outside to stand in tree pose until he had calmed down, and a student advisory board, rather than a principal, meted out discipline when fellow students misbehaved. In short, the Oakland Community School structured an educational environment for poor children of color that was similar to how education was provided in more wealthy schools. It achieved top-notch results. Though this was an educational strategy that would in some ways seem to be self-evident, such interventions were rarely seen in traditional public schools. They were, however, widespread in the Black independent schools that flourished during the period.[15]

In 1975, one particularly notable educator, Marva Collins, took $5,000 from her teacher's retirement fund and used the money to open a private school called Westside Preparatory School. It was located in Garfield Park, an inner-city area of Chicago that was as poor as was the East Oakland neighborhood where the Oakland Community School opened. Collins specifically recruited students who were poor and struggling academically, euphemistically saying she was most interested in recruiting students to her school who were "dirty and smelly." She explained that "when children are poor, self-esteem and excellence are their ticket to being the very best." This was the gift she wanted to give to those students who she believed needed it the most. Both she and her methods proved so successful that in 1980 president-elect Ronald Reagan courted her to become secretary of education. She declined his offer. She thought she could do more in the classroom than as an administrator because, as she said, "Once you teach children how to think they don't need school. If I had my way, I would only teach children science, philosophy, and math because when they learn philosophy they can ask their own questions and find their own answers." In 1988 President George Bush approached her, again asking that she consider setting education policy for the nation. Again, she declined. When President Bush pressed, asking why she did not serve the nation in that position, or even agree to take federal funding to ease the financial pressure she was under running a private school for low-income children whose families couldn't always pay, she responded, "Mr. President, with all due respect, my people never could have failed so miserably without the government's help. I believe in the saying that he who eats my bread does my will." [16]

Collins began her career teaching school in Alabama for two years, then moved to Chicago in 1959. She quickly became frustrated by both the conditions she saw in the segregated inner-city schools in which she taught and the overall low levels of expectations held by both teachers and principals. Saying that she wanted the same education for all Black children as she wanted for her own, she opened her own school. Westside Prep was initially located on the top floor of the brownstone where she and her family lived. At first she only had six students, four children from the neighborhood, plus her own two. [17]

In describing how she came up with her teaching techniques,

she said she knew from fourteen years of teaching that students needed to read, write, and think, and so those pursuits were at the core of her school's curriculum. In addition, she used the Socratic method and exposed them to the "great classics because they expose you to complex thought." Her success with students labeled as "unteachable" by others led to profiles in *Time* and *Newsweek* magazines and television appearances on *60 Minutes*, among other programs. She was as much a motivator as she was an educator, once telling an interviewer, "Every child in our school must tell us what they will do to make their community better, their city better, the world better. Anyone can be locally good, but what do you have to do to make the world better?" [18]

Of course, given her consistent success with educating Black children who were poor and labeled by public schools as impossible to teach, Collins was repeatedly approached about reproducing, if not franchising, her methods so that both she and students outside of Chicago could benefit. In the late 1980s, she turned down the chance to earn $30 million by working with funders who wanted to open one hundred Marva Collins schools across the country. She did so because she said that while the money would have of course altered the lives of her family, not to mention her school, she couldn't go forward with the plan because "I have integrity." She went on to explain that the challenge would be finding enough teachers who were trained in her particular methods and could reproduce her startling results. Unfortunately, despite her not sanctioning them to do so, some unsavory characters used her name without asking. She ended up "in litigation with several people who have started schools in my name only for the fame of it, but the children are doing poorly. It's easy to say you want to replicate this, but people don't want to do the work. You can't give a child a worksheet and say do it. You have to lead the child to excellence." Collins did offer workshops to interested teachers, and did have some success along those lines, but as the one-woman show that she truly was, it was her personal involvement that guaranteed transformational results.

In 1990, Collins agreed to work with over thirty public schools in Oklahoma. Harvard University's Ron Ferguson tracked the progress in eight of the schools. Four of the principals accepted, promoted, and implemented her techniques and strategies with teachers. The principals of the four other schools said they were on board but did not actually do much to promote her methods among the teachers. The results after one year were astounding. The four schools that embraced her structure had an average increase on the Iowa Standardized Test of over 172 percent. One school almost tripled its test scores. The four schools that did not properly use her methods had an increase of only 10 percent. Ferguson concluded that her high expectations made a huge difference.[19]

At the end of 1996, not satisfied with only impacting the educations of students with the money to enroll in her private school, Marva decided to go back into the Chicago public schools with the explicit goal of helping three of the one hundred and nine schools placed on academic probation that year. She specifically asked for the three lowest-achieving schools, in the worst areas, and with the lowest levels of parental involvement. This last qualification was important because, as she said, "The parent is wonderful in an ideal situation, but if I am going to save these children I can't say I can't help these children because of the parents."[20] Similar to the Oklahoma cases, two schools decided to implement the Marva Collins methodology while one school decided not to follow through. After just four months of working with her, the two schools (Beidler Elementary and McNair Elementary) that followed her program had an increase of over 85 percent on mandated state tests, while the other school had an increase of only 10 percent. Beidler and McNair both doubled their test scores in at least one area, and Beidler came off probation.[21]

Collins believed that the Chicago public school system as a whole simply refused to teach many Black children who were poor and instead labeled them as learning disabled. She said that one sure way to improve the education of and for Black children was to "stop talking about what's wrong with Black children who can't learn because if you give them to me for a year, I guarantee you my last life I will give them back to you different children. I would love nothing more in my life than to show that there is nothing wrong with our children." The students who graduated from Collins's Westside Prep were getting scholarships to Northwestern, Yale, and Harvard, and almost 90 percent graduated from college. She said, "The greatest gift of my life is seeing children holding wonder in their eyes like a cup." It is a tremendous shame that more children were not able to drink from her cup as well.[22]

That same sentiment was shared by yet another educator who showed what was possible in urban areas if given the right tools, resources, and teachers. A Philadelphia school named the Ivy Leaf School was begun by a woman named Liller Green. Green was the youngest of five daughters and began reading when she was just a little older than three. As a child growing up in Athens, Georgia, in the 1930s, she was sent by her parents to a one-room preschool run by Mrs. Rosabelle Strickland, a graduate of Spelman College who alternated play periods with blocks of what Green referred to as teaching time, during which the toddlers received academic instruction. Green recounted in an interview that all of the children who attended that small, all-Black school "completed the first-grade curriculum before school age and were fully prepared for school" by the time they were five.

Liller Green and her family moved to Philadelphia when she was seven years old. She attended public schools in the city, earned a master's degree in social work, and met and married William Green when she was in her twenties. In 1965, when her daughter Jan turned three, she wanted her to have a similar preschool experience to what she had known back in Athens, Georgia. She could not find a place for Black children in Philadelphia that offered that kind of structured, rigorous program. Most of what was available to her was a higher form of babysitting. After trying out a few less than successful options, in 1967 Liller and William used their savings and a bank loan to co-found the Ivy Leaf School as a half-day preschool program. One of their informal tag lines made clear that they saw their school and mission as a corrective to the substandard experience of a racist American society: "Before society told children that they can't, we have demonstrated to the children and their parents that they can." Five-year-olds at the school regularly tested as reading on a first or second grade level, and seventh and eighth graders were reading at the college level. Overall, 90 percent of students at the school were reading above grade level.[23]

After its founding, the school expanded rapidly, and the curriculum was organized "to provide experiences that will maximize potential" so that students "will not be disadvantaged by the racism in society." Toward that end, the school focused its curriculum both on mastery of academic basics and on what Green described as "cultural pride and history" as a means of helping her students to succeed. Green believed that such self-esteem-enhancing activities were particularly valuable since she thought it was important to tell the children that "they're eagles and despite barriers, they can soar as high as they want." By 1987, the Ivy Leaf School had almost eight hundred students from kindergarten through eighth grade and had become one of the country's largest independent Black private schools. She described the growth of Black private schools as "a sleeper that just keeps growing all around the country." Green said the school owed its success to the fact that it was first an academic school and then an Afrocentric one. The school's mission statement bore out those priorities, declaring, "Within the framework of a comprehensive academic curriculum, which emphasizes the mastery of academic skills, in which the history and culture of African peoples are taught, Ivy Leaf School seeks to prepare students to become effective and productive leaders of the future."[24]

Like Marva Collins's school and many of the hundreds of others across the country, the Ivy Leaf School quickly developed a long waiting list despite the fact that admission came with a price tag. Other prestigious secondary prep schools in the Philadelphia area, like Baldwin, Springside, and Chestnut Hill Academy, requested that the school refer its top eighth-grade performers to them, promising full scholarships to those they enrolled. Liller thought that the success of her school wasn't widely known because "there is little attempt by anyone to study the success stories in the Black community." Such success stories in regard to independent Black education were, for a time, numerous, and most were achieved by adherence to the philosophy espoused by the Greens at the Ivy Leaf School: "We believe that all students can learn. Students are helped to acquire skills in the ability to think critically, to appreciate the arts and humanities, and to develop practices . . . necessary for maintaining a healthy environment."

This pattern, in which either an individual parent or a group of Black parents turned their backs on traditional public schools completely and began to either homeschool their children or open educational cooperatives or schools based on an ideology of Black liberation, was repeated in cities around the country, especially those under desegregation orders and thus facing the divisive option of sending Black children to previously white schools. Of course, according to Liller, the Ivy Leaf School would welcome white students. White families sometimes brought their children by for a look, but invariably they declined to send their children to the school. She said she didn't know if it was because it was majority Black or not.[25]

Trickle-Down Education and
Profiting from Black Poverty

Dr. Joan Davis Rattcray, president of the Institute for Independent Education, started her enterprise in the mid-1980s specifically to gather statistics about private schools founded and operated by leaders of color. She was also interested in consulting with them as to curriculum, standards, and assessment. During her research, she found about four hundred Black independent schools, most of which had begun between the mid-1960s and early 1970s when President Nixon was in office. In addition, she found at least forty similar schools primarily in urban areas for Latino children, and about a dozen for American Indians. All told, such schools served roughly 45,000 students. Although these schools had differences in terms of curriculum, ideology, and focus, there are striking similarities in their emphasis on academic rigor, high expectations, and structure, and in the fact that they were staffed, attended, owned, and operated almost entirely by non-whites. As Rafferty is quoted saying in an article about the growth of Black private independent schools, "Public schools are putting children into such a chaotic situation, whether it's busing or desegregation, that parents want to get them to a place where they feel at home." She went on to affirm the fact that "Black academies provide a nurturing environment and counter the notion that quality education can be achieved only outside the Black community." Not surprisingly, for parents, sending their children to such schools was preferable.[26]

The vast majority of Black independent schools were opened in densely populated urban areas, and the majority of students served were poor. As a result, there were constant struggles to keep the doors open, and they often had to be creative as to payment methods. Ivy Leaf, for instance, began a practice whereby it would hire parents to work part time at the school in lieu of paying tuition. Despite the hardship of turning to a private school solution, given that Philadelphia's high school dropout rate was approaching 50 percent and that many students who graduated from inner-city public high schools were functionally illiterate, such schools were a godsend for Black parents who could afford them or managed to make a way. The standard of high expectations helped such schools do much more with much less. For example, Ivy Leaf five-year-olds used first- and second-grade readers, and by the age of eleven students were expected to write complex research papers, as did one young man whose paper was titled "How Psychologists Determine When a Person Is Mentally Ill and Some of the Most Effective Treatments." This was far and away more demanding than much of what was taking place in public schools where urban Black children were usually educated.

The success of such schools soon attracted the attention of those who saw a way to advance their own financial and ideological agendas. Where some Black parents saw an opportunity to lead and innovate in methods of Black education by founding independent schools (that could and should have become a model for how the public education system might come to properly educate poor children of color), others, usually not from similarly blighted communities, saw dollar signs—and an opportunity to move the resources earmarked for poor children of color into the hands of schools and districts that were white and affluent. These less noble aims would become a major contributor to the dismantling of public education systems.

Taken as a whole, during this period of time—the mid-1970s through the early 1980s—the northern struggles around racism and education born of segregation were not enshrined in law but were nonetheless as significant if not as lucrative as any scheme thought up by southern segregationists. By then, there were new voices and figures interested in urban education, but their strongest arguments circulated around the potential for financial gain tied to the education of Black children. The business community formulated an all-out assault, and it found an ally in a Reagan administration focused on privatizing education as a means of breaking the grip of big unions and clearing the way for corporate profits. There was quite a bit of profit ripe for extraction from northern apartheid schools. One particularly popular scheme was built on—though differed from—the tactics pioneered during the era of segregation academies in the 1950s and 1960s—school vouchers. Vouchers allow public school children to take taxpayer-collected funds and apply them to the fees associated with private schools and academies. The updated strategy involving vouchers was not based specifically on racist ideologies or on the historical practices of the segregation academies, where taxpayer funds were apportioned solely to white parents in order to educate their children in segregated schools. Yet the intended outcomes did share the goal of dismantling tax-supported public education in urban areas. The cause and effect of vouchers were fundamentally similar to the dynamics in the urban South during the period when segregation academies were a familiar feature.[27]

In 1955, Milton Friedman, a "free market" economist and professor at the University of Chicago, published an essay called "The Role of Government in Education" in a book paradoxically titled *Capitalism and Freedom*. He argued that the only legitimate role for government in regard to public education was to provide the funds, in the form of vouchers, that would enable parents to send their children to the school of their choice. He did not think federal or state governments should be in charge of the oversight or running of schools, or have a role in structuring curriculum. In his thinking, vouchers should replace the funding of public schools and be good for use at any approved school, public or private, religious or secular. He imagined that the government oversight of the voucher program would be "minimal, on par with health inspection at restaurants," and he and others who supported vouchers framed them as an "opportunity" for low-income parents to send their children to public or private schools and escape the struggling public schools in poor urban areas.[28]

While vouchers might have actually helped a few more children receive a better education, that was hardly their primary purpose. A 1984 voucher bill described vouchers as a way to "introduce normal market forces" into education and to "dismantle the control and power of" teachers' unions. By 2006, Friedman was much more clear, saying vouchers were really a step toward "abolishing the public school system." This idea of school choice—the use of tax dollars to expand the options for where Black and poor parents could send their children—would come to undergird a number of late-twentieth-century educational experiments aimed at poor urban communities. Among these experiments were policies that expanded support for public charter schools, alternative licensing plans for teacher training, and magnet schools. Most were at least initially aimed primarily at neighborhoods like those where the Ivy Leaf School, the Oakland Community School, and Westside Prep were located. Instead of choosing to support and expand the footprint and reach of such schools employing practices with proven track records of successfully educating those the public school systems were leaving behind, this new free-market segrenomics—*school choice*—was offered up as the prescriptive cure for centuries of racist policies and actions. An untested ideology, Friedman's ideas would become central to the educational futures of urban Black and Latino families who, whatever else is true, were once again subject to an educational organization and structure far different from any championed for American schoolchildren who were affluent or white, or both.[29]

Today, at least thirteen states and the District of Columbia allow the use of educational vouchers. They first came into widespread use in 1989 in Milwaukee, Wisconsin, where a Black woman named Annette Polly Williams forcefully championed their use for her city's Black school district, which was under a desegregation order. Though the idea for vouchers came from an economist who wanted to dismantle public education, Williams, a passionate advocate of public schools, initially agreed with those who said they were a way of giving Black parents options outside of the failed and failing educational system in urban America. However, a few years before she died, she repudiated their use, her role in championing them, and the government officials and philanthropies she worked with to implement them in poor, Black communities. She came to believe that their ultimate goal of ending public education in the United States would devastate, not help, the parents, children, and communities about which she cared most deeply. Despite this change of heart, at her death most of her obituaries referred to her as "the mother of school choice."

Born in Belzoni, Mississippi, in 1937, Williams served for thirty years in the Wisconsin State Assembly. Though clearly popular with her Black constituents, whites did not view her as particularly impactful or influential as a legislator until 1989. That is the year she announced that she was joining political forces with the socially and fiscally conservative Republican governor Tommy Thompson. The issue that united them was the creation of a statewide school voucher program. While a controversial decision, she said that she supported vouchers because she had once served on the board of the Urban Day School, a nondenominational Black independent school run by Racine Dominican Sisters and led by Sister Sarah Freiburger, who had taught in the Freedom Mississippi Schools. Sister Sarah believed that schools could be a positive force for inner-city children, and during the time when Williams was on the board, the school achieved high-flying results similar to those attained by Marva Collins's Westside Prep, the Oakland Community School, and the Greens' Ivy Leaf School. Over 80 percent of the children the school educated were Black and poor. Having already lost faith in the racially and economically segregated and funded public school system in Milwaukee, Williams was convinced that taxpayer support for schools like Urban Day were the best chance poor Black children had to finally receive a quality education. She believed vouchers were the best way to ensure such schools would consistently receive the funds they needed to thrive. As she explained, "My fight is for . . . my Black children . . . to be able to access this system and get the best that this system offers."[30]

At least initially, Williams saw the fight for vouchers as a way to aid in bringing about Black educational equality, saying, "We wanted the children to stay in their own community and have the resources there. We had been fighting for years to improve the public schools, but it was falling on unresponsive ears." She said the idea for vouchers took off once she and others who supported her began asking about a way to empower Black parents fatigued with the low-performing schools in Milwaukee who wanted to "initiate what they think is best for their children." Aware that many Black activists believed that Friedman's faith in the free-market power of school vouchers would ultimately weaken instead of strengthen the public school system on which so many of them depended, she said she made a point of drafting the legislation to ensure "low-income families are the only ones that can participate in this program because those are the students and families who need help the most and who always get left out." Frustrated by noncompliance with state and federal orders to racially desegregate their schools, she believed the lack of a quality education for poor Black children was approaching a crisis. Low-income families in Milwaukee in the 1970s and 1980s found their children were still largely confined to low-performing schools and, if they spent their formative years in subpar institutions, rarely qualified educationally to attend better schools later on even if they could get in. Though she did so for very different reasons, Williams found herself in agreement with Milton Friedman that the best hope for public schools to educate Black children was to put the public funds for a child's education in the hands of the parents and let them spend those funds at a private school if their child's public school wasn't satisfactory. She determined that, despite the risks, it made sense for her to support vouchers, even if she had to work with conservative politicians to do so.[31]

Given her reasoning and background, for proponents of vouchers and school choice, Williams became the perfect spokesperson. She was not an outsider in relation to Black communities, and she had a good argument for why Black parents should trust her and these new policies. She was also convincing. In short order, Williams became a star of the conservative talk circuit, and her forceful support for vouchers became personally lucrative as well. According to one of the numerous obituaries announcing her death in 2013, in 1994 the money she made in speaking fees, $58,000, far outpaced her $35,070 salary as a legislator. During the height of her fame, she collected "honorariums as high as $5,000 for speeches about school choice at the Hoover Institute, the California State Republican Convention, and the National Conservative Summit." However, after 1997 she began to voice her concern that the rapid expansion of the voucher program in Wisconsin was doing far more to benefit white children, who were using the program to attend Catholic schools, and further impairing desegregation efforts. An education activist named Howard Fuller replaced her as the Black spokesperson for choice. According to the president of one of the philanthropic organizations supporting and funding Wisconsin's voucher program, the money and support shifted to Fuller because "he was a more charismatic speaker and a uniquely powerful symbol: a former superintendent of a big city school system declaring that only choice could save our children. And he didn't have Williams' abrasive personality or reservations about expanding vouchers."[32]

As the speaking engagements and media attention came to an end for Williams, she complained in 1998, "Howard . . . is the person that the white people have selected to lead the choice movement now because I don't cooperate." Her disenchantment with school choice only grew. In a 2011 interview with *Milwaukee Journal Sentinel* columnist Eugene Kane, she explained that her change of heart had to do with how it seemed to her as if affluent whites were benefiting more than the low-income students and communities of color that had been the early focus. She said, "The program was designed for low-income families; it was supposed to lift them out of hardship. Families who make that much money already have good schools or they have the ability to move to another neighborhood to get a better school." Williams went on to tell Kane that she had of course heard the concerns when she helped to shape the legislation that would become "school choice"—the cries from the opposition that it might eventually be expanded by politicians who wanted to damage the public school systems and teachers' unions and were not primarily concerned with helping poor urban children learn. She explained that at the time she just didn't want to believe it.[33]

In her last interview on the subject, in 2013, Williams said that choice supporters "have definitely undermined the intent of the (original) legislation" by expanding it to cover married couples with two children making up to $76,800. She believed that "The upper income people, they push the low incomes out" because "as soon as the doors open for the low income children, they're trampled by . . . [those with a] high income. . . . The upper crust have taken over." Williams had fought to create a program for low-income students attending alternative city schools like Urban Day, the school that did so much to shape her perspective. However, the program had grown to serve more than 20,000 Milwaukee students, making it the second-biggest school district in the state, and most of the students who were helped where neither Black nor poor. By the time she died, 75 percent of private school students getting a state voucher had already been attending the same school, which is to say that they were able to use their taxpayer-funded vouchers to continue attending a segregated private school. Most important, by then many studies showed participants did no better than their public school counterparts. However, that revelation didn't really matter, because voucher supporters had begun to describe them not as a better but rather as a cheaper way to educate children, a characteristic to be valued in this new free market of education.[34]

As students enrolled in the voucher schools, charter schools, and other "choice" programs, enrollment in the traditional Milwaukee public schools plummeted. In 1998, the district had about one hundred thousand students. A decade later, enrollment in public schools dropped just below eighty thousand. Vouchers, charters, and choice were rapidly eroding the public education system. According to educational historian Diane Ravitch, before the 1980s, because so many people viewed so-called school choice plans as thinly disguised ways for whites to avoid sending their children to school with Blacks, the issue of school choice remained out of the mainstream until the election of Ronald Reagan. However, once elected, and given his deep belief in Friedman's ideas about the free market, deregulation, and privatization, Reagan pushed openly for school choice and particularly for the implementation of vouchers. To aid in making them more widely available, Reagan appointed Milton Friedman as one of his advisers. However, President Reagan's legislative proposals for vouchers "were not intended for all children—as Friedman had urged—but for low-performing students, to make the voucher idea politically palatable." In his second term, Reagan backed away from mentioning vouchers in particular, instead changing his focus and language to promote "public school choice," which he thought made Milton Friedman's free-market ideas sound even less threatening.[35]

Despite efforts to enhance the popularity and support of free-market ideas at the highest levels of successive presidential administrations, Congress has repeatedly pushed back against efforts to bring about the legal changes required to allow a taxpayer-funded expansion of vouchers and so, at least at the federal level, schemes to bring about the implementation of voucher programs have begun to slow. However, deep-pocketed billionaires, such as our current secretary of education, Betsy DeVos, continue to champion their use and expansion. This reminds us that, as pointed out by educational sociologist James Ryan, "Education policy, at the moment, is largely something that happens to urban districts, not something that comes from them." That is certainly how many Black, Latino, and poor people living in urban areas continue to feel as they find paths to non-apartheid education blocked at every turn. It is not, however, clear that such communities will soon see an end in sight, as Friedman-inspired school privatization efforts continue to proliferate.[36]

Joseph Bast, president of the free-market champion Heartland Institute, believes that "complete privatization of schooling might be desirable, but this objective is politically impossible for the time being. Vouchers are a type of reform that is possible now." Another opinion writer states, "This deeply dysfunctional educational landscape—where failure is rewarded with opportunities for expansion and 'choice' means the opposite for tens of thousands of children—is no accident. It was created by an ideological lobby that has zealously championed free-market education reform for decades, with little regard for the outcome." The trickle of education from those who are wealthy, privileged, and well connected down to communities with less social capital continues apace.[37]

5

EDUCATION DREAMS AND
VIRTUAL NIGHTMARES

In December of 2016, President-elect Donald Trump announced that he would tap the Michigan multibillionaire Betsy DeVos as his nominee for the Department of Education. She was confirmed in February 2017. DeVos was a longtime school choice activist in the free market–inspired vein of Milton Freidman, and upon hearing the news of her nomination, public school teachers, unions, and advocates mounted a vigorous campaign to oppose her confirmation. Protesters pointed to her involvement in the expansion of unregulated charter schools in Michigan, to her support of school vouchers, and to comments of hers that critics saw as hostile to public schools. Journalist Rebecca Mead, writing in the *New Yorker*, summed up the dismay over her nomination by saying, "DeVos has never taught in a public school, nor administered one, nor sent her children to one." In addition to concerns over her lack of personal involvement with traditional public schools, there were further questions about her support for free market–inspired forms of public education such as vouchers and virtual charter schools.[1]

In a 2013 interview with *Philanthropy Magazine*, DeVos said her ultimate goals in education reform encompassed not just charter schools and voucher programs, but also virtual education. She said these forms were important because they would allow "all parents, regardless of their zip code, to have the opportunity to choose the best educational setting for their children." Also in 2013, one of the organizations that she founded, the American Federation for Children, put out a sharply critical statement after New Jersey's school chief, Chris Cerf, declined to authorize two virtual charter schools. The group said the decision "depriv[es] students of vital educational options." Yet another group DeVos founded and funded, the Michigan-based Great Lakes Education Project, has also advocated for expansion of online schools, and in a 2015 speech available on YouTube DeVos praised "virtual schools [and] online learning" as part of an "open system of choices." She then said, "We must open up the education industry—and let's not kid ourselves that it isn't an industry. We must open it up to entrepreneurs and innovators." DeVos's ties to—and support for—the profoundly troubled virtual school industry run deep.[2]

At the time of her nomination, charter schools were likely familiar to most listeners given their rapid growth and ubiquity. However, the press surrounding the DeVos nomination may have been one of the first times most became aware of a particular offshoot of the charter school movement—virtual or cyber schools. Despite flying somewhat under the mainstream radar, online charter schools have faced a wave of both negative press and poor results in research studies. One large-scale study from 2015 found that the "academic benefits from online charter schools are currently the exception rather than the rule." By June of 2016, even a group that supports, runs, and owns charter schools published a report calling for more stringent oversight and regulation of online charter schools, saying, "The well-documented, disturbingly low performance by too many full-time virtual charter public schools should serve as a call to action for state leaders and authorizers across the country." The jointly authored research was sponsored by the National Alliance for Public Charter Schools, the National Association of Charter School Authorizers, and 50Can, all groups that lobby state and federal agencies to loosen regulations to allow more robust charter-school growth. As one of the report's backers said, "I'm not concerned that Betsy DeVos supports virtual schools, because we support them too—we just want them to be a lot better." Such an upswing in quality seems highly unlikely to happen anytime soon. They are yet another trickle in the stream of apartheid forms of public education flowing down from the wealthy and politically well connected to communities that are poor, of color, or both.[3]

This chapter looks at the impact of the educational choices, such as virtual education, supported by an expanding group of governors. In Pennsylvania, Michigan, South Carolina, Ohio, and Florida, poor students from rural areas as well as those in underfunded urban schools that primarily educate students who are Black and Latino today face a new response to the question of how to solve the riddle of race, poverty, and educational underachievement. Increasingly, despite little supporting evidence, a growing number of states and local school districts no longer believe that the solution is merely about infrastructure, class size, funding, or hiring more teachers. In states with high levels of poverty and "hard to educate" Black and Latino students, virtual schools are on the rise. Such schools are not growing nearly as fast in school districts that are white and relatively wealthy, nor are they the educational strategy of choice in most private schools. As much a business strategy as one promoting learning, virtual education allows businesses to profit from racial inequality and poverty. Sadly, this particular cure to what ails our education system more often than not exacerbates the problems.

Though supported by Democrats as well, the expansion of virtual charter schools accelerated as Republicans increased their margin of control in governor's mansions and state legislatures across the country. At the start of 2016, Republicans occupied thirty-two of the nation's fifty governorships, ten more than they did in 2009. During that same period of time, Republican control of state legislatures doubled. What that means is that by 2016, Republicans controlled more legislative chambers than they did in the entire history of their party. The same political winds

that have shifted to blow so many Republicans into office have, at
the same time, pushed virtual education to the forefront of educational policy for a certain segment of our nation's youth. This
chapter looks at how this came to be.[4]

Hoping That Every Student Succeeds

In December of 2015, Congress sent the long-awaited overhaul of
the federal government's education bill to the White House for
President Obama's signature. Called the Every Student Succeeds
Act, the new bill updated the previous educational act signed into
law in 2002 by President George W. Bush, No Child Left Behind.
When introducing that new act, Bush said that it was a means for
our nation's schools to begin to seriously combat what he termed
"the soft bigotry of low expectations" that had so often stood in
the way of ensuring the success of America's children who were
poor, of color, special needs, or in any way struggling to achieve
academically. President Bush promised the nation that No Child
Left Behind would require that by 2014, 100 percent of all public school children could perform at grade level as measured by
standardized tests in the areas of math and reading. However, by
2012, President Obama's administration and much of the rest
of the country realized we as a nation were far from successfully
achieving the previous president's promised outcomes. Obama's
education bill made no grand promises such as those found in the
previous law, and in many ways was most notable for the fact that,
unlike No Child Left Behind, with its push to give the federal
government authority to prescribe and enforce educational standards, curriculum, and consequences from Washington, the Every
Child Succeeds Act by and large returned such matters to the control of the states and local governments.

Proposals for addressing issues of racial equity and fairness have not tended to benefit the poor and non-white when left to states to decide. In regard to educational equality, according to the progressive Republican watchdog organization American Bridge 21st Century, beginning in 2010 the Republican candidates for governor in Wisconsin, Michigan, Pennsylvania, Kansas, and Ohio rode a cresting wave of Tea Party support to elected office. They all campaigned on promises of massive budget overhauls that would cut taxes for both wealthy individuals and businesses. Once elected, in order to deliver on those promises, one governor after another eyed the funding pots set aside for public education as a way to pay for their budget priorities. By 2014, the legislative overhaul was complete, and the impact of the electoral shifts meant that changes were not just a matter of states' and local governments' agreeing about the best ways to fund the education of children who were poor and non-white. No, with this shift in the political landscape, the very nature and meaning of education underwent a change as well. Republican governors hewed closely to their party platform on education, which, in sum, aimed to shrink federal oversight of education; increase parental choice and flexibility; allow federal dollars to follow children to the school of their choice; expand school choice by increasing the number of charter schools; return greater control to parents, teachers, and school boards; and defend and increase options for home schooling. In regard to education, the shift was away from government regulation of public schools even while the proposed alternatives required taxpayer dollars.[5]

As educational historian Diane Ravitch has pointed out, the educational reforms championed by these legislators seek to

eliminate the geographically based system of public education as we have known it for the past 150 years and replace it with a competitive market-based system of school choice—one that includes traditional public schools, privately managed charter schools, religious schools, voucher schools, for-profit schools, virtual schools and for-profit vendors of instruction. Lacking any geographic boundaries, these schools would compete for customers.[6]

Virtual schools and their growth in both number and significance were not part of the public discussion surrounding the repeal of No Child Left Behind. Still, in reality, as it became more and more clear that the new education bill would pass, interest groups, state legislatures, and educational nonprofits interested in the lucrative, easy expansion of virtual education all sprang into action. Many knew that states would now have more power to propose the expansion of such schools, allegedly as a way of confronting the challenges facing states in need of creative ways to address the educational deficiencies of their lowest-achieving students, who were usually poor and often of color.

In April 2015, the Alabama State Legislature voted up State Bill 0072, known as the Virtual School Options for Local Boards of Education Bill. It required that, "at a minimum, each local board of education" adopt a policy for providing a "virtual option for eligible students in grades 9–12." In Maine, two virtual academies opened in 2014 to specifically educate students in the state's "poorer districts" and in May of 2015 the state explored the feasibility of opening a state-run virtual academy. In June, state education officials in Illinois announced that they would begin to test out limited online learning options during snow days for a three-year period. Following their analysis at the end of the test period, they held open the possibility of more wide-ranging implementation. The Virginia Department of Education piloted a new program during the 2015–2016 school year in which students spent 100 percent of their time in a cyber school, never setting foot inside a school. This flurry of activity was brought on by the ease and speed with which these new computer-based schools could expand and by the fact that the financial rewards were simply too great for cash-strapped politicians to ignore.[7]

By 2015 virtual schools had gone mainstream, aided in part by the fact that between 2008 and 2014, 175 bills that expanded on-line schooling options passed in thirty-nine states and territories (including the District of Columbia). As a result, today there are public schools in every state that offer some form of online course-work, and in five states—Alabama, Arkansas, Florida, Michigan, and Virginia—students are actually *required* to take at least one online or partly digital class if they want to graduate from high school. In thirty states and Washington, D.C., there are fully on-line schools available.[8]

Despite all of the state- and federal-level support for these new education methods, all of this growth has happened without a similar amount of verification of the efficacy of virtual educa-tion. Over the past decade, we have heard more about the failure of Massive Open Online Courses, or MOOCs, to make a memo-rable impact on the style in which college instruction is delivered than we have about the success or failure of virtual education at the K–12 level. Colleges might get all the attention for going on-line in part because big brand names like MIT and Harvard now offer virtual courses for free around the world, but K–12 online schooling has, over the past twenty years, become a major player in the educational arena. As a result of MOOCs and other de-velopments overshadowing this conversation, little attention has been paid to where in the country this profitable switch has grown most rapidly: areas with high levels of racial and economic in-equality fueled by segregation. In districts that are rural and poor, and overwhelmingly with Republican governors and legislatures, in states like Florida, Alabama, Mississippi, and South Carolina, or in urban districts like Philadelphia, virtual schools are quickly becoming the format of choice despite politicians' having little grasp on how cyber education impacts achievement for the most vulnerable students.[9]

According to a 2012 *Philadelphia Citypaper* article, "Who's Killing Philly Schools," in a district comprised of 80 percent

Black and Latino students, the vast majority of whom are below the poverty line, cyber schools accounted for fully educating more than a third of the children in 2014. The goal is for that number to rise to at least three-quarters, if not more, in subsequent years.[10] However, between 2011 and 2014, 100 percent of the children enrolled in Philadelphia-area cyber schools who took state achievement tests failed. The record of Pennsylvania's fourteen cyber charter schools was so abysmal that the state of Pennsylvania denied all applications to open new cyber charter schools in 2013 and 2014. Their poor track record has not derailed the long-term plan of increasing the numbers of students who take classes via virtual education, however.[11]

Cyber education grew during the term of Pennsylvania's Republican governor Tom Corbett. Elected in 2010 and serving only a four-year term, his policies exemplified the organized effort on the part of political and business leaders to spearhead the shift to online learning. His first step was taking funding away from "brick and mortar" schools. In his first full year in office, he cut funding to the Philadelphia School District by $198 million, a 20 percent cut. Then, in 2011, he reduced public school funding by another $900 million, or 10 percent. Those cuts, plus more the next year, meant that by 2013 thousands of teachers were laid off and almost 70 percent of Pennsylvania's school districts increased their class size, 40 percent cut extracurricular activities, and 75 percent cut instruction. The impact of his educational leadership was devastating for schools and communities throughout the state, and districts targeted by Corbett's cuts felt them intensely. Dozens of schools closed. Thousands of teachers and school support staff were laid off. Art and music became scarce, along with nurses and guidance counselors. School buildings became so unpleasant that virtual education almost seemed like a respite.[12]

In one particularly telling real-world example from 2016 of how such cuts affected students in the "brick and mortar" district, high school junior Jameria Miller talks about why she starts every morning running through the school to get a good seat near the front of the room in her first-period Spanish class. It's not because she is just excited about the class. It's because the school is cold. As she explains, "The cold is definitely a distraction. We race to class to get the best blankets." What she means is that because the classroom where she begins her day has uninsulated metal walls, Jameria's teacher hands out blankets to the students on a first come, first served basis. It's the only way for them to stay warm. Miller's school in the William Penn District is situated in Philadelphia's "inner-ring" suburbs and serves a student body that is majority Black and overwhelmingly impoverished. Though concentrating in the cold is hard enough, Miller says the hardest part of her daily ordeal is the knowledge that life isn't like this for students in other districts. She means students in wealthier districts. "It's never going to be fair, they're always going to be a step ahead of us. They'll have more money than us, and they'll get better jobs than us, always." She says she doesn't believe that either funding or systemic school improvement will ever truly equalize: "What I'm about to say might not be very nice, but rich people aren't going to want [funding fairness]. They want their kids to have better things so that their kids can get a jump start in life and be ahead of everyone else. And, as long as people feel that way, we all won't be equal. We won't receive equal education ever, because education is what gets you success." Her district is not the only one in Pennsylvania so affected.[13]

Since 1998, Philadelphia schools—the largest city and school district in the state—have been run by the governor-appointed School Reform Commission. In the summer of 2013, in order to address a $350 million hole in its budget, the commission passed what was termed a "doomsday budget." Thirty schools were closed that year. In 2014, Thomas Knudsen, chief recovery officer for the School Reform Commission, told a reporter writing a story for *Salon* that the commission wanted to "close 40 schools and an additional six every year thereafter until 2017." At that point, he believed the district, which at its height had over 180 schools, would be down to 20 to 30, and those would be placed into "achievement networks" where public and private groups would compete to manage them. This news led the *Salon* reporter to describe what once was our nation's tenth-largest school district as being in its "death throes." The district wasn't to be saved, or even managed, by the Reform Commission as much as dismantled.[14]

Despite such severe money worries and their negative impact on "brick and mortar" schools, virtual educational sectors thrived during the same years. According to a 2011 *New York Times* article, five Pennsylvania cyber charters received $200 million in tax money in 2010–2011, and Agora Cyber Charter, which is run by the for-profit company K12, took in $31.6 million in 2013 alone from state taxpayers in Philadelphia. By 2015, cyber schools received over $60 million in per-student payments from the chronically starved and often bankrupt school districts. To make matters worse, the companies who run online and virtual schools are also consistently accused of financial impropriety. In 2011, the *New York Times* conducted a months-long investigation into virtual schools. By way of summing up its overall findings, the article begins by showing how, in the realm of education, what is good for business is not necessarily good for the students those businesses claim to educate:

> By almost every educational measure, the Agora Cyber Charter School is failing. Nearly 60 percent of its students are behind grade level in math. Nearly 50 percent trail in reading. A third do not graduate on time. And hundreds of children, from kindergartners to seniors, withdraw within months after they enroll. By Wall Street standards, though, Agora is a remarkable success that has helped enrich K12 Inc., the publicly traded company that manages the school. And the entire enterprise is paid for by taxpayers.[15]

The amount of money involved, as well as the potential profit, is significant.

One of the largest companies providing virtual education, Agora Schools, was on track to earn $72 million in 2011, a number it has bested each succeeding year from 2011 to 2014, when out of Agora's $849 million in profit, $117 million came from its virtual schools division. And those profits are for just one company, in just one area of a crowded field of online education providers. In order to help build a market for their services, these companies often target children via huge advertising buys on Nickelodeon and Cartoon Network, as well as on teen sites such as MeetMe.com and VampireFreaks.com.[16]

In addition to its seeming inability to properly educate students and the unsavory targeting of children with its product, it is worth noting that Agora's parent company, K12 Inc., was founded by a man who had served federal time for financial improprieties. His name is Michael Milken. Milken not only came to symbolize 1980s-era Wall Street greed and excess by serving as the inspiration for the Michael Douglas character Gordon Gekko in the 1987 movie *Wall Street*; he also spent almost two years in a federal penitentiary for securities fraud. Once released from prison, he joined forces with another junk bond dealer, Ron Packard, who specialized in mergers and acquisitions for Goldman Sachs in the 1980s. Together they invested $10 million into K12 Inc. and formed a company with the goal of profiting from the $600 billion public education "market." They have been dogged by financial improprieties. In 2012, K12 settled a federal lawsuit for $6.8 million. The suit alleged its executives inflated stock prices by misleading investors with false student-performance claims. In the summer of 2016, the company agreed to pay $168.5 million to settle alleged violations of California's false claims, false advertising, and unfair competition laws, though the company admitted no wrongdoing. No matter; by 2016 Milken had a net worth of around $2.5 billion, according to *Forbes*—almost all of that money from contracts with public schools.[17]

Pennsylvania has the second-highest cyber charter enrollment (after Ohio), and it accounts for about 17 percent of the national cyber charter school population, which across the country numbers over 220,000 students.[18] In terms of instruction, students usually take lessons at home, so the virtual school operators have no classrooms to maintain, staff to hire, or heating bills to pay. Teachers are paid less, and student-teacher ratios are massive, sometimes as high as fifty students for each teacher. But, despite the widespread belief in their affordability, in Pennsylvania the district pays cyber schools as much per child as it pays to educate students in brick-and-mortar schools. In 2016, most of Pennsylvania's cyber schools had dismal results. According to the state's School Performance Profile website, only three—21st Century, PA Cyber, and PA Virtual—had a score above 60. The state considers 60 and below to be substandard. None of the cyber schools scored higher than 70, which is the state's minimum passing score for all schools, and some cyber schools in the study scored down in the 30s. Such schools are neither inexpensive nor effective, yet they continue to expand.[19]

In addition to questions about how effective cyber schools are in terms of a return on investment for taxpayer dollars, an issue of particular concern is the sector's emphasis on serving so-called high-risk students who don't have the parental and other support structures that research shows are necessary to make the most of the model. Poor, rural, and urban districts are prime candidates, since cyber educators have explicitly stated that it is their business strategy to go after kids who—because it is believed that they do not have motivated parents—would demand the least from their educational experience. Students in foster care and Native Americans schooled on their tribal homelands are two categories of students targeted by virtual school providers in Florida.

Targeting the most economically vulnerable students ultimately yields cyber education businesses increased profits resulting from the segrenomics of apartheid schools. The undereducation of the poor and people of color is a business opportunity that generates great profit for businesses but provides little in the way of quality instruction.[20]

Toward that end, it is important to take a few steps back and at least notice that, despite the near-universal enthusiasm for projects that give technology to educationally vulnerable poor children of color, computer-aided instruction, when not deployed in an informed, responsible manner, actually *widens* the gap between the financially and educationally privileged and everyone else. Nonetheless, over the past ten years, public school districts have invested millions of dollars in various types of online and computer-aided learning and instruction programs, and few are able to show the educational benefit of their expenditures for a majority of students. Those who benefit most are already well organized and highly motivated. Other students struggle and, according to researchers studying students in a variety of digital settings, might even lose academic ground.[21]

Supporters of online learning say that all anyone needs in order to access a great education is a stable Internet connection, but only 35 percent of households earning less than $25,000 have broadband Internet access, compared with 94 percent of households with income in excess of $100,000. In addition, according to the 2010 Pew Report on Mobile Access, only half of Black homes have Internet connections at all, compared with almost 65 percent of white households. In its 2016 report on Internet usage, Pew related that a whopping 94 percent of Latinos used mobile phones to access the Internet, generally a much more expensive and less-than-ideal (if not altogether ineffectual) method for taking part in online education. In short, the explosion of this type of educational instruction, though on the rise, may leave wanting the very students who need public education while at the same time offering businesses providing Internet access an opportunity to reap significant rewards.[22]

As but one example of how touting the benefits of cyber education goes hand in hand with profits for businesses, we need look no further than South Carolina. There, the growth of cyber education in the state got an advantageous boost in 2014 when the governor at the time, Nikki Haley, announced a new education budget and asked the state legislature for tens of millions of dollars to provide WiFi service to rural schoolchildren. It was a precursor to the expansion of virtual education. Once approved, the 2015 education budget provided "$29 million for improving bandwidth to school facilities, bolstering wireless connectivity within school walls, and furthering the push to ensure that every student has a computer or tablet." These changes were enacted because, according to the press release announcing the allocations, "modernizing technology and improving bandwidth will give students greater access to educational content and will help improve critical computer skills their future employers will demand." An additional $4 million was also provided for teacher technology training. Schools facing difficulties hiring could also offer courses in a "blended" setting, with students being taught online while sitting at a desk in their traditional school. Schools pay $3,500 for an entire classroom to take a virtual course—far less than the cost of a teacher. The allocation of those funds also set the stage for the aggressive expansion of online learning to a cohort of students who would benefit most from high-quality, in-person instruction.[23]

The same year that Governor Haley released her technology-enhancing budget, the National Education Policy Center issued a 2015 report finding that, "despite the considerable enthusiasm for virtual education, there is little credible research to support virtual schools' practices or to justify ongoing calls for ever greater expansion." Though the authors concede that the available data are limited, which may make their findings less than definitive, "there is not a single positive sign from the empirical evidence presented here." Nonetheless, Governor Haley and others like her insisted that this particular form of free-market public education would help the state's children who were poor and without high-quality schools. She told the state's citizens that an increase in cyber education was, in the language of school choice advocates, tantamount to "taking a stand against the idea that where you are born and raised should influence the quality of your education."[24]

On the day that Governor Haley made her announcement, Patricia Levesque, CEO of the Foundation for Excellence in Education, an organization that former Florida governor Jeb Bush founded, released a statement through Haley's office praising the new South Carolina budget. It enthused, "The K-12 Education Reform Initiative's emphasis on literacy and technology has potential for long-term positive results for schools and children." She added, "We applaud the governor's action to build a foundation of infrastructure and resources for growth in these crucial areas for education."[25] The announcement made clear that, though she didn't mention it herself, Haley was working in concert with a group of Republican governors first organized by Florida's Jeb Bush.

Jeb Bush and the Rise of Virtual Education

In 1994, when Jeb Bush made his first, ultimately unsuccessful bid to become the governor of Florida, he was asked at a campaign stop what he would do for African Americans during his first term as governor. His answer was "Probably nothing." Journalists often point to Bush's response as the probable reason he lost that election. Others suggest that the fallout from that one interaction led him to embrace the reform of public education as a tool for closing the educational achievement gap that so negatively impacted

Black and Latino students. He thought that his efforts would play well with voters of color. Whatever the reason, soon after this defeat, Bush founded a chain of now defunct charter schools that helped to shore up his civil rights agenda (as so many so-called educational reformers do, he described the efforts to shape a racially equal educational future as the civil rights movement of our time). The next time he ran for governor, in 2002, he won with overwhelming support from Black voters in the state. He had come to be known for his education agenda, which advocated for an aggressive expansion of charter schools, including those offering a virtual education.[26]

After leaving office, Bush's desire to continue his work in education led him to create the Foundation for Florida's Future. He hoped to nationally expand the kinds of reforms that he had backed in Florida. One of the first activities the foundation undertook was reaching out to other similarly inclined Republican state education leaders to form a new group he called Chiefs for Change. Then, in 2010, along with former West Virginia governor Bob Wise, Bush launched an initiative called Digital Learning Now, which promoted the benefits of "virtual schools" providing online instruction. In a 2015 article, "The Big Jeb Bush Charter School Lie: How Florida Became a Cautionary Tale for the Rest of the Country," Jeff Bryant reports that between 2000 and 2010 the number of charter schools in Florida more than doubled, with the largest concentrations taking root in the most urbanized corridors of the state. Bryant charts the ways that, during that same period of time, the nature of the influence of Bush and his foundation also changed. It grew. Starting in 2009, Bush used the resources and network of his Foundation for Florida's Future to create a sister organization, the Foundation for Excellence in Education. This second organization was founded "in response to requests for assistance from lawmakers and policymakers who were interested in advancing reforms," according to the organization's website. In other words, the new organization existed to "lead a more robust and focused effort to advance specific education leg-islation through direct lobbying and electoral activity," another way of saying its purpose was to lobby legislators and campaign to convince voters to support educational reforms that would benefit private industry.

As might be expected, according to a *New Yorker* article by Alec MacGillis, companies soon came to see Bush's Foundation for Excellence in Education as an ideal platform through which to promote a range of products to state education officials. By 2010, when Bush convened a "Digital Learning Council," in addition to elected officials, he included virtual school executives from around the country. One of their first orders of business was to issue a report urging states to adopt industry-friendly measures, such as eliminating limits on virtual-school enrollment. Mac-Gillis writes that in Maine, according to a 2012 investigation by the Portland *Press-Herald*, foundation staff members essentially wrote legislation backed by the Republican governor, Paul LePage, to expand virtual schools. When Maine's education commis-sioner wrote to the head of Bush's foundation, Patricia Levesque, to let her know "I have no 'political' staff who I can work with to move this stuff through the process," Levesque replied, "Let us help." According to emails obtained by the watchdog organization In the Public Interest, Levesque pitched the state commissioners on behalf of the companies that Bush's organization represented. Maine was not the only state to benefit from the group's lobbying work. In July 2011, Levesque "encouraged Chris Cerf, who was then the New Jersey commissioner [of education], to accept an of-fer from Dell of a demo 'teacher dashboard,' a digital classroom-management system." When interviewed on the subject, Cerf said, "Public education is a public enterprise, but it's also true that, like all public entities, it also relies on collaborations." Whatever the meaning of his cryptic response, Cerf went into business with the company.[27]

One of the first victories scored by the Digital Learning Council was in 2011 when Utah's legislature passed a bill based almost entirely on its blueprint. It expanded opportunities for high school students to take online courses. As Stephanie Mencimer reported for *Mother Jones* in 2011 when covering how this change came about, Jeb Bush visited the state a few months before the vote in order to make the case for virtual schools to state legislators and to address Governor Gary Herbert's Education Excellence Commission. Further, as Mencimer talked with various educational stakeholders she learned that "when supporters feared that Herbert might veto it, Bush was on standby to make a governor-to-governor call" to shore up Herbert's resolve. Once Utah's bill passed, other such victories followed. Florida, Ohio, and Wisconsin quickly passed laws allowing online-education companies to access more public funds. Some even required public school students to take online classes in order to graduate. Following Ohio's Republican governor John Kasich's signed legislation authorizing online schools, Bush issued a public statement praising the vote and the politicians who'd ensured that "more students in the Buckeye State will have the opportunity to achieve their God-given potential." Today, Ohio remains one of the largest providers of online education for its students.[28]

The language around the expansion of virtual or cyber schools is couched as an opportunity for students to move away from a "one size fits all" model and as being especially useful for students who are poor and of color and who are often failed by traditional brick-and-mortar schools. While the truth of that line of argument is contested by their consistently poor performance, we know that replacing traditional public schools with the cyber school variety is lucrative. By 2012, Bush's Digital Learning Now initiative had earned revenues of $10 million, much of it in the form of tax-deductible donations from education companies. Those companies sent representatives to the summits, where foundation officials set aside time for them to have "donor meetings" with the Chiefs for Change. In 2012, the National Education

Policy Center studied virtual schools and found that their students lagged in math and reading proficiency and had lower graduation rates than those in traditional schools. Nonetheless, they continue to grow, and elected officials and educational entrepreneurs continue to tout such forms of learning as the silver bullet capable of saving public education for the poor in America. In December 2014, Bush's Digital Learning Council issued its third report card detailing the "10 Elements of High Quality Digital Learning." On the list was a call for state policymakers to "hold schools and providers accountable for achievement and growth." Which is to say, accountability falls on the businesses and companies most interested in growing and marketing their educational businesses; instead of parents, teachers, or communities determining the educational growth of students, companies that provide digital learning are themselves responsible for ensuring that the enterprise continues to prosper.[29]

It is worth noting that, for years, Bush worked closely with Betsy DeVos to expand school choice policies across the country. She served on the board of his Foundation for Excellence in Education. Now, the programs the two crafted together are likely to serve as models for federal policymaking. Governor Bush, when asked about DeVos's nomination, said, "I cannot think of a more effective and passionate change agent to press for a new education vision, one in which students, rather than adults and bureaucracies, become the priority in our nation's classrooms." The students most impacted by these policies are rarely asked what they think about such interventions. They are rarely asked what they think at all.[30]

Black and Latino children and their parents and communities have reason for concern about the rapid and unchecked growth in cyber education. It tends to impact them most. When Florida's severe budget cuts in 2011 made it difficult for schools to meet class-size rules and left them too cash-strapped to hire more teachers, some schools in the Miami-Dade district required seven thousand of their students to take online classes in virtual labs with only noncertified teacher's aides available to provide assistance. Students did not know of these new arrangements until they showed up for school one day, and parents were neither asked about nor informed of this change. Of the district's roughly 344,000 students, 324,000 are Black or Latino. These types of educational arrangements simply do not take place in districts that are wealthy and have low numbers of students of color.[31]

It is then surprising that, to a large extent, the success of the shift to digital learning has been aided by rhetoric that positions education as a basic right of citizenship, a civil rights mountain still in need of scaling. Nonetheless, to refer back to Stephanie Mencimer's *Mother Jones* piece, "beneath the rhetoric, the online-education push is also part of a larger agenda that closely aligns with the GOP's national strategy: It siphons money from public institutions into for-profit companies." She continues to say that the tangible result of such efforts is to undercut "public employees, their unions, and the Democratic base. In the guise of a technocratic policy initiative, it delivers a political trifecta—and a big windfall for Bush's corporate backers." What it rarely delivers is a quality education, never mind one that comes close to the sort found in the wealthy, white school districts to which the Bush and DeVos families would send their own children.[32]

In many virtual school settings, students rarely even hear or see their teachers. At some cyber charter schools, students need only sign in to the school website and/or communicate with a teacher once every three days to prove they're actually attending. In Wisconsin, a state legislative audit found that 16 percent of the virtual teachers surveyed had contact with individual students as little as three times a month. Other schools in the state outsource duties such as paper grading to contractors in India, making it difficult for the teachers to meaningfully explain to students the basis for the grades they received.[33] While virtual education is a growth industry in Wisconsin, it is important to note that the state has the largest achievement gap between Black and white students in the country and ranks last in reading-comprehension tests among Black fourth graders. Milwaukee, one of the largest cities in the state and home to the highest number of Black students, is the biggest contributor to Wisconsin's racial achievement gap. Four out of five Black children in Milwaukee live in poverty.[34]

While much of the sector's growth can be seen as being tied to states with Republican governors and legislatures, it was greatly aided in 2013 by the Obama administration when it launched the ConnectED Initiative, a five-year plan to connect nearly all U.S. students to high-speed wireless systems in their schools and libraries, earmark funds to train teachers to incorporate digital technology and devices into their lesson plans, and "unleash private sector innovation" in order make it easier for educational technology providers to offer personalized educational software, online education opportunities, and online textbooks to entire school districts. If such policies and practices actually worked to educate students who are undereducated, that might not be cause for concern. However, given all of the information that we have, we must conclude that they do not. It is then hard to understand why there is such a push to expand them. At the very least, it would make sense to also expand policies that would make it possible for schoolchildren who attend schools that lack heating in the winter to sit comfortably in their classrooms without resorting to huddling under a blanket.[35]

For too long, the price paid by some of our nation's children for the financial gain of a handful of adults has simply been too high. As we embark on the presidency of Donald Trump and wait to see what his department of education will do over the course of his presidency, we already know that a majority of state legislatures and municipal governments headed by Republicans have trod an educational path leading away from a clearly successful focus on equalized funding and racial and economic integration to one that is accepting of the status quo: racial segregation and economic isolation. Where once we as a nation pledged to wage war on high levels of segregation in our schools, today we not only accept this injustice as an unavoidable fact but allow our government to empower corporations to benefit from the very segregation we once swore to eradicate.

6

STEALING SCHOOL

In 2011, a Cuban immigrant named Hamlet Garcia and his wife, Olesia, enrolled their five-year-old daughter, Fiorella, in a largely white and affluent school in the Philadelphia suburbs of Montgomery County, Pennsylvania. Before the move, the child was to have attended a lower-performing school in Philadelphia. The couple says that they were having marital problems that became severe enough for Olesia to move out of their Philadelphia home and take their daughter with her to her father's house in the suburbs. In March of 2012, the couple reconciled, and Olesia and Fiorella moved back to Philadelphia, though Fiorella finished the year at the suburban school. In April of 2012, the school district contacted the couple to dispute their residency, and that August they were told they were facing arrest. The criminal complaint sworn out against them said the Garcias "stole" $10,000, which was the per-pupil cost of one year at the Montgomery County public school their daughter had attended. The dollar amount made the charge a felony, with a potential prison sentence of seven years. Rather than face the ordeal of a trial and the possibility of conviction, the couple accepted a plea bargain and agreed to pay the district close to $11,000. The case also cost the couple an additional $70,000 in legal fees. When interviewed, Garcia said, "I was just in disbelief that this was happening in America over the education of a 5-year-old child." He continued, "I pleaded with the superintendent. I said, 'Look, we're good parents. We're good citizens. I'm a business owner. I never did anything. I always walked the straight line.'" His pleas fell on deaf ears. Education is no longer seen as a valuable commodity just because it promises social mobility and lucrative employment. It is also a possession with a specific dollar figure attached, owned by the wealthy, and, all too often, denied to those who are not. For that reason, cases of so-called educational theft like that of the Garcia family exemplify the impact of segrenomics on communities in search of quality education. Just as underperforming, highly racially and economically segregated urban schools constitute a lucrative opportunity for some in the business of education, high-performing schools in wealthy areas are a valuable asset worth protecting with incarceration, if it comes to that.[1]

Given cases like the Garcias', it is then perplexing that federal, state, and local authorities are rarely as aggressive about protecting taxpayer money from businesses or individuals who steal the educational funds earmarked for the expansion of charter schools in communities of color. Such theft is a widespread problem. In May of 2014, two nonprofit groups issued a research report titled "Charter School Vulnerabilities to Waste, Fraud and Abuse." Jointly authored by Integrity in Education and the Center for Popular Democracy, the report warned that the lax federal oversight of the rapidly expanding charter industry has led to the theft of more than $100 million due to fraud, mismanagement, and outright theft. A few months after that study was released, a subsequent wave of news reports described federal raids and arrests at the offices of charter schools and charter management organizations in Connecticut, New Mexico, Indiana, Ohio, Louisiana, and Illinois. These actions were taken following investigations into activities such as theft of money and equipment, bribery, kickback and stock manipulation schemes, and the misappropriation of funds by charter school administrators who used taxpayer dollars to purchase real estate for their personal use, take luxury vacations, and treat friends and associates to fancy meals. Unlike the funds stolen by charter school founders and administrators, the varied roads that lead to the conviction of lower-income parents reveals a tight connection between substandard educational systems, racism, poverty, segregation, and a criminal justice system that harshly punishes poor, non-white people in a way disproportionate to the nature of their offenses when compared to the large-scale fiscal abuse perpetrated in wealthier, whiter communities and by some segments of the charter school industry. If quality education gushed forth in communities that were poor and of color, instead of trickled down from the wealthy to everyone else, this simply would not be happening. This chapter looks at that double standard. In one instance, parents in search of quality education are surveilled, prosecuted, and at times jailed, while at the same time, charter school operators steal millions of dollars because of the lack of consistent regulation of the industry as a whole.[2]

Between 2012 and 2014, parents in Connecticut, Kentucky, Pennsylvania, and Missouri were all arrested and stood trial for enrolling their children in better public schools outside of their districts. They were all charged with stealing education. This particular phenomenon is now so common that on either coast—and in many places in between—school districts have in the past few years begun to hire special investigators to follow, photograph, and film children as they go from home to school and back again. This surveillance helps school officials determine if all the students who show up day after day are legally permitted to attend the schools. The desire to keep poor, non-white children out of wealthy schoolhouses has even spawned new businesses. Districts in Florida, Pennsylvania, California, and New Jersey that did not want to spend the money to hire full-time investigators have contracted with companies promising lower-cost ways of verifying student addresses. With names like VerifyResidence.com, such companies, according to one website, provide "the latest in covert video technology and digital photographic equipment to photograph, videotape, and document" children going from their house to school. For school districts willing to invest even more, that company offers a rewards program that awards anonymous tipsters with $250 checks for reporting out-of-district students. The consequences for parents and students caught in this web are devastating and can include tens of thousands of dollars in fees, jail time, and felony convictions that preclude them from voting and gaining future employment.

That is what happened in the spring of 2014 when a judge in Connecticut sentenced a Black mother, Tanya McDowell, to twelve years in prison for "stealing an education" for her kindergarten-age son. Education officials in Connecticut said that her son should have enrolled in the city of Bridgeport, not the wealthy town of Norwalk. McDowell and her son were homeless when she was arrested for educational theft. They split their time between a homeless shelter in Norwalk, the home of her babysitter—Ana Marquez—in Norwalk, and sometimes, if there was no room elsewhere, in the backseat of her minivan. In order to even enroll her son in school, she used her babysitter's Norwalk address, which was in a public housing complex. When school officials discovered that the kindergartener was not what they considered a legal resident of Norwalk, they could have simply asked McDowell to remove him from school. That is what they had done with the twenty or so other students found to be "illegally" enrolled that year. But officials decided to prosecute this Black, single, homeless parent on first-degree larceny charges that carried a maximum sentence of up to twenty years in prison.

School district officials readily admitted that they treated McDowell far more harshly than they did others because they wanted to make an example of her. They didn't want their community to be seen as welcoming to other parents who might want to provide their children with an education to which they were not entitled. In that regard, Bridgeport is a microcosm of the many cities where the migration of wealthy whites and their tax dollars to the suburbs has had devastating consequences for the people left behind. As such, this case makes clear the lengths to which some

would go to make sure the drawbridge allowing access to their
schools is quickly and securely pulled up behind them after they
are safely ensconced on the other side. In relation to urban education, school reform, and the difficulties involved in navigating the
caste-defining realities of apartheid education, this case and the
situation of Bridgeport's schools in general are a distillation of history made present and point out the urgency of our need to find
solutions.

The educational impact of poverty and racial and economic
segregation on Bridgeport—Connecticut's largest city—has been
evident since at least 1961. At that time, in a series of articles la-
menting the lack of focused attention, financial support, and viable public policy solutions from state and federal officials, the
reporter noted, "What frustrates us is that in this crowded, un-
planned, unlovely city, there is so much to be done that no one
can tell where to start." Another article published later that same
week in 1961 reported that when state educators came to Bridgeport to evaluate the local high school, they praised the teachers
but chastised the city for a lack of financial support, specifically
noting that "students were forced to pay for their own books, science equipment, globes, and maps." The officials reported, "This
situation makes a mockery of a free public education," conclud-
ing, "If Bridgeport were a poor community in a poor state in a
poor nation, this condition might be more easily understood."
Bridgeport's schools in the 1960s were only beginning their trans-
formation into an abysmal state; the trickle of whites moving out
to other towns and cities with their tax dollars was not yet the
rushing river it would become a few decades later.[3]

However, since 1960, Connecticut has, in a sense, warehoused
its poor in this one city surrounded by towns that are among the
richest in the nation. By the 1990s, 20 percent of the residents
and a quarter of the children there lived in poverty. As is so often the case, poverty breeds other ills. According to pastor Kenneth Moales Jr., a former school board member, "In the city of

Bridgeport, we have 18 schools that are failing. Of those, 13 have been failing for over 10 years." The children in Bridgeport are educated in a system with few students who are white or wealthy. It is a school system long understood to be a failure. With that history as context, it is easy to see how a homeless Black mother might risk everything to ensure a quality education for her child, as well as easy to understand the reasons why authorities would struggle mightily to keep her out. If she were allowed to stay, others might follow. The fears on both sides are as much about policy as they are about economics. However, economics is the driving force.[4]

The Bridgeport public schools spend around $8,000 per pupil each year. That number is far less than what is spent in wealthy districts in Connecticut and elsewhere. A 2014 *New York Times* data analysis of wealth and school achievement found that Bridgeport's sixth graders were lagging nearly two grade levels behind their Norwalk peers just fifteen miles away. Also in 2014, the U.S. Department of Education found that Connecticut spent 8.7 percent less per student in its poorest school districts than it did in its most affluent ones. It was not alone in having skewed spending priorities, nor has the trend abated. In 2016, nine states had large disparities between what they spent in wealthy districts and in those that were poor: Arizona, Illinois, Missouri, Nevada, New York, Pennsylvania, Rhode Island, Vermont, and Virginia. When asked about his views regarding how these choices impacted the education of poor children, former secretary of education Arne Duncan said, "Children who need the most seem to be getting less and less. Children who need the least seem to be getting more and more. There is something unfair, educationally unsound and . . . frankly . . . un-American in what is happening." The truth of his assertion about how American or not it is for the wealthy to hoard educational funds for their own children and deny them to poorer students of color is, at the very least, up for debate. However, what we know for sure is that Tanya McDowell was charged with "stealing" $15,686 in educational services for her son. That is the amount, almost double what is spent in Bridgeport, that Norwalk schools spend per pupil each year.[5]

Despite the fact that there had previously been no penalty for so-called theft of education, the Norwalk school board president, Jack Chiamontc, in answering the question of why they seemed so intent on prosecuting this one woman, replied, "There has to be a penalty for stealing our services. Right now, there is none." In setting such a precedent, perhaps school officials believed they would have an easier time scapegoating a homeless, Black, single mother. Their thinking persisted despite the fact that her homelessness should have protected her and her son. Under federal law, children can continue to attend classes in the school district where they began their education if the family becomes homeless at some later point. That made no difference whatsocver. Norwalk's mayor, Richard Moccia, when asked to explain why the family's homelessness didn't lead his administration to follow the law, did not so much answer the question as restate the facts before offering his opinion when he said, "This woman . . . was using an illegal address in a public housing complex, has a checkered past and despite all the protestation that she's concerned about her son, if she had done things right, this would havc nevei happened." Mayor Moccia did not specify what exactly he wishes McDowell had done more right. And she and her son were not the only casualties of the case. When McDowell enrolled her child in Norwalk's Brookside Elementary School, Ana Marquez, McDowell's babysitter, signed a notarized statement saying the child lived in her public housing unit. In their quest to establish the inviolate boundaries of their schools, school officials passed that statement to Norwalk Housing Authority officials, who then began eviction proceedings against Marquez for fraud. It would not just be McDowell and her son who would pay a high price for trying to obtain a rigorous education—one that would have been almost impossible to obtain within the Bridgeport city limits.[6]

An average Black student in Bridgeport attends a school with five times the poverty rate of a school attended by the average white student in Connecticut. Two-thirds of the city's children are born into families on public assistance. More than half of the neighborhoods in the city have unemployment rates reaching as high as 50 percent. These are the conditions that led to McDowell's impossible choice about how to meet her son's educational needs. As a result, the vigor with which prosecutors pursued McDowell attracted national attention. The Connecticut chapter of the NAACP both hired a lawyer for her and issued a supportive statement that said, "The criminalization of parents trying to enroll their child in a better quality school simply to give their child a chance for a better life is wrong and should be resolved through civil, not criminal means." The online petition site Change.org collected over 27,000 signatures urging an end to her prosecution. Public sentiment seemed to be moving in her favor, but then McDowell was arrested on drug charges as a result of an undercover police sting. To the extent that the national outcry over her treatment might have had an ameliorating effect on a harsh sentence, following the drug conviction, prosecutors, believing they now had the moral high ground, pressed for a speedy conclusion. They joined the drug and "school theft" cases and won the right to have them tried together. Given mandatory sentencing minimums, McDowell faced the potential of serving over twenty years in prison. Instead, she opted for a plea that resulted in a twelve-year sentence with parole eligibility after five years. While she serves her time, her son lives with his grandmother in Bridgeport and attends school in that district. He is said to suffer from frequent nightmares.[7]

Though the sentencing in this case is extreme, McDowell and her family are not alone in attracting national attention for attempting to navigate structural barriers impeding Black children from receiving a quality education. The so-called crime of educational theft is growing and expanding by leaps and bounds. The same year that McDowell began serving her sentence, a federal judge sentenced another single Black mother, Kelly Williams-Bolar of Cleveland, Ohio, to ten days in jail, three years of probation, and eighty hours of community service. Though the governor would subsequently pardon her, she too was convicted of "stealing" an education for her children. Sadly, her father was also swept up in the frenzy and was arrested on fraud charges for letting his daughter use his address. In trying to fight the prosecution, he lost his house and ultimately died in 2012 while still in prison. The whole case is yet another example of the ways that education—and access to a quality, non-segregated, non-apartheid kind of it—has become a marker of a socially limiting caste system. Her "crime" was using her father's address to enroll her children in a predominately white and wealthy school district in which she did not reside. His "crime" was helping his grandchildren.[8]

Williams-Bolar, who worked as a teacher's aide for many years, was aware of many "boundary-hopping" kids, or students who were zoned for one district but attended school in another. She knew that it was both illegal and discouraged. She never believed it was prosecutable. However, she made the choice to try to find a more stable situation in 2006 after there was a break-in at her home in Akron. Though no one was there when the robbery took place, she was nonetheless deeply concerned about her daughters, then ages thirteen and nine. As she explained, "I've got two girls and they're growing up. I couldn't have them walking home alone from school." She says this was the first time it occurred to her that she might be able to use her father's address. Not only were the schools where he lived better but, because he was retired, she said, "I knew that he would be home to look after the girls."[9]

Though Williams-Bolar says the educational quality of the schools in Copley-Fairlawn were not the primary reason for her decision, the difference between the educational record of Akron's schools and that of the Copley-Fairlawn School District, where her father's house was located, is stark. In the 2010–2011 year, Akron public schools met "state-prescribed performance goals on just 5 of 26 categories of performance—such as high school graduation rates and standardized testing scores for reading and math—while Copley-Fairlawn School District met all 26 of its state benchmarks." The only way for students to attend a school in the Copley-Fairlawn district is for them to either reside within its borders or pay a $9,000 annual tuition. Williams-Bolar, who in 2012 earned roughly $28,000, couldn't afford that kind of fee and so listed her father's address on her daughters' enrollment forms. They attended school in the district for two years. Though she couldn't have known it, the decision to enroll her children in Copley-Fairlawn came at a time when the district was in the midst of an aggressive war against parents who tried to "steal" their kids' educations. To its administrators and many of its parents, people like Williams-Bolar simply looked like thieves, literally stealing their school without having to contribute anything to the tax base to pay for the provided services. The residents of those districts say it's not right for them to be expected to subsidize the education of a child whose parents don't pay taxes in the district. They worry about the impact of outside enrollment on class sizes, test scores, and special education programs. They believe these feared changes justify increased vigilance about keeping out families who do not pay taxes, even though at times the methods involved border on something more than extreme.

In order to fight back, the school district deployed a range of tactics to protect what it viewed as an increasingly valuable commodity. Among other things, officials hired private investigators to track parents, and in 2008 they announced a $100 "bounty" to anyone who turned in an illegally registered family. As Williams-Bolar understands it, she was caught because a private investigator hired by the school district had sat outside her father's home for months, monitoring her comings and goings. He assembled photographic evidence that she was not a Copley resident and did not often spend nights at her father's home. Though she fought the charges, she was eventually indicted for grand theft and forgery.

Her father was convicted of fraud. After her conviction, she served nine days in jail, and the terms of her parole forbid her from drinking and required her to submit to drug tests and to report monthly to a probation officer. She also had to perform eighty hours of community service and pay $800 in restitution, as well as the cost of Summit County's prosecution against her. Upon her arrest, supportive groups and organizations set up online petitions and, together with one organized by a Massachusetts woman named Caitlin Lord, garnered 180,000 signatures calling for Governor John Kasich to pardon her. He did so, but the conviction still remains on her record.

The account of Williams-Bolar's youngest daughter, Jada, comparing the school district to which she had been assigned with the one to which her mother and grandfather were able to send her for a few short years, harkens back to the pre–*Brown v. Board* era of sanctioned segregation. She remembers, "We had things that I never would even think an elementary school would have. We had a computer lab. We had the garden outside. We had our own greenhouse." As Jada recalls the move back to the Akron schools, she says, "It was a huge difference. It was huge. We didn't learn that much. It was disruptive in classes. There were no resources. It was completely different, and I felt like I wasn't learning anything at all."[10]

Tellingly, wealthy whites do not end up with felony convictions when they are accused of educational theft. Consider the case of Mark Ebner, a Columbus, Ohio, parent who illegally enrolled his children in a neighboring suburban school district. The Ebner family's primary residence was a $1 million property just outside the suburban district's borders. When Ebner found out that private investigators were tailing him, he reportedly arranged for a house swap with relatives inside the district. He then sued the district for spying on him. The same year that Williams-Bolar and family were engulfed in their court case, the Ebners were able to use their wealth and privilege to evade the grasp of the criminal justice system, and their children continued to benefit from attending a higher quality school. The situation of Williams-Bolar would not be the last time that families who are struggling financially would find the schoolhouse doors in wealthy districts firmly shut in their faces.[11]

In Rochester, New York, Yolanda Hill used her mother's address to register her kids in the academically strong suburban district of Greece, where her mother lived. She had herself lived in the district the year before, but after losing her home to foreclosure, she was forced to move to the less expensive town of Rochester. Wanting to keep her children in the stronger district and give them the opportunity to maintain their social networks, Hill chose to keep them enrolled in the Greece school district. She was charged with third-degree grand larceny and first-degree offering a false instrument for filing. Both of the charges are felonies. Officials found out about Hill from Kevin Degnan, a former law enforcement officer who worked for the Greece school district. He spent mornings and afternoons staking out bus stops and the house in Greece where Hill said she and her children lived. He discovered that they commuted to Greece by bus every morning, and so he turned them in to school officials.

In Broward County, Florida, the school board put up posters that read, "False address can lead to arrest." School registration forms also warn parents that lying about where they live can lead to a perjury charge and jail time. In Grosse Pointe, Michigan, a wealthy suburb of Detroit, three thousand parents signed a petition demanding that the school board spend the necessary $8,000 to verify the registration information of each of the nine thousand students in the district. Officials acquiesced, but at the end of the investigation they found only forty nonresident students. If found to be guilty, parents in that state can be jailed for up to twenty days. In Washington, D.C., parents can be jailed for up to ninety days for stealing education, and in Oklahoma perpetrators can be jailed for up to a year.[12]

In 2015, the school district in Orinda, California, made national headlines when officials hired an investigator to spy on the seven-year-old daughter of a nanny. Both lived together near the school, in the home of her mother's employers. School officials allowed the little girl to stay in the district school only after her mother agreed to make the couple she worked for "official caregivers" for her child, which allowed her employers to enroll her in school. In the Fremont Unified School District in California, the district has created an anonymous tip line and can impose up to $5,000 in fines for any parent found to be skirting the residency requirement. The district also has caseworkers who conduct residency checks at the beginning of each school year. This is true despite the fact that Valerie Williams, director of pupil services in Fremont, says the number of students removed for hopping boundaries each year is fairly small. In Atlanta, a mother of three faced up to eighty years in prison after being charged with sixteen counts of falsifying school documents so that her kids, all honor students, could attend better schools in the city rather than in her home district of Cobb County, Georgia. And the Bayonne School District in northern New Jersey promises parents a $200 bounty when they provide credible information that leads to a student being kicked out. None of the parents snared in these schemes are wealthy, few are white, and most are single mothers of color who are doing what they can to provide a quality education for their children. They have to risk either turning themselves into criminals or enduring financial ruin to achieve it.[13]

This is a well-defined, multipronged, and life-altering assault on parents who are poor, of color, and desperately seeking access to high-quality education for their children. For them, due to lack of money, the schoolhouse doors are closed and they risk time in jail for their actions. Meanwhile, the same ethos of vigorous oversight, surveillance, and prosecution is lacking in relation to the staggering sums of money stolen by growing numbers of charter school managers and operators in states throughout the country. By and large, this money and the schools funded by it are supposed to be used primarily to educate urban children who live in school districts like the ones parents risk prosecution in order to escape. Within the charter school sector, unscrupulous educational providers regularly steal millions in taxpayer funds because of a startling lack of mandated oversight from local, state, and federal officials. These providers are not followed, harassed, or stalked with the laser-like focus directed at poor parents in struggling school districts who want to enroll their children in higher-performing schools.

Despite financial abuses, and during a time when the prosecution of economically vulnerable parents is expanding apace, both major political parties continue to support the largely unregulated expansion of charter schools. As a result, the cycle of hoarding and plundering educational funds earmarked for poor and working-class children of color continues uninterrupted, as it has since the nineteenth century. Again and again, these families learn that race, segregation, and educational policy in this country work against, not for, low-income Black and Latino communities. At the same time, the wealthy and political elite learn that race, segregation, and educational policy works for them. It shores up their caste status, bespeaks moral authority, and ensures financial gain—for some—all while whole communities fall further and further behind. Perhaps our failing to collectively notice this social arrangement, where increasingly thick walls are erected around certain districts, both allowing and keeping out students based on race, ethnicity, and economic status, can help to explain how it came to be that in April 2015 the United States Congress voted 360 to 45 to pass the Success and Opportunity through Quality Charter Schools Act (H.R. 10). The bill was authored with the express purpose of strengthening "the Charter School Program and [to] allow successful charter school models to be replicated nationwide to support choice, innovation, and excellence in education." The bill did not include provisions requiring a strengthening of innovative surveillance techniques to catch charter school cheaters and criminals who were stealing both educational funds and futures. It's only fair that we strengthen regulation and oversight of this industry to at least match the levels at which we enforce theft policies targeting poor parents of color. There is no other way to make it clear that class and skin color are not merely the segrenomic entry fees to a new kind of free-market education system that generates vast profits by exploiting economic and racial inequality.

The Theft of Public Funds

Everyone who met him said Christopher Clemons was charming, competent, and seemingly stable. He was the founder and chief financial officer of a highly regarded charter school, a magna cum laude Ivy League graduate of the University of Pennsylvania, and had also earned an MBA from the Massachusetts Institute of Technology. He arrived in Atlanta and had strong credentials indicating a well-vetted background via the education reform movement. He'd served as chief financial officer of a Boston-based nonprofit that works to create high-performing charter schools across the country. Perhaps all of those seeming markers of trustworthiness explain how it was that Clemons was able to steal so much for so long. In May of 2016, authorities sought his arrest on charges of embezzlement of school/taxpayer funds and fraud. By then, the school's new principal had found numerous cash transfers to Clemons and other staff; tens of thousands of dollars in cash withdrawals; and charges at places like Hooters and Twin Peaks, and for strip clubs with names like Goldrush Showbar and the Cheetah Lounge. In some cases, the charges totaled more than $5,000 on a single date, with the largest single strip club charge coming in at over $12,000. These charges to Atlanta's Latin Academy Charter School's account should have set off some type of alarm. State education officials and corporate executives from Teach for America and Coca-Cola sat on the school's board. Someone should have noticed. No one did. Instead, the theft continued for years. In the end, the final total amounted to more than $600,000. It was all taxpayer money. Clemons fled the state after the losses were discovered. The school from which he stole was, as a result of his actions, so financially troubled that board members closed it. Soon after, the boards of two other Atlanta area charter schools Clemons founded reported that more than $350,000 in additional funds were also missing.[14]

Nearly two hundred children attended the hastily closed school that, given its focus on classical educational practices such as the study of Latin, was supposed to prepare the low-income children who attended the school for a college education. This story is but one of a growing number of cautionary tales for those supporting the rapid, and often lightly regulated, expansion of charter schools. As a newspaper account emphasized following the revelation of the theft, "Latin Academy, with its all-star board, and experienced leader, seemed on track to thrive. But behind that facade of apparent success, the school spent millions of tax dollars with little public scrutiny and operated with a lack of public input foreign to many traditional public schools." The $600,000 embezzled by one man at one school pales in comparison to the total amount in taxpayer dollars that is disappearing from school coffers nationwide.[15]

In May 2016 we learned that the management company for two for-profit charter schools in Jacksonville, Florida, was accused of grand theft, money laundering, and aggravated white-collar crime. Newpoint Education Partners, which operated the San Jose Academy and San Jose Preparatory School, both in Jacksonville, was indicted for fraudulently billing different vendors hundreds of thousands of dollars for supplies, equipment, and services. Prosecutors said Newpoint had been working to launder the stolen money since 2011. The management company collected millions in public education funding annually for running schools in at least three Florida counties. One of Newpoint's schools in St. Petersburg, Windsor Prep Academy, ran up a $1 million deficit and also had to return a $75,000 grant because the company's managers couldn't tell authorities how the money was spent.[16]

For some, charter schools seem to function as something akin to ATMs, with no maximum daily limit attached. In Philadelphia alone, between 2005 and 2011 the U.S. Department of Education opened fifty-three investigations into charter school fraud, resulting in twenty-one indictments and seventeen convictions that implicated twenty of the city's ninety charters. Federal prosecutors there indicted the CEO and the board president of the New Media Technology Charter School, alleging the pair had stolen more than $500,000 in school funds and used the money on other business ventures, including "a private school, a health food store, and a web design firm." At one point, the two hired a marketing consultant for their health food store, gave him an office in the school, and paid him with school funds. At the Philadelphia Academy Charter School, founders solicited bribes and kickbacks from school vendors, submitted fake invoices for reimbursement, and "hired a contractor to help destroy computer records that might implicate them." The former CEO admitted to stealing roughly half a million dollars from the school by, in part, "raiding school vending machines for the coins collected there." Unfortunately, Philly is not the only city with this record. In 2010, L. Lawrence Riccio, the founder of a D.C.-based charter school, was investigated by the FBI for financial misconduct, including having the school pay for his international travel and charging it for purchases at Victoria's Secret and at a wallpaper shop in France, where he owned property. In California, Steven Cox, the founder of what was once California's largest charter school chain, the California Charter Academy, was charged with multiple counts of grand theft after a state audit failed to account for roughly $23 million in taxpayer funds. Cox and at least one other employee used school funds for personal benefit, "including $18,000 for Jet Skis, $11,000 for Disney-related merchandise, $9,000 at the Disneyland Health Spa, and $42,000 to pay personal income taxes." He also diverted more than "$500,000 into other ventures, including a company called Xtreme Motor Sports, and spent more than $ 1 million hiring family members and giving them retroactive raises." [17]

Preston Green, an urban education professor at the University of Connecticut, warns that the underregulated growth of these publicly financed, privately run institutions is more than just a drain on taxpayer dollars and could result in a type of financial "bubble" in Black, urban school districts. Many Black parents, he says, are unhappy with the state of traditional public education in their communities and view charter schools as a better alternative. But along with such schools comes the potential for educational theft, and it is not a stretch to suggest that these transactions could create a type of educational financing bubble not unlike the subprime mortgage debacle that led to the 2008 recession. Indeed, in the run-up to that financial collapse, we as a nation learned quite a bit about the inner workings of subprime mortgage lenders who steered borrowers into risky loans and targeted home buyers, particularly Black and Hispanic borrowers, with excessive fees. It was incredibly lucrative for some, but was equally unsustainable. Green says charter schools have engaged in practices that are successful because they take financial advantage of the fears of "vulnerable parents who lack the political power and financial resources to advocate for change in the existing system." He goes on to note that because of the desire for more educational options, poor communities of color are more likely to support policies that create the conditions for more "charter school bubbles." According to the research study, this is happening because "supporters of charter schools are using their popularity in Black, urban communities to push for states to remove their charter cap restrictions and to allow multiple authorizers. At the same time, private investors are lobbying states to change their rules to encourage charter school growth." The result is what he describes as a policy "bubble," where the combination of multiple authorizers and a lack of oversight can end up creating an abundance of poor-performing schools in particular communities that need high-quality education more than most communities do.[18]

The leaders of such schools find ways beyond theft to be entrepreneurial. Green cites examples such as charter schools in Milwaukee that handed out $100 gift cards, purchased with taxpayer funds, to students and parents. They were given to those who successfully encouraged other students to enroll in the school and to stay long enough to qualify the school to collect state educational funds allocated on a "per student enrolled" basis. In one such school, the Urban Day School, an electronic billboard hung above the front office informing members of the school community: "Hey parents! Refer a student and earn $100 cash!" Officials at the school said the gift card campaign was cost effective because it could raise the school's official enrollment level and, along with it, the corresponding level of state aid. Another school in that city, Capitol West Academy, offered families who referred a child who then enrolled the chance to enter their name in a drawing for a $100 gift card. Windlake Elementary School jumped into the fray and began offering a $50 grocery store gift card to anyone who referred a student. For the "winners" to be eligible for the card, the recruited student had to be present at the school on September 19, the day enrollment numbers were reported to state authorities. All told, by means legal as well as those illegal, charter schools are a cash cow for many of their operators.[19]

Over the past few years, as Black and poor parents were jailed for "stealing" education for their children, we have seen a flood of FBI raids on charter schools all over the country. Agents burst unannounced into schools and carted off documents that they hope will lead them to some of the missing money and aid them in their prosecution efforts. Unfortunately, stolen charter school

funds are rarely returned. Yet the number of such schools continues to grow. Indeed, they remain popular with our political and
financial elite. For example, while not mentioning the staggering
amounts of missing money, former secretary of education John
King has called charter schools "good laboratories for innovation." As a result of a rhetoric focused primarily on educational innovation and not on the innovative ways that some operators are
finding to both legally make as well as steal money in the United
States, the number of public charter schools has grown from
1,542 in 1999 to almost 6,000 in 2016. And, of course, in some
cities the percentage is much higher. New Orleans' public school
system is now almost completely comprised of charter schools. In
Detroit, almost 60 percent of public schools are charter, and in
Washington, D.C., upwards of 50 percent of schools are charters.
And as the number of charter schools across the country continues to grow, the doors to almost four thousand traditional public
schools have closed in the past ten years. The popularity of charter schools, and their ability to fill a long-held educational need in
poor communities of color, speaks primarily to the deeply frustrated desire on the part of Black parents for public schools to provide their children with a quality education. Though it is tragic
that there are so many willing to profit from that desire, there are
some who have long supported the aims, goals, and outcomes of
charter schools who are now starting to notice the extent to which
money, more than good works or closing achievement gaps, seems
to guide many operators.[20]

For example, Rebecca Fox Blair, a charter school administrator and founder of one small school in Wisconsin, shared in an
interview that she was discouraged by how the charter school
movement is changing to focus on moneymaking potential rather
than on so-called innovative teaching. She noticed this shift in
2010 when she attended a national charter school conference.
She recalled, "It's all these huge operators, and they look down on
schools like ours. They call us the 'mom and pop' schools." It is

clear that what education writer and editor Stan Karp has referred
to as the "huge transfer of resources and students from our public
education system to the publicly funded but privately managed
charter sector" has made the potential profits more than a little
tempting. One example is Michael Sharpe, a former CEO of the
FUSE charter school in Hartford, Connecticut, who admitted in
court that he had faked his academic credentials in order to hide
the fact that he was a two-time felon, had been previously convicted of embezzlement, and had served five years in prison as a
result.[21]

In Detroit, Michigan, another city with a burgeoning charter
school movement, the presence of such schools has led to lucrative
contracts for private operators at the same time that traditional
public schools are starved for funds. According to Tom Pedroni,
an associate professor in the college of education at Wayne
State University, "One school bought useless wetlands. Others
overpaid—by a lot—for their school property. And another gave
its administrator a severance worth more than a half million dollars." Two-thirds of the National Heritage Academy schools across
the state "pay as much in rent as tenants in Detroit's Renaissance
Center, with its expansive views of the Detroit River," Pedroni
said. Charter schools are an opportunity for an educational gold
rush as much as they are an answer to an educational crisis in poor
communities of color.[22]

In addition, for all the talk of how we need to improve public
education for lower-income students of color, one of the primary
forms of so-called help has, as a sector, cost taxpayers dearly in
terms of looted, plundered, and misappropriated funds. In one
state after another, investigations have brought to light activities such as theft of money and equipment, bribery, kickback and
stock manipulation schemes, and the misappropriation of funds
by charter school administrators. Though necessary, these complicated investigations into charter school finances are not inexpensive and, in addition to the stolen funds, constitute an added

cost to taxpayers. Toward that end, at least one group has already filed suit, alleging that federal policies supporting the rapid and unregulated expansion of charter schools violate the rights of non-white students.

Filed with the U.S. Department of Education's Office for Civil Rights in May of 2015 by a civil rights organization called the Advancement Project, as well as with the Justice Department, the complaint charges that the federally backed practice of closing traditional public schools and opening charter schools in their place has so harmed students in Newark, New Jersey; Chicago; and New Orleans that "African American children's hopes of equal educational opportunity are being dashed" and their civil rights impeded. What these districts all have in common are Black and Latino enrollments of over 80 percent, along with poverty levels consistently over 70 percent. Put simply, these are children who can least afford to have the tax dollars allocated for their education stolen or their right to a quality education disrupted.

According to Green, who authored the report suggesting that the charter school industry is arguably at the point of a financial meltdown on par with that of subprime mortgages, lawsuits such as these may ultimately represent our best hope to burst this charter school bubble before it gets much further out of control. Civil rights lawsuits alleging unequal treatment are one way to have some of this unchecked, lightly regulated growth slow, if not fully halt. He adds that we may be approaching a period when we will start seeing state constitutional challenges, like in Washington State, where in the spring of 2016 a coalition of public school educators, administrators, and labor unions challenged the constitutionality of the state's original, 2012, charter law, which was then overturned by the Washington Supreme Court. Their lawsuit charged that the new law allows "unelected charter school operators" to spend public money without adequate public oversight or accountability and that the new law funds charter schools with lottery money, diverting funding from the state general fund, the main source of funding for the state's K–12 public schools.[23]

As Green concedes, the most worrisome scenario is a community that ends up with few traditional public schools, insufficient oversight by both charter management organizations and elected officials, and no significant pressure to get charter schools to perform well. He could also add that such a system, in a worst-case scenario, would probably also vigorously prosecute parents who made an attempt to circumvent residency laws in order to access a well-run, well-regulated school system that consistently provided a high-quality education. If we continue on the current trajectory, that would be the present and future of education in far too many communities.[24]

7

THE AGE OF RESISTANCE

In the summer of 2015, a group of middle-aged and elderly Black community members in Chicago announced they were going to wage a hunger strike. This, they said, was the only way left open for them to draw attention to their struggles with educational officials working with the Chicago public schools. Maybe, they hoped, publicly starving themselves would elicit a response from school administrators who they said ignored, disrespected, and denied them a governing voice in the education of their sons, daughters, grandchildren, and neighbors. Calling themselves the Coalition to Revitalize Dyett High School, the twelve participants demanded that district administrators reopen a beloved neighborhood high school. It had been closed because of chronically low scores on standardized tests.

A statement released by an advocacy nonprofit named the Network for Public Education made it clear that standardized tests were impacting education in Chicago beyond just the one school. It charged that in low-income communities of color, such tests were used to "rank, sort, label, and punish" Black and Latino children, that though the exams were often extolled as a means to allow education officials to document racial and economic achievement gaps, they often instead became a justification for a larger agenda aimed at further destabilizing poor communities of color, a conclusion reached because "thousands of predominantly poor and minority neighborhood schools—the anchors of communities—have been closed" as a result of the scores. Surely those sentiments resonated with the hunger strikers as, according to one, "the city has sabotaged our community, which we know is undergoing gentrification. Why would they close the only neighborhood high school left for our children?"[1]

At the same time that the drama surrounding the Chicago high school was unfolding, groups of white and Asian parents and students were also responding quite forcefully to the ways that federally mandated tests circumscribed their lives. They were publicly protesting by joining in with what came to be known as the opt-out movement and beginning to take a stand to tell schools that their children would not take state and federally prescribed high-stakes tests. In the spring of 2015, New York State had one of the highest test-refusal rates in the nation when more than 20 percent, about 240,000 students, opted not to take the state exams. The use, overuse, purpose, and practicality of testing has spawned a sustained movement in communities that were wealthy and in those that were poor, both educationally and economically. However, despite the testing being a common enemy, so to speak, against which both communities could organize, for students of color in failing schools testing was just one of a number of concerns against which they began to organize.[2]

This chapter explores community activism and protests against educational policies and practices communities believe to be harmful to their educational futures. Across the country, those most impacted by segrenomic-dependent educational schemes and practices are raising their voices to push back. Some decry how tests are used to circumscribe their futures or impact the teachers and schools in their communities. Others direct their activism toward ending abusive disciplinary practices found in poor schools, though almost completely absent from those that are wealthy. In both instances, people whose lives are harmed by educational policies are finding ways to resist. In wealthy white communities, lessening the frequency of standardized tests is the goal of protest. In communities of color, in addition to decrying the frequency of tests, the conversation has expanded to include critiques of how tests are used to pave the way for school closures, shrinking education budgets, community destabilization, and abusive discipline practices in schools. For students, protesting is one of very few ways in which they are able to add their voices to discussions about educational policies impacting their schools.

Do standardized achievement tests unfairly advantage white, Asian, and wealthy students and disadvantage everyone else? According to a group of educational advocacy organizations and civil rights groups, such as the NAACP and the Advancement Project, the answer is yes. In 2012, they jointly filed a complaint with the U.S. Department of Education pointing out that Black and Latino students in New York score below whites and Asians on standardized tests so consistently that, although they are almost 70 percent of the overall student body in the system, they make up only 11 percent of students enrolled at elite public schools. As a result, the complaint argues that New York City is in violation of the 1964 Civil Rights Act because schools rely on a test that consistently advantages one racial group over another.[3]

Opinions differ as to why, on K–12 achievement tests and college entrance exams, lower-income students as well as Black and Latino students consistently score below privileged white and Asian students. These gaps persist despite decades of research and numerous studies attempting to explain and close them. One theory posits that students with grandparents who have graduated from college always score higher, suggesting that the tests unfairly penalize students who are the first in their family to attend college. Whatever the explanation, it is difficult to reconcile why we rely on such tests when there is plenty of evidence showing that they heavily advantage some districts and students and greatly disadvantage others.[4]

While the standardized testing gap between people of color and whites and Asian Americans is bad, it's nothing compared to the gap between the poor and the wealthy. A 2014 study by the

Annie E. Casey Foundation found that the gap for achievement test scores between rich and poor had grown by almost 60 percent between the 1960s and 2014 to be almost twice as large as the gap between white students and children of other races. The playing field is far from level when we continue to use tests that we know at the outset will show that wealthy students do better than less wealthy students and that white and Asian students outperform everyone else. But the research shows us that the issues are with how we use these tests. That is the history of standardized tests, which—according to Columbia University professor Nicholas Lemann's history of the Educational Testing Service, *The Big Test: The Secret History of American Meritocracy*—were first developed in the 1940s as a way to exclude Jewish students from Ivy League campuses. Kaplan, today one of the largest test-preparation organizations, got its start when Stanley Kaplan resolved to come up with test-taking techniques to "beat the test" and ensure that such students did well in admissions to elite schools.[5]

Today, acknowledging the inherent racial and economic inequity of standardized achievement tests, hundreds of colleges have already stopped requiring the SAT for college admission decisions. However, the same cannot be said for K–12, where scores on standardized tests are used for everything from admitting students to prestigious public schools to placing students in gifted programs, relegating them to remedial ones, allocating federal funding, evaluating teachers, and closing schools. In response, a growing number of parents, school boards, teachers, and civil rights organizations are beginning to question the fairness of our overreliance on standardized tests.

In 2014, over three hundred groups, including the NAACP Legal Defense and Educational Fund, signed a petition to ask Congress to ban the use of such tests. Nothing came of the petition, and, as a result, parents and students in low-income communities of color are more often than not left to their own devices when searching for the most productive path to protect themselves from the financial and emotional consequences of high-stakes tests—and the uses to which they are put. They ask why there is not more money to fund proven methods that will help their children learn. They want to know why test scores are used to hurt their children, close their schools, and add to the instability in their communities. In the twenty-first century, standardized tests are a key feature of how wealthy educational investors and school reformers ensure that highly racially and economically segregated apartheid school districts remain lucrative. This has been true since President Bush announced his intention to use them this way.[6]

At the 91st Annual National Association for the Advancement of Colored People Convention held in 2000, President George W. Bush announced what would almost amount to a declaration of war on unequal education and explained the necessity of using standardized tests as a primary tool in the nation's arsenal. Though he used no such phrasing in his speech announcing No Child Left Behind, in many ways the bill's promise to devote the full resources of the United States government to the project of equalizing the racial and economic achievement and opportunity gaps in public education was, at the least, an acknowledgment of what it would take to accomplish such a feat. In addition to the bill's shining a light on the ways that race and poverty shape educational outcomes, it introduced standardized testing as a key component of how communities of color might actually achieve educational equality. But before focusing specifically on the test, Bush began his remarks by acknowledging that there was a tense history between the Republican party and organizations focused on Black freedom, but he said, "For our nation, there is no denying the truth that slavery is a blight on our history and that racism, despite all the progress, still exists today. For my party, there is no escaping the reality that the party of Lincoln has not always carried the mantle of Lincoln. . . . Transcending our history is essential."

The president went on to tell the assembled group that it was time that the nation, in a nod toward such transcendence, made a new commitment to those who found themselves living in what he called "prosperity's shadow." He added, "The purpose of prosperity is to ensure the American Dream touches every willing heart . . . we cannot afford to have an America segregated by class, by race, or by aspiration." As he called on America to close the "gap of hope between communities of prosperity and communities of poverty" the audience rose to applaud. As he extolled the efforts of previous generations of "men and women once victimized by Jim Crow [who] have risen to leadership in the halls of Congress" they cheered. When he acknowledged that we had to do more to enforce civil rights laws and pledged that his administration would do so because, he said, today, "instead of separate but equal, there is separate and forgotten," the group erupted in full-throated and appreciative affirmation. Finally, he got to his point, and the oft-quoted "tagline" of the speech. He said that we had to "confront another form of bias: the soft bigotry of low expectations."

With that pronouncement, the president pivoted to his core concerns for the day—the fact that poor children who are also Black and Latino are not as well served by our nation's educational system. In particular, he noted that there then existed "a tremendous gap of achievement between rich and poor, white and minority" and a form of discrimination that produced a group of Americans "imprisoned by illiteracy, abandoned to frustration and the darkness of self-doubt." He announced that he was linking the unfinished struggle for civil rights to the unfinished struggle for educational equality and making a commitment to hold the nation accountable for ending the centuries of educational inequality that had so long existed. He pledged to call out those educators who fail our nation's youth and to also provide parents with a broader array of educational choices. Testing was central to this plan, as objective criteria and tools, he said, were the most potent weapon we had to finally turn the educational tide toward justice. He added:

All students must be measured. We must test to know. And low-performing schools, those schools that won't teach and won't change, will have three years to produce results, three years to meet standards, three years to make sure the very faces of our future are not mired in mediocrity. And if they're unable to do so, the resources must go to the parents so that parents can make a different choice. . . . Education helps the young. Empowerment lifts the able.[7]

President Bush linked the new No Child Left Behind bill with parental empowerment and the politically popular and financially lucrative school choice movement. Not only would tests alert educational officials to yawning gaps between students based on race and economics, but they would also be responsible for determining which schools would remain open, which testing companies should be hired, and whether districts needed to spend the money to hire outside consultants. By 2008, President Obama upped the testing stakes with the institution of another educational bill called Race to the Top. That bill opened the door to the use of testing to evaluate and potentially fire teachers and to hold them personally responsible for the shortcomings of their students.

It is doubtful that either president could have imagined that by 2015 parents and students; suburban and urban; white, Asian, and Black; wealthy, middle class, and poor; those who had choices as to where their children attended school and those who did not would rise up to vigorously protest both the amount and uses of testing. For some parents, the issue was the individual well-being of their children; for others, it was the way that tests led to school closures and created an environment rife with harsh disciplinary practices. Some parents decried the effort to distill the essence of true learning down to an easily manageable test score, while others complained of the undue stress and strain such tests put on the still-forming psyches of young children. Some opposed the very idea that a test, a snapshot of performance on one day, could come to shape the future of an individual, an entire school, a whole neighborhood.

Far from the first or only action that those fed up with the over-reliance on testing cited, an opening salvo in the developing battle took place in November of 2013. The secretary of education at the time, Arne Duncan, ignited a firestorm of protest when he told a gathering of the Council of Chief State School Officers that he believed much of the pushback against the administration's imposition of a new round of mandatory tests called the Common Core was occurring because "white suburban moms are discovering that their children are not as brilliant as they thought and their schools are not as good as they thought." While he apologized for the remark within a day or so, the white, suburban-led organized resistance to overtesting has continued to grow. And it's not just parents who are concerned and pushing back against what they believe to be burdensome levels of testing. Students have joined the fray as well.[8]

In 2015, over one hundred students in Bloomington, Indiana, staged a walkout from their classes to protest their fatigue with the regime of standardized testing. Instead of attending school that day, one of the organizers, Ankur Singh, planned a screening of a film called *Listen*, a feature-length documentary he said shows that "behind every one of those test scores is a living, breathing child who has dreams and aspirations that may or may not align with what's being measured on standardized tests." Between 2014 and 2016, parents and students alike organized similar walkouts, protests, and demonstrations in communities from Maryland to Massachusetts. In some schools in California in 2015 over 50 percent of students opted out of standardized tests. On the whole, parents and students who opt out of standardized tests are white or Asian and range from middle class to wealthy. State legislatures, as well as the federal government, are responsive to these constituents. According to an article on CNN's website, in 2015 New Jersey lawmakers approved a measure requiring schools to accommodate parents who opt out of testing by providing alternative activities, such as independent reading, for their children. Also in 2015, in Indiana, the state's superintendent recommended that parents homeschool their children during the testing weeks instead of having them take the tests. However, in perhaps the most significant endorsement of their concerns, in October 2015, President Obama posted a video message to Facebook calling for schools to reduce the amount of standardized testing taking place in classrooms.[9]

The response to complaints coming from communities of color about testing in particular, or education in general, is not always as positive, nor are those communities' educational concerns solely about the tests themselves. Instead, for Black and Latino students in underfunded districts, student activism often revolves around the use of high stakes testing to dismantle their public schools and also includes a focus on how they are harshly disciplined in schools and classrooms.

In her award-winning book *Unequal City: Race, Schools, and Perceptions of Injustice,* educational sociologist Carla Shedd points out that many of us who are educators, researchers, politicians, and cultural critics spend little time talking *to,* as opposed to *about,* young people when doing work on topics that impact that demographic. She says,

> Teenagers have remarkable vantage points on the cities they live in—not only on how their city functions but also on how it does not. They are a walking experiment in the effects that city agencies—in this case, the board of education and the city policing apparatus—can have on a generation of people who are especially vulnerable and may even be harmed by the policies and procedures that seek to ensure their safety. It is long past time to let their voices be heard.[10]

When we listen to the concerns of students educated in America's apartheid schools, we get a full accounting of the specific ways they believe their humanity is under attack as well as advice for what should be done to fix education policy. One of the most impactful student groups is named the Philadelphia Student Union (PSU). It was founded in 1995 by a group of young people who were concerned about not receiving the quality of education that they deserved. According to its website, the group's guiding principles are organized around a belief that not just parents and guardians, but also students themselves, would have to be involved in setting policy if school reform were ever going to be successful. In the past few years, it has expanded across the country, opening chapters in Newark, Chicago, and Detroit.

Though it was founded in 1995, it wasn't until 2001 that PSU began to attract widespread local and national attention as one of the leading and most vocal organizations at the forefront of the fight against the takeover and privatization of the schools in Philadelphia. In response to mounting deficits and continued low student performance on standardized tests, the Commonwealth, as the state of Pennsylvania is often dubbed, announced it would wrest control of Philadelphia's system from local authority. In preparation, the first step state officials took was to commission a study from an educational management organization—Edison Schools. Education officials asked Edison to conduct an evaluation and to make recommendations for how to improve the educational conditions in the city. Edison's report proposed that the city's one hundred lowest-performing schools, as well as most central administration functions, should be taken from city control and contracted out to a private provider. Its conclusions were hardly surprising. At the time, Edison's business model relied on managing failing or struggling schools. It recommended that its company be given the job.

Before Governor Mark Schweiker could proceed with these or

any other recommendations, Mayor John Street negotiated with him to work out a compromise. The mayor wanted more control over the appointment of new district leadership, and, in return, the deal he endorsed eliminated the plan to turn the running of the school district's central office over to a private company and committed the state to providing the district with a one-time infusion of $75 million. What that meant was that administrative jobs were saved, though schools and students were still threatened. Working in concert with the governor, in late 2001 Street suspended educational democracy in the city and replaced the publicly elected school board with a five-member School Reform Commission. Governor Schweiker appointed James Nevels, a businessman from the suburbs, as chair. Nevels immediately began implementing what became known as the "diverse provider" model. This meant that the commission identified forty-five of the district's most-troubled schools and assigned them to private providers, including Edison Inc. and others. Of course, these were the schools where children were struggling most immediately with poverty and other forms of social and economic instability. Having lost faith in the adults charged with educating them, the students themselves stood up and pushed back.[11]

The opposition to the educational plans supported by elected officials was as immediate as it was fierce. Joined by Youth United for Change, the Philadelphia Student Union staged protests, marches, candlelight vigils, and blockades of the school district's headquarters to show its opposition. The results were impressive. On November 20, 2001, eight hundred students from Philadelphia gathered at the state capital in Harrisburg for a day of protests. Their primary demand was that the governor withdraw his support for any plan involving Edison Schools' taking over the struggling school district of Philadelphia. According to the group's website, the students were deeply concerned because, as far as anyone outside of the company could confirm, Edison had little to no track record of success. They were also against the plan for the state to take over the school district and disband the school board.

Hundreds of students walked out of class in protest of the pending takeover, and hundreds more staged a rally both at the school district headquarters and at City Hall. At the district headquarters, the students held hands, encircling the entire building. This, organizers said, was to symbolize their desire to keep private companies out. Despite their efforts, plans for the state takeover of the district and for Edison Schools to take over twenty or so of the lowest-performing schools in the district continued apace. In response, a few weeks after their first action, more than a thousand high school students from all over the city descended on City Hall, staying there for almost three hours. Building upon those earlier actions, the PSU has launched campaigns for changes on a wide variety of school issues, including school underfunding, which has left Philly students without counselors, nurses, or after school programs; pushing back against the increase in charter schools; fighting for funding at the state level; pushing for the School Reform Commission members to be elected rather than appointed so they are accountable to students and parents; school policing; and ending the school-to-prison pipeline.

Though schools in Philadelphia were not returned to local control, one of the things that came out of all this was that the group and its tactics expanded to other cities where similar changes were under way. This included Newark, New Jersey. Similar to students in Philadelphia, the Newark chapter of the Student Union rose to prominence as it refused to quietly accept the fact that the school district was under state control. The state provided what the Student Union believed was a lack of adequate funding for traditional community schools, preferring to fund the growth of charter schools run by free market–inspired organizations or private companies using taxpayer dollars. Tanaisa Brown, who in 2015 at the time of the strike was seventeen years old and the secretary of the Newark Student Union, explained, "Our schools are crumbling . . . so we want our education to be fully funded, and that's what we're fighting for today." She added, "Some of these reformers never really think about how they may affect the students individually. They're just thinking about their personal benefit." She ended with, "I think students stepping up to the plate are showing that they do care about urban education, about their schools, and about learning through a school that helps them emotionally as well." [12]

When asked by a reporter what she and the other students hoped to accomplish, one seventeen-year-old student named Olivia Owens-Culver said, "Most people walk around this world, thinking that they can't get nowhere . . . but us, as young people, we have a voice. We need to speak for ourselves." This protest ended up being one of the largest student protests in Newark's history, as students from various high schools marched while waving signs with messages like "Save Our Schools" and "We Have Rights." The group's president, eighteen-year-old Kristin Towkaniuk, told the crowd, "We did not come here . . . to play a game. . . . We're done playing games with our education." As the students locked arms, Towkaniuk led the crowd in a chant of "We have a duty to fight. We have a duty to win. We must love and protect one another. We have nothing to lose but our chains." [13]

The charges of district starvation lobbed by students, parents, and activists consistently point out the substandard condition of the buildings in which students are expected to learn. Today, one American city stands out in terms of the decayed and chaotic nature of both its buildings and the educations found, and not found, in them. That city is Detroit. The state of traditional public schools in the district offers a clear example of the run-down, underfunded, apartheid educational conditions students are protesting. The buildings have decayed to the point of being unsafe, failing by every statistical measure, and the district is consistently threatening to cross the line from minimal solvency to outright

bankruptcy. As an example of what they see as problematic, teachers, students, and parents report heating systems that do not
work, leaky roofs, unsafe levels of mold, odors described as rancid,
and cockroaches as long as three inches that scuttle about "until
they are squashed by a student who volunteers for the task." One
teacher reported "rodents out in the middle of the day, like they're
coming to class." In 2000, Detroit public schools had close to
150,000 students, but by 2016 that number had dipped drastically
to fewer than 45,000. While in recent decades large numbers of
people left Detroit for either the suburbs or other states, many of
those who stayed chose to enroll their children in charter schools,
which more than half of school-age children from Detroit now
attend. According to the National Alliance for Public Charter
Schools, about 20 percent of school-age children in Detroit attended charter schools in 2006. By 2014, less than ten years later,
that number had shot up to 55 percent, and it continues to rise.
The 2009 appointment of an emergency manager to take charge
of the struggling school district has not turned the finances or
achievement around. "We're on our fourth emergency manager
here," said Craig Thiel, a senior research associate for the Citizens
Research Council. "They each seem to be borrowing from the
same playbook: figure out a way to get through the current year,
end the year without going insolvent, and then push costs onto
the next year in the hopes that things will improve in some way." [14]
In order to address these failings, many people in Detroit said they
wanted a locally elected school board to make the decisions about
district schools as well as an end to state-appointed emergency
management. They also called for more immediate intervention
to address the deteriorating state of school buildings. No voices
are raised more loudly than those of students attending the city
schools. [15]

   In April of 2016, at Martin Luther King, Jr. High School,
between forty-five and fifty students walked out to protest

conditions. Detroit student leaders talked to the *World Socialist Web Site* about their cause: "There are rodents and there is no
pest control. . . . It's either too hot or too cold." Another student
added, "In most of my classes . . . there are less than half the books
we need. . . . I have no books in world history, Algebra II, vocals,
and student government. . . . In my main structured class, phys-
ics, we have no books and have to download the material online."
In response to a question about why she was out there that day,
she answered, "We are fighting for our education, for victory. It's
not just a fight for teachers, it's not just a fight for students, it's
a fight for education." Ashley Ray, another Detroit student, addressed the reasons for the student protests, saying, "Education
is the most important thing, and for anyone to try and take that
from us is wrong." Though not receiving much attention, student-
led movements for a quality education continue to spread across
the country.[16]

In Chicago and Portland, Oregon, students have joined together to form student unions. In those cities, as was true elsewhere, they did so to protest budget cuts, teacher layoffs, school
closings, and high-stakes testing. The Chicago group got its start
after the Chicago Teachers Union strike in 2012. Then, a Chicago high school student named Israel Muñoz says he began to
wonder, "Where is the student voice in this? Why haven't we been
consulted when it comes to any decisions regarding education?"
He began to think that if the teachers had a union, then it only
made sense that students should have one too. When interviewed
for an online article, Muñoz and Ian Jackson of the Portland Student Union both stressed that it was important for the students
to develop a voice and empower themselves if they wanted to see
change come. Muñoz remarked, "Young people are given this
notion that if you want to make a change you have to wait until
you're eighteen so you can be an adult and you can vote." He adds,
"But the reality is that someone's age shouldn't determine whether

or not they can speak out, whether or not they want to make a change, whether or not they want to organize to make that change a reality." [17]

From New York to Chicago to San Francisco, whether in relation to traditional public schools or to charter schools, students are organizing both to complain and to offer solutions and policies that they believe are more humane and go far beyond concerns with the number, use, and frequency of taking standardized tests. As one of the youth organizations in California argues on its website, the creation of a "two-tiered education system has left a significant number of students with very few options for their future, and essentially condemned to another generation of low-wage work or prison." [18] They say that these inequities are perpetuated and intensified by a range of aggressive, unregulated, and biased disciplinary practices that disproportionately impact low-income Black and Latino children, thus "depriving them of their fundamental right to education and in many cases pushing students permanently out of school and into the juvenile and criminal justice systems." [19]

One of the leading educational locations where harsh discipline takes place is in many of the free market–inspired and taxpayer-supported charter schools popular in poor urban school districts. Support for the damaging perspectives against which students are arguing, one that advocates what is known as "zero tolerance" in terms of violating any expectations or school rules, was summed up in an April 2015 think piece written by the founder of the Success Academy chain of charter schools, Eva S. Moskowitz. She published her views in the *Wall Street Journal*. Though offering no support for her thinking, Moskowitz says she believes "zero tolerance" discipline policies are linked to higher learning outcomes. According to her charter chain's 2012 code of conduct, there are over sixty infractions—including bullying, spotty attendance, dress-code violations, littering, and failing to be "in a ready-to-succeed position"—that might lead to a violation.

Enough violations, and students are suspended. Because of these policies, the suspension rates at Success Academy Charter schools are almost three times higher than those in regular New York City K–12 public schools. Moskowitz defends her school's policies, saying, "Anyone who wants students to succeed in life should focus on better education, not on more lax discipline." She says others who support such lax policies are in opposition to scholarship and are moving in opposition to what is recommended as a best practice. However, there is a lot of scholarship, not just students, that disagrees with her.[20]

Educational researchers who study school discipline policies point out that restorative justice may substantially reduce disruptive behavior, enhance learning, promote positive school climate, and destroy the school-to-prison pipeline that exacerbates inequality and disadvantage for minority students.[21] Though Moskowitz refers to such practices as a "campaign to diminish the school discipline needed to ensure a nurturing and productive learning environment," the U.S. Department of Education, the U.S. Department of Justice, civil rights and civil liberties organizations, researchers, foundations, and advocacy coalitions all agree that suspensions and expulsions are used excessively in urban schools, often for such minor infractions as "talking back," and that such practices should be reduced. Indeed, based on research conducted by a wide range of organizations, such as the American Academy of Pediatrics, the American Psychological Association, and the School Discipline Consensus Project of the Council of State Governments, it is clear that zero-tolerance policies are harmful. In turn, restorative justice policies are supported by those organizations, as well as, perhaps most important, by the children who actually attend the schools. Though they have an overwhelming amount of evidence on their side, some educators and administrators nonetheless continue to utilize policies that put them at a severe disadvantage. In response, students of color attending urban schools feel the need to band together and sometimes even unionize. For them, discipline in both traditional public schools and the free market–inspired public charter schools is often as negatively impactful as excessive test taking is in schools that are predominantly wealthy and contain few students who are Black and Latino. Their activism is a form of self-protection. It is sorely needed.[22]

The students are getting results. If not so much in the areas of reducing testing, increasing budget allocations, or getting their districts out from under state control, they are at the forefront of making change possible for future generations in the area of harsh disciplinary measures. For example, in 2015 in Chicago, high school–aged activists helped to pass state Senate Bill 100, which prohibits schools from adopting so called zero-tolerance disciplinary policies. In NYC, student activists who attended low-income, low-performing schools were instrumental in pushing the Bill de Blasio administration toward supporting "The Roadmap to Promote Safe Schools," which was his plan for providing training in de-escalation techniques to police and school safety officers, as well as promoting restorative justice techniques in a bid to end overly punitive school discipline policies. It focused in part on the problematic role of school safety officers in public schools.[23]

A familiar presence in low-income urban schools, though far less present in well-resourced schools, school resource officers are a form of security guard who work in public schools. In practice, some say, they are worsening the situation and hastening how quickly children become embroiled in the "school-to-prison pipeline" rather than curbing its impact. Thanks to inconsistent training models and a lack of clear standards, critics contend school officers are "introducing children to the criminal justice system unnecessarily by doling out harsh punishments for classroom misbehavior." As an example of why students are focusing so specifically on discipline in their schools, one need look no further than a videotaped May 2016 encounter between a school safety officer and a high school student in Philadelphia. Brian Burney, a member of the Philadelphia Student Union, says he was headed to the third-floor bathroom between classes when he was confronted by a school police officer and was told he didn't have the proper hall pass. Burney says, "We got into an argument. I threw an orange at the wall, but not at the officer. He punched me in the face. He knocked me down, brought me down to the ground, and put me in a chokehold." Burney sustained a concussion during the struggle, which school officials said was caused by him banging his own head on the ground, not by the attack perpetrated on him by the safety officer. Burney said, "School officers, they're just dealing with us like criminals. It's sad that a lot of the students are accustomed to this." Sadly, that is a sentiment that seems to be all too true.[24]

Maria Fernandez, the senior coordinator for the Urban Youth Collaborative, a citywide coalition of New York City students of color fighting for comprehensive education reform in city public schools, also has a story to tell about school safety officers. She recalls the day when, as a sixteen-year-old public school student in New York City, the "student safety officer grabbed me, threw me on the stairs, twisted my arms, called for more cops, and then handcuffed me. I had to go to court. I had bruises all over my body. I felt worthless." Motivated by this event as well as others, in 2012 Maria became a lead organizer of a group called Journey for Justice, a national intergenerational alliance of parents and students "working to fight back against the privatization of education and to stop the disruptive school closures in communities of color." In recalling the violence directed at her in school that day during a hearing with education officials about excessive force in public schools, she asked, "Are Black students or students with special needs more disruptive, or more dangerous than their white peers? No, our *response* to these students is the danger!"[25]

The group she works with, the Urban Youth Collaborative, is

specifically interested in making sure district schools in NYC rely far less on the use of harsh disciplinary practices like zero-tolerance policies, which they say involve the police in minor incidents and lead to school-based arrests, referrals to juvenile detention, and sometimes even incarceration. They also advocate for the elimination of suspensions for the vague category of "defying authority" and call for the funding and implementation of district-wide restorative justice approaches to discipline instead of suspensions as well as the elimination of the position of school safety officer and of their right to handcuff students on school grounds. Though the sight of handcuff-wielding police officers arresting students is rare in wealthy schools with few students of color, in poor schools it is regrettably common.

Though Fernandez's experience was in New York City, it mirrors a viral video of an incident in South Carolina that made its way around the Internet in the fall of 2015. It showed a white police officer brutally attacking a young Black girl sitting in her classroom seat. On the video, we see the school safety officer storm into the classroom, grab the student, and hurl her to the floor before picking her up, handcuffing her, and leading her from the room. Her name was Shakara. Another student who yelled at the officer to stop was also attacked and led from the room in handcuffs. Her name was Niya. They and not the officer ended up facing criminal charges for "disturbing the school." Across the country, that same charge is leveled at students who receive summonses for a similar charge, "disorderly conduct." This charge can encompass everything from "refusing an order to leave a classroom to being excessively loud." As a result of such incidents, outside of free market–supported school reform circles, few agree about the educational utility of such harsh disciplinary methods. Black and Latino students are doing something about it. Though these measures are a clear step in the right direction, they may be a case of too little too late as, having already seen enough, many Black parents are leaving schools entirely behind.

There's No Place Like Home

Given the problems in districts like New York, San Francisco, Newark, and Detroit, it should perhaps not be too surprising that across the country, in order to try to keep their children safe, many Black parents are voting with their feet and opting for home-schooling. According to the National Home Education Research Institute, by 2015 Black parents were homeschooling an estimated 220,000 children instead of sending them to schools where they were often undereducated and harshly disciplined. Black families are one of the fastest-growing demographics in homeschooling, with—according to the National Center for Education Statistics—Black students making up an estimated 10 percent of the total homeschooling population. At present, that group makes up only 16 percent of all public-school students nationwide. One such student's parent is Vanessa Robinson, who pulled her son, Marvell, out of public school in San Diego following a number of incidents where students at his elementary school regularly harassed him.

While white homeschooling families generally cite religious or moral disagreements with public schools in their decision to pull their children out of traditional classroom settings, in a 2012 article published in the *Journal of Black Studies* called "African American Homeschooling as Racial Protection," Temple University professor of education Ama Mazama surveyed Black homeschooling families from around the country. She found that most chose to educate their children at home at least in part to avoid school-related racism; she notes, "We have all heard that the American education system is not the best and is falling behind in terms of international standards. But this is compounded for Black children, who are treated as though they are not as intelligent and cannot perform as well, and therefore the standards for them should be lower." Mazama acknowledges that homeschooling is controversial because, particularly for "African Americans[,] there is a sense of betrayal when you leave public schools in particular because the struggle to get into those schools was so harsh and so long, there is this sense of loyalty to the public schools. People say, 'We fought to get into these schools, and now you are just going to leave?'"[26]

In a 2015 *Atlantic* article on the rise of homeschooling among African Americans, Paula Penn-Nabrit, who homeschooled her children in the 1990s, acknowledges that concerns with betrayal of the type Mazama describes hit particularly close to home. Indeed, in her case they involve her own family. Her husband's uncle, James Nabrit, was a central figure in the Washington, D.C., case that was bundled into *Brown v. Board* and actually argued *Brown v. Board of Education* in front of the Supreme Court alongside Thurgood Marshall. When Penn-Nabrit and her husband finally decided to pull their three sons from public school, she said, "A lot of people felt that because my family was intimately involved in the effort to integrate schools, that for me to pull my children out of schools was a betrayal of all that work." She said that, in the end, she concluded that ultimately *Brown v. Board* actually had nothing to do with what she as a parent might think her child needed. Rather, "that decision meant the state can't decide to give me less than, but I can decide I want more than." In 2003, Penn-Nabrit published her first book, *Morning by Morning: How We Home-Schooled Our African-American Sons to the Ivy League,* as a resource for other Black parents who might want to replicate her success with homeschooling. Her eldest attended Princeton while her youngest son went to Amherst College.[27]

For students who are poor and of color, America's schools are in crisis. The infrastructure, ideology, progress, and promises all fall more than a little short if the goal is equality. As the structure has crumbled, the rationale for why has focused far less on the structure or system itself and much more on the failures of those it is designed to educate. We focus far more on how and why it is that

America's urban youth can't learn and have families that don't value education, as well as why Black children in particular are so damaged that many believe that to do well in school, to aspire at all, is akin to "acting white." At the same time, as we play a cynical game of blame the victim, we are short on solutions.

Support for current segrenomic educational policies crosses traditional party lines, and their expansion found favor in the federal policies begun under President Clinton, refined under President Bush during his eight years in office, and greatly expanded during the Obama presidency. But even as political, economic, and social leaders continue to support increasingly narrow educational policies that do nothing to lessen the caste-creating apartheid schools, Black community members protest them by resorting to hunger campaigns in order to attract attention; Black and Latino youth ask education officials for protection from the intended and unintended consequences that are raining down on their heads, hearts, and bodies; and some parents make the choice to leave the public education system behind entirely. These communities are engaged, organized, and mobilized to make relevant the educational systems that seek to make their futures irrelevant. In the process, they may save us all.

CODA

Trickle-Up Education

In the spring of 2010, Facebook founder and multibillionaire Mark Zuckerberg donated $100 million to the public school system in Newark, New Jersey. The long-troubled district, like so many others in highly segregated urban areas, had been annexed by the state in 1995. State investigators had documented long-standing and pervasive corruption in the school system, along with an almost total neglect of the educational needs of the district's students. The final report concluded that "the longer children remain in the Newark public schools, the less likely they are to succeed academically." By 2010, however, it was not clear that state governance was any more effective in bringing about educational change. The new state-controlled management developed its own record of ineffectual—if not criminal—leadership. As a result, almost twenty years after Newark schools fell under control of the governor's office, no more than 30 percent of third through eighth graders were reading or doing math at grade level. The high school graduation rate was only 54 percent, and more than 90 percent of graduates who attended the local community college required remedial classes. Newark was simply failing to educate its students, the majority of whom where poor and of color.[1]

Zuckerberg's $100 million solution was a matching grant requiring then-mayor and current U.S. senator Cory Booker to raise another $100 million in order to have full access to the gift. Confident in their ability to succeed, and in order to achieve maximum publicity for the philanthropic windfall, Booker, Zuckerberg, and Governor Chris Christie all appeared on the wildly popular Oprah Winfrey show to announce the gift. Zuckerberg explained that the largesse he had decided to put forth was inspired by wanting to find a way to address educational inequality in urban districts—and he wanted to have something substantial to show in five years. The trio promised that by 2015, Newark schools would be a shining example of how philanthropy; state, local, and federal education officials; education reform devotees; consultants; and community members could work together to once and for all show the world how possible it was to turn a district from chronically struggling to thriving. In the end, by most measures, the entire effort was an extremely expensive failure, perhaps the most expensive an American city has ever seen.

In the battles over how to fix America's schools, pundits and policymakers often return again and again to discussing the people perceived to be most directly responsible for learning: teachers. Can teachers alone solve educational inequality? This question lives at the heart of contemporary discussions about the role, race, and background of teachers in low-income communities in the United States and abroad. To be clear, there is no solution to the problem of educational inequity that does not include teachers. Unfortunately, teachers are rarely asked to take a seat at the education reform table alongside the wealthy and well connected when it is time to fund innovations in urban school districts. The experiences, beliefs, and practices of teachers whose work is primarily among poor children of color are not central to the educational schemes purported to be in the best interest of children. Instead, those who neither teach nor have experience with poor communities or those of color make the lion's share of the decisions relative to educational policies. The powerful group of decision makers—from elected officials to corporate reformers—believes that high test scores will provide access to opportunity. Freedom, equality, and opportunity, while first cousins, are not all the same thing. Opportunity without equality will never lead to freedom. Virtuous teachers know better.

If insanity really can be defined as the committed repetition of failed behaviors with the expectation each and every time that the outcome might be different, then there are quite a few involved with the education reform movement whose actions most surely demand a professional evaluation. Doing more of what fails will never lead to success. The educational experiments and plans devised by the wealthy in concert with the political elite fail the majority of the children of color who are the supposed beneficiaries. In response, more and more frequently, teachers who share an affinity with and often but not always the racial and economic background of students from struggling communities are finding ways to insert themselves into an educational conversation that, for the most part, has historically excluded them. Their work is a particular form of resistance that does more to emphasize what is right with Black children than to focus on what is wrong with Black communities. It is not an answer in and of itself, but it is important.

While the previous chapter looked at the organized resistance and pushback of Black students, young people, and communities to the privatization and educational reform efforts that starve schools of necessary resources and impose impossible disciplinary standards on them, this chapter looks at how college graduates of color and sometimes those from impoverished backgrounds have chosen public school classrooms as their battleground. They are using the easy access to urban classrooms provided by Teach for America to positively intervene in the lives of students. More than just teaching students to take tests, these teachers believe that those among them who understand their students' backgrounds can do far more to facilitate educational, cultural, and economic change than can almost any other single intervention. However, as Teach for America has embarked on a global growth strategy, providing its particular brand of teaching to poor and disenfranchised students in over forty countries around the globe, it does not seem interested in learning from the critiques many of its own teachers have offered. It still traffics in apartheid education, and "segrenomics" still mars its path.

In 2015, Dale Russakoff published the result of her five-year investigation into what happened to the $200 million that was supposed to save Newark's struggling schools. Her book, titled *The Prize: Who's in Charge of America's Schools?*, found that the largest amount of the gift—almost $90 million—went toward labor costs, most of which involved the state's finally honoring long-ignored union contracts for teachers. Close to $60 million went to the aggressive expansion of charter schools in the city. In order to accommodate such growth, district officials also had to downsize the traditional school district, and there were costs associated with that as well. Consultants, some charging as much as $1,000 per day, accounted for another $20 million, and about $24 million went to a variety of local, more modest initiatives, such as $3 million for a literacy initiative to purchase books for district youth so that they could start their own home libraries, $2 million for start-up costs associated with opening four new district high schools, $1.5 million to expand after school programs and other similar types of initiatives. Most of the participants working to implement new policies and directives associated with the Zuckerberg gift neither lived in Newark nor had many significant relationships with members of that community. As a result, most of the new ideas were implemented without input from parents, students, or local administrators. Parents and community members openly rebelled.

One of the first signs of trouble came early in the process. Parents found out over the summer that instead of sending their children to the closest school, often one to which their child could walk, going forward students would have to go online and choose a school that could be located almost anywhere in the city. The computer, not their preferences, parents were told, would have the final say. Given that Newark was a district made up of neighborhood schools and that most kids, as had their parents, walked between home and school, this change, parents argued, could put students in dangerous situations. They might have to cross into crime-ridden neighborhoods where gang-related violence and drug dealing was known to erupt. Needless to say, not all parents were sure those in charge actually cared about the safety, much less the education, of their children.[2]

By 2015, the year when Newark was to have been able to show the world its successful model for systemic educational change, Zuckerberg instead found himself talking about what he, not the children of Newark, had learned over the preceding five years. He said he now knew that community input and involvement mattered, noting, "It's very important to understand the desires of a community, to listen and learn from families, teachers, elected officials, and other experts." He added, "We now better understand why it can take years to build the support to durably cement the changes needed to provide every student with a high-quality education." It was an expensive lesson all around. Indeed, those who saw the five-year experiment in urban education reform as a success rarely noted the negative financial impact the half decade had on the district. Despite what most, including Zuckerberg, acknowledge as a well-meaning and expensive yet failed effort, some supporters of privatization and charter school expansion still claimed victory because many more students were enrolled in charter schools than had been previously. Yet this fact says little about how students were faring, and the initial goals had been far more grand than simply increasing the number of charter schools. Owing to the increased numbers of students and the dollars that followed them from traditional public schools to charter schools, the expensive experiment deepened the financial crisis in the traditional public school district, which was still responsible for educating the vast majority of children in the city.[3]

Though not in any way officially involved in the supposed educational overhaul being discussed at the highest levels of state and local government, there were Black teachers in the city who saw themselves as involved in the fight to provide a transformative education to the students of Newark. They learned an important lesson as well. Their tactic, rather than beginning with redrawing district lines, hiring consultants, or opening charter schools, instead focused on individual students in particular schools. Their approach was to teach each child what he or she needed to know in order to thrive. Though profoundly different from the efforts of the professional education reformers who flocked to Newark between 2010 and 2015, they were no less focused on achieving comprehensive change. Russakoff interviewed three such teachers for her book: Princess Williams, Dominique Lee, and Charity Haygood. They told the reporter that they met over an eighteen-month period with the goal of trying to turn around one of the poorest and least academically successful elementary schools in the entire state. It was called Avon Avenue Elementary. When they began, this group of educators believed that committed teachers could do more to transform the educational futures of Newark's youth than all the other strategies championed by the wealthy and politically connected. They all began their teaching careers working for Teach for America.

As Booker, Zuckerberg, and Christie vowed on television to create a national model for turning around failing districts within five years, Williams, Lee, and Haygood channeled legendarily successful Black teachers like Marva Collins at Westside Prep in Chicago and William and Liller Green from the Ivy Leaf School in Philadelphia. They resolved to commit their entire teaching careers—not just a few years—to Newark's schools and the low-income children there. Williams found creative ways to nudge her students past their self-doubt and inconsistent motivation. She said that she spent quite a bit of time thinking about how she could "push them to be more excellent, never to accept mediocrity, otherwise they hit a ceiling." For example, she shared that if a child liked to braid hair, she would say, "That's a great skill for a surgeon." She had begun the effort believing that a teacher who was born and raised in the community in which she taught, and who was committed to bringing forth educational excellence, was the most important ingredient in any recipe aimed at boosting achievement. However, what she discovered was that poverty mattered. It trumped her motivation. At one point, Williams had a class of twenty-six kindergarten students, fifteen of whom were being monitored by the state for either neglect or repeated exposure to domestic violence. Such social realities led one of the Avon school teachers to say, "Our children's nervous systems are designed from birth to be in trauma mode. . . . I don't think we understood that at first." Initially, the group believed what Teach for America as an organization also believed: "If you just work hard enough, we can fix it." But by the end, they understood that much more than dedication and hard work was required.[4]

Williams, Lee, and Haygood began their teaching careers working for Teach for America after its founder, Wendy Kopp, transitioned out to co-found a new global organization called Teach for All. However, seemingly resistant to the lessons learned from its American variant, the new organization persisted with the perspective that smart teachers are all that is necessary to overcome poverty. In an article in *The Nation* on the Teach for America offshoot, Teach for India (TFI), a reporter, George Joseph, follows a new teacher during the early days of her new career. Like most Teach for America recruits, she was placed in a classroom after only five weeks of training. She does not speak the same language as the children in her classroom. She is struggling. As Joseph points out, instead of recognizing her own limitations regarding her inability to be understood by the thirty-four boys sitting in the hot classroom, "she yells until her voice is hoarse." When asked how she thinks she is doing at her new post, she blames the children, saying they are inattentive. Teach for India was started by a young woman who, but for her Indian heritage, has a life story that sounds quite a bit like Wendy Kopp's.[5]

Shaheen Mistri began her forays into education reform for the poor from a privileged economic background. She attended Tufts University and, like many college students, wasn't sure exactly what she wanted to do with her life. Then one day, on a summer visit back home in Mumbai, she experienced an epiphany while sitting in a taxicab. She recalls in her memoir, "Three children ran up to my window, smiling and begging, and in that moment I had a flash of introspection. I suddenly knew that my life would have more meaning if I stayed in India." She dropped out of college and set about her new goal of finding ways to positively impact educational inequality. Like the teacher who yelled at her classroom full of students, she says, "At 18, I did not think of the quality education I'd forego by leaving Tufts, nor the fact that I didn't speak a word of Hindi." Although born in India, she had actually grown up in various European countries, and her family spoke only English. Nonetheless, as she recalls, "I just knew that India was the place where I would make my life."[6]

India is perhaps more dramatically shaped and defined by income inequality than is even the United States. There, desperately poor and often hungry children live "shouting distance" from wealthy families with parents who paid for private school and children cared for by nannies and transported in chauffeur-driven cars. For the children of the wealthy, Mistri recounts, the local airport might represent the potential for a luxury vacation, while to the poor, "the dark narrow winding pathways of the low-income community around the airport was the entire world." It is then little wonder that the education system in India has been rife with problems that rival, if not surpass, those in the most destitute urban school districts in the United States, where it is not uncommon to find schools where roofs leak, heat does not work in the cold of winter, mold runs rampant, and the holes in the infrastructure are so large that vegetation grows inside the school through the cracks. Similarly, in Indian schools teachers have reported that the poverty, violence, and disciplinary practices children are exposed to at home often make their way into the classroom. For many students, drinking is a problem in the community, and students as young as ten are exposed to pornography because their elder siblings watch it at home. Physical abuse in the community is commonplace and accepted as a part of life. Teach for India students sometimes come to school with signs of having been recently beaten, and their parents simply tell the Teach for India teachers that they should feel free to beat their children as well.[7]

In much the same way that Teach for America's founders discussed the issue of poverty in United States schools as little more than an unfounded excuse implying that poor children can neither learn nor thrive academically, similarly, Teach for India and the other Teach for All member organizations also believe that relating issues like poverty to educational inequality reinforces the wrongheaded belief that poor children are simply incapable of reaching the educational heights achieved by more wealthy students. Instead, Teach for All organizations have as one of their core values the belief that all children have "potential just waiting to be unlocked" and say that their organization, no matter where in the world it is located, will help in this effort by providing the young teachers with a "valuable understanding of the challenges facing the underserved populations" and "provide political leadership aimed at devoting more resources to solving the problem of educational inequity." Though the organization does not so much as promise to equalize access to education, it tells recruits that they will gain valuable leadership experience. In addition, instead of advocating for governments to increase funding to poor children to help address the systemic impact of poverty, a former

Teach for India fellow explained, "We don't think it would be fair to ask companies to pay higher taxes for education. The problem is not one of funding, but how that funding is spent." Perhaps then it is not surprising that, like Teach for America, Teach for India advocates for the increased use of standardized tests, the introduction of cheaper forms of instruction, like virtual classes, and increased private-sector participation in Indian education.[8]

Finally, with a mind-set similar to that of those behind the proposed reforms in Newark who believed that change should come from the top and bypass community input to the greatest extent possible, when *The Nation*'s Joseph asked a trio of Teach for India's teachers, Selna, Nikhil, and Priya, how much they worked with the surrounding community to push for better school conditions long-term, Priya said, "Those [policy] decisions are made at the top anyway. So what is the point of community engagement?" Pressing the point, Joseph asked if these community views were perhaps why Teach for India teachers should live in or around the neighborhoods in which they were working and possibly agree to stay at the schools for longer than two years. One of the fellows responded that TFI wouldn't be as marketable or popular with those changes in place. These views show that these teachers have well learned the lessons of Teach for America even as the organization has grown to encompass the globe.

Wendy Kopp launched Teach for All at Bill and Hillary Clinton's family foundation, the Clinton Global Initiative, in 2007. At the time, she said that the goal of the new organization was to support global entrepreneurs who wanted to build movements similar to Teach for America in their own countries. Within the first ten years, Teach for All franchised Teach for America's model on six of the seven continents. According to Teach for All's website, much like Teach for America, this global variant is financed through a mix of corporate, foundation, philanthropic, and state funding in individual countries, and all those who sign on agree that fixing education is urgent because "in rich and poor countries alike, where children are born often determines the quality of their education, and, ultimately, their future opportunities." Also similar to Teach for America, providing leadership opportunities for teachers who joined the program is highlighted more than is the purported help they will bring to struggling students. It promises recruits, "During your two-year teaching commitment, you will join Teach for All alumni across the globe who are working to expand opportunity for children, whether in education, policy, or other sectors." Though it could not promise that the children in the classrooms would necessarily benefit, the fact was foregrounded that any interested teachers, in any of the countries, would most certainly do so.

In India, as in the United States, some teachers are trying to resist Teach for India and its rapid incursion into that country's public education system. They are not getting very far. As one such teacher—Firoz Ahmad, a primary-school teacher in Delhi—says in the *Nation* article, "We are trying to push them off and we are trying very hard, but they have very powerful people behind them." He adds that he worries that what will happen in the future is poor children will begin to be targeted, trained, and educated into service roles or entry-level positions. Though he does not use the terms, he is concerned that the nature of the apartheid education some children receive will consign them to a particular caste, or that the education they are provided will equip them only for life outside of the middle class with no way to move up the social ladder. As a result, as is also true with some forms of education in the United States, schools in India are beginning to sort students into groups. Some are marked for vocational training and others for more rigorous types of instruction. As Ahmad reports, "We are quite afraid they are going to use early screening and labeling to screen [students] into vocational courses . . . purely *economic* schooling." Whether in the United States or elsewhere, there are vast sums of money to be made by organizations that sort, selectively educate, and give privileged young adults leadership opportunities and financial benefits poor children will rarely see. It still remains to be seen if the model will actually foster educational equality at a systemic level. In the United States, so far it has not.

As I reach the end of many years spent teaching, thinking, and writing about education, I have come to understand that teachers are but one piece of a complicated puzzle. In the past, Black teachers who successfully educated generations of Black children to and through college were able to do so when they worked with Black community members and parents, and when they also creatively controlled the instructional strategies, curriculum, disciplinary methods, ideologies, and assessment strategies. However, as Zuckerberg reflected following the conclusion of his failed $100 million experiment in Newark, wholesale change requires all community stakeholders to at least convene at the same table. That is the only way to ensure educational systems and strategies do not benefit entrepreneurial investors more than they do poor children. Our system will need to be almost completely overhauled and rethought if it is to serve those who are presently the victims of our American brand of apartheid education. As it currently exists, it is a system based on the segrenomic financial ideology and thus requires high levels of segregation and poverty to function.

The conclusions I draw when I look at the past and present trajectory of how our system of public education has functioned are outlined in these pages. However, I want to end this book with the voices of young people—young educators who continue to believe that education will lead to freedom and who have pledged to do their part to be involved in that future. They are the products of the types of dysfunctional school systems that are chronicled throughout this book. They have been subjected to the American brand of apartheid education. Unlike many of their peers, they survived. We need to hear from them more if we want to bring about systemic change. The educational organizations that have an increasing influence on our school system today were founded largely by elite and privileged whites whose aims and experience differ significantly from the goals and backgrounds of young people like Dwight and Nora. The voices closing this book make clear that the eager, well-intentioned college students deeply interested in fixing our country's broken education system are not the issue; rather, the problem is the relentless focus on the bottom line—a focus that precludes the education of our children from being the real priority.

Dwight and Nora are both people of color who initially attended underserved schools and were then able to transition to wealthy private schools. They both went to college and successfully earned bachelor's degrees. Dwight went further, earning a law degree. From their stories, we get a deep sense of the distance between the elite students who founded and continue to steer educational reform organizations and the realities of the neighborhoods and schools that make their work possible. Dwight did not see many white people in his neighborhood and classrooms during his formative educational years. That changed when he got to middle school and was identified by A Better Chance as a student who would thrive in a prep-school setting. Nora's educational experience was different, as she often attended school with whites. Neither Dwight nor Nora had any awareness that during the early phase of their educations a highly funded movement was flourishing with the explicit goal of addressing the educational futures of students like them: students from modest backgrounds attending dysfunctional schools with a host of academic, administrative, and behavior problems. I hope the lessons from their histories provide a blueprint for our collective educational future. It is time we let educational insights like theirs begin to trickle up to those currently setting education policy in the United States.

Dwight

I was not the kind of student anyone would have assumed would end up going to college at a school like Princeton University. I grew up in the South Bronx. My neighborhood was all Black, a mix of African Americans, Afro Caribbean (including Latinos), and some West Africans. My father was a "freelancer," by and large. He was a security guard, and sometimes a van driver for different companies. My mother has been a nurse's aide since I was a baby. That's what she does. She set the example of getting up early and being consistent.

Not just in my neighborhood, but even in school, I didn't see any white people. I don't really remember any white teachers. I didn't see white people until I joined the prep program that got me into high school. My classrooms were all Black. I remember in kindergarten getting into a fight over someone throwing stuff at me. When I was in third grade, I chased a guy in a hallway and it ended in a fight. But for the most part, I never really had to deal with bullying and stuff like that because my family was affiliated with the Bloods street gang. I never got picked on because the Bloods dominated my neighborhood. People knew who I was affiliated with.

I think there were two things that, in retrospect, I noticed about my background. One was that there were no books in my house. I think my mother may have had a Bible, but there were no other books in my house. Also, I remember my father was consistent with checking my homework every day when I was a child, up until he moved out of the house. From kindergarten through third grade, he would ask me if I did my homework. Overall, though, there was no educational background in my family. My father stopped school in the ninth grade. My mother finished high school. But generally, there wasn't a culture of understanding the importance of education. I think the goal was getting a high school diploma. We've since progressed and now we think college degree.

Other people noticed that I was smart first. There were two stages. One was fourth grade, when they started doing citywide and statewide standardized tests. Suddenly, my test scores were important. I remember in middle school they would read off the names over the loudspeakers of those who finished in the top 10 percent. I was in the 99th percentile. It became clear to the teachers that I would be in the top class, which wasn't really a big deal to me.

Most of what I remember about my teachers was not that great. Still, I was in the number one class. If there were ten classes, there was tracking in the sense that we tested the best so we were put in the top class. I think if anything it created a safer classroom environment, and typically the students in the number one class, their parents, and their families were more engaged. You didn't have to deal with behavior problems. The trick, though, is that you have to go to recess and lunch and walk home with the same kids who are being more neglected by the system. Mostly I just played basketball with people, which was actually the main reason why I went to school. I just wanted to play basketball during recess. There were guys who would play sports. There were girls who would jump rope. Then there were the guys who were in gangs and the girls who were looking at the guys in gangs. Those were the social circles that I remember.

Because some of my family members were in gangs, I was able to not have to be in the gang, because it's like if your family is not in a gang, you run the risk of being picked on every day at the school. I would see kids, usually high school–aged, that would stand outside of our middle school and follow kids to beat them up. Not even because of any sort of personal relationship—just wanting to see the world burn, like sheer anger. I remember being followed home one day. They decided to turn back when they realized the block that I lived on. I also had a relationship with the guys on my block, the drug dealers and stuff. I remember one day playing basketball and a guy got in my face. Before I could react, a guy punched him in the face and beat him up to protect me. These dealers are the same guys who, once they realized that I was doing something else academically, would encourage me.

My father's a boxer. My mother grew up in the streets and was very comfortable there. My sister was in a gang. I used to fight, myself. We were close to the drug dealers. We had so many ties. There were downsides to that. We had to leave the state multiple times because somebody got killed and we were affiliated with that incident. There were multiple times in which it brought relief and too many times in which it brought stress.

I had one teacher in eighth grade whom I still have a relationship with. When she found out I was going to a boarding school, she was so happy for me. She loved her job. She was there every day. My science teacher was pregnant, and she missed a lot of my eighth-grade year. My history teacher was trying to write a book or something like that. We had other teachers who weren't there so often. It seemed like we had substitutes every day.

When I got tapped for City Prep and A Better Chance, it sounded great to me. I've met a lot of people, from my neighborhood and similar neighborhoods, afraid of change and afraid to try something new. For me, it was cool. At that point, I hadn't even seen campuses. But once I went on a tour of boarding schools, it was such a no-brainer. There's a standardized test, the SSAT, that you take for these schools. The test scores separated me from my friends in City Prep who didn't end up going to boarding schools. I kind of had my pick of the litter. I got into Exeter, Lawrenceville, and the other boarding schools. I picked Lawrenceville because of the school colors. They were red and black, and red was the color for the Bloods street gang. The other thing was, a recruiter called me from Lawrenceville and he sounded like a Black person. It turns out that he was from Brownsville, Brooklyn, and had a similar background. I gravitated toward that. I liked that there was now a voice and a face at the school.

The Lawrenceville School was difficult. Socially, it was a bit difficult, but there were people like my friends James and Jamal, who came from similar backgrounds. We kind of just gravitated toward each other. We created a home outside of home. But, academically, I was suddenly getting Cs. I still got As in math, but I was getting Cs. I was like, "What's going on?" Because I'm somebody who got As my entire life. That is something that stuck with me when I became a teacher. I never wanted my students to feel that shock of realizing that they've been undertaught for so long.

I've always been focused on Black communities. I've tried to broaden that, to think more of humanity as a whole rather than being concerned about just Black people. But I think just seeing a disparity, thinking that a kid like myself can come into a private school with Cs because of how different the resources, talent of teachers, and everything else is upsetting. I mean, at Lawrenceville, we had $17,000 microscopes. You can imagine the impact of my going to that school, because I still remember the number. I don't think we had books and computers and everything else that added up to $17,000 in my public school. Seeing that, I wanted to pay it forward.

I think I did well because people took a special interest in me. I don't care how intelligent you are, if you don't have a couple of people to point you in a certain direction, it doesn't matter. I thought, even if I can do that for a year, if I can take that one kid and push them forward, that would be enough. When I learned about Teach for America and the easy way in which you can get into a classroom, for better or for worse, I was like, this will work for me. I could jump in and teach a classroom even though I didn't major in education. It was actually the number one job preference that I had. Throughout college, I intended to join Teach for America.

After I graduated from Lawrenceville and then Princeton, I taught fifth, sixth, and seventh grade math in a D.C. public charter school. My school was a mess. Initially, I literally only had half the classroom to teach in. There was a flimsy, foldable barricade put up. I taught math on one side, and the science teacher taught science on the other side. At the same time. We would both have about fifteen to twenty kids in our class. The school, in order to remedy the lack of facility space, merged classes, resulting in one class of fifth- and sixth-grade students and one class of sixth- and seventh-grade students. To me, this was the most devastating thing psychologically to some of the sixth graders. The top-performing sixth graders were put with the seventh graders. The low-performing sixth graders were put with the fifth graders. Some sixth graders were in the same class as their younger siblings. Some of their siblings were testing better than them. I didn't allow it in my class, but I know what's going on in recess: "You're dumb. Your little sister just did this and you failed."

I always loved the students. People ask me why I left teaching. It wasn't the kids. It was the administration. I had three principals my first year. Every month there was a new philosophy, a new direction, or a new pedagogical goal. As if these changes were going to make us strike gold. Kids need consistency. We're constantly shifting the target on them, and it's hard for the teachers too. In the middle school, we had two experienced teachers and two first-year teachers. I was the only person that was not from a historically Black college. We had people from Spelman, Morehouse, and Howard, and then me from Princeton. All Black.

I learned that it's not necessarily the race of the teacher that will make them a success. One teacher grew up well-to-do and did not know how to handle the environment. The teachers would talk bad about kids. They also had problems with the kids, but I didn't. I think it was in part because I was sort of "bad" in school. I was the type that would not give you respect unless you earned it. I already knew that there was going to be a bunch of little kids like me in that classroom. I went in there first thing and gave them my background: "I'm from the Bronx. I grew up poor and around violence. The world doesn't care. But I have love for you."

I was very close with my kids. The school didn't have a nurse, security guard, library, or gym. We didn't have a lot of things. Fights would break out in the hallway. I would tell my kids, "Keep doing your work," and go break up the fight. I would come back and they would still be doing their thing. Part of it was manipulation; I convinced them that there were spies in the classroom.

In my second year, I taught my kids about Black empowerment. It was part of why I wanted to move to D.C. The kids would say things like, "Your hair is nappy." I would ask, "What's wrong with curly hair? Who taught you that that wasn't beautiful?" We were always a unit. Beginning of the day, I'm walking around the classroom asking the students how was their morning. If a kid acted up, I would wait until everybody walked out, pull him aside, and say, "Listen here, young boy, you're not going to talk to me like that." Because I know he's going to be intimidated by me in a one-on-one situation, but if I call him out in front of his boys, he's going to puff his chest. I was too young of a teacher to deal with that power dynamic. Too many teachers give threats they can't follow through on: "I'm going to suspend you for a week." No, you're not. Then the kid is going to go to the principal's office, come back strolling, and you lost credibility. I would tell my administrators, don't come into my classroom and try to regulate. This has to be my space. I didn't believe in suspensions. I was like, "We're going to deal with all of this in-house."

If I could wave a wand, which is just saying not worry about the budget, not worry about politics, and fix urban schools, I would cap class sizes at twelve. I would require teachers to either live in the community or do community service and meet a certain quota of hours, because I think the biggest issue we have is that teachers and police don't recognize the kids that are there. It's hostile territory for them. They don't recognize the parents. But it's different if you see the kids in the supermarket, you see the parents at church. It's like suddenly these are humans as opposed to data or obnoxious people.

Certain kids need differentiation, and you can't really pull that off. What you end up doing is teaching to the middle. You hope that you can keep the smart kids busy with something else and you hope that the less-talented kids just stay quiet. That's what you end up hoping for. If you had twelve, you could address all of the students' needs. I think the school day should be extended, but not academically. I think the academics should end at maybe 2:00 p.m.—which is when kids are done anyway—and then there should be extracurricular activities. Too many schools don't have extracurricular activities anymore. If you take away music, sports, and other things that kids can feel proud of, you take them out of the classroom. I would also extend the school year. Schools should be year-round with two-week breaks at the most.

Smaller class sizes, extended school year, extended day, and teachers involved in the community. Those are the four things that I hope to influence one day in politics. However, I don't think that anybody should be in the leadership position out of ambition. I think you should have a calling, and people should have faith in you. If I do well enough in my career, whether it's law or education, and people say, "I believe that you can help us," I would love to be like an elected official. My goal is to practice law and then try to go back into the classroom, teach for a few of years, move up the ranks administratively, learn what I need to learn, and then open my own school. I want to take kids as they are. Don't focus on building prisons. Build more schools. See what happens when you actually have enough teachers.

Nora

I grew up in Springfield, Massachusetts, which is a post-industrial city in Massachusetts. It's the third largest city. It's in western Mass. It's next to Holyoke, which is also a very large city. I went to kindergarten in Connecticut, because I was young, and my mom didn't want me to wait to start. I was four, but I was turning five in November, and my mom was like, "You already know how to read." My mom was very adamant. She told me, "You're going to know how to read before you go to school, you're going to know how to write your name." So we went to Connecticut so I could go to school.

Then I came back, and for my first two years in elementary school, we lived in a suburb right outside of Springfield. It was called East Longmeadow. It's mostly white. Sort of a working-class, middle-class mix. I absolutely hated it. I liked school, but I didn't like going there. I was the only Black student, the only student of color that wasn't in the busing program from Springfield. There were three Black kids and one Dominican kid in my class. Basically, I was grouped with those students, and so those were the only friends I had. The white students would tease us. They wouldn't talk to us. It was very traumatizing. When we moved back to Springfield, my mom was like, "We're not doing white schools anymore. I have to keep coming to the school. I have to keep talking to these people. This is ridiculous."

We moved back to Springfield, but my schools were predominately Black and Puerto Rican. There were some white students, and I was just really not cool with any of them. I kept thinking, you look like the little white girl that would pull my hair and push me off the swings in the playground. White friends? For what?

I spent the rest of my time in schools in Springfield. I was basically tracked into all the honors and AP courses. My parents both work in corrections, so I would say we're generally solidly middle class for whatever that word means for Black people. They could afford the Catholic school I went to. It wasn't a super ritzy private school; it was just a regular, working-class school. I wasn't learning anything. It wasn't one of the super prestigious schools. It was just an alternative. This was a time when middle school started to become sort of the worst part of the public education system. This was especially true in our district. My mother started complaining that I didn't have any homework. You're not learning anything. She started wondering what the point was of her paying so much money for bad education.

My stepdad grew up in Hartford, Connecticut. He grew up very poor. His father was a West Indian immigrant, but he died when my stepdad was very young. My stepdad had a lot of brothers and sisters. It was just them and his mother in probably one of the worst neighborhoods in Hartford. When he was growing up, he was involved in gang life. That was kind of just the norm. Not necessarily the sort of drug and gun culture of gang life, but just the street gangs, just roaming around, getting in trouble. He was very, very poor, but his mother was very big on education. She always would go to school and handle his business. He didn't go to college, though.

In my public high school I was in the talented and gifted program. Even within that I was tracked. This is kind of when I started to become aware of educational systems. My first two years I loved my school. I was very excited and proud to go there. We did all kinds of stuff. We did a section on the Harlem Renaissance in our English class. We went to Harlem on a bus trip. We went to this jazz museum. We took a tour of Harlem. We just walked around and took pictures, and all kinds of stuff. It was really cool. We did another session on world religions. Instead of how in most schools teachers say this is your unit, you read this book, you take this test, then you move on to the next unit, we had multiple levels of assessment for each group of "learning targets." In my world history class, we studied the conflict in Israel and Palestine and the role of

the West in that conflict. My sophomore year we read the autobi-
ography of Malcolm X, and we went to visit the mosque that he
built in Springfield and spoke with the people there. It was a very
project-based, community-oriented school. This was lofty stuff for
ninth graders.

I loved the school. We all felt like there was so much to learn.
It was still majority Black and Puerto Rican. However, there were
quite a few more white students there. In any case, the district re-
voked the pilot status of the school, which meant that all the autonomy they had, similar to a charter, over their budget and their
contracts was no longer there. When I got there in 2008, we were
its third class. This is also around the same time that the majority of the schools in Springfield became level-four status, which
is whatever terrible name each district gives to schools that don't
meet their adequate yearly progress. This was all around the same
time. Basically, that year, one of the high schools in Springfield,
Commerce High School, became level four, which meant that
they had to fire half of their teachers and their principal and re-
staff. Then, they had to allow the district to come in and basically
have more control. The other option was to close the school, and
another option was to close it and reopen it as a charter school.
They chose to fire the teachers. But most of those teachers were
tenured, and the union was pissed, so they started shuffling them
elsewhere. That meant that we got teachers at our school that
didn't want to be there and didn't believe in the model of learning; some of them were point-blank awful teachers. Literally like,
"Here's a worksheet. Fill it out. That's your learning for today,"
type teachers.

We were all pissed. This was my junior year of high school. I
was tracked into AP English, but the regular English class had this
awful teacher. She had tenure. She was white and had tenure, and
it took them four months to get rid of her, so my classmates lost
four months of actual learning. Then, they brought in someone
else, but she was like, "I can't do this." So they brought in someone

else. He didn't work out. So then they brought in someone else. Within one year, they had four English teachers. They were all bad. Then in honors chemistry, with my chemistry teacher it was the same thing. She was just plum awful. Eighty percent of my classmates were failing the course. I think maybe one person had an A. Then, a similar thing was happening with math. More than half of my classmates were failing the course.

As a way of trying to address the problem, the school held a mass meeting. They invited all the parents. I wasn't worried. I was doing all right. My mom would kick my butt if I didn't do all right. I'm always going to just figure out how to get the A, even if I don't know what's going on. I'm with my parents, and my friends' parents, and they started talking about, "This is what we're going to do, and this is our new plan to fix things." The chemistry teacher stands up and says, "Well, the majority of our students are failing this course because they don't do their homework." The parents ask if they are getting the questions wrong or just not handing it in. She says we are just not handing it in. The parents then ask, "Okay, how are they doing on the exams?" She says, "The majority of them are failing the exams." So the parents say, "Don't you think that if they're not handing in the homework, they don't understand what you're teaching?"

Basically, the teachers start blaming the students, and that starts to become sort of like our story as a class. We are the problem class. We're all failing. At the same time, that year, they start suspending people like crazy. I had one friend who got suspended for multiple things in one day. They started suspending people for all kinds of stuff. So much so that we started joking, like, "Well, okay, if you talk out of turn, suspension." It was just like everywhere we turned, everyone was getting suspended. We started joking about it, because it was ridiculous.

I told my mother I didn't want to stay at the school. I told her if I stayed I would probably start to get in trouble. Then I had a problem with the chemistry teacher. I basically blew up on her in class, and she kicked me out. My mom came up to the school and handled it. I had a problem with another teacher. The school tried to suspend me. Just a number of things, but I knew I needed to transfer out. Finally, she told me "Okay, you've made your point clear. I can see that whatever is going on at this school is not what we thought it was going to be." We started trying to figure out how I could transfer. I transferred to the High School of Science and Technology, which, by all accounts, was a lesser performing school, but I knew people there. I knew that I wouldn't have this administration breathing down my neck all the time.

It was a school that aimed for 100 percent college acceptance. That just meant that everybody applied to community colleges so the school could claim college acceptance. No one was like, "All right, we're going to push you to apply to an Ivy League. We're going to push you." When I told my guidance counselor I wanted to apply to an Ivy League school, she said, "I don't think that will happen for you. I don't think you will get in." She told me my SAT scores were very low, which was not true. I left that school and I went to yet another school, but I had a blast of a senior year. I had some good teachers and some substandard teachers, but I did have teachers who pushed me. I felt supported. Granted, the majority of the other students didn't feel that way. But because I was in the AP classes, I got good treatment.

Overall, though, it was a tough environment. We were on lockdown often. There were regular brawls outside of school. People were arrested all the time. There were police officers in and out of the school. They were just there all day, pretty much. It was a different school environment for me, but I didn't mind it.

I joined Teach for America because I wanted to teach kids in neighborhoods like mine. I started the summer after my senior year in high school working with a learning program. I taught during both my freshman and sophomore summer breaks with a collaborative in Boston and Cambridge. This past summer I taught with Uncommon Schools in Boston.

I think that in the beginning Teach for America made some mistakes. You don't just go into a school and sort of say, "I'm TFA. I'm here. I know what I'm doing. All of you all are terrible, which is why I'm here in the first place." You say, "Okay, what can I learn from the people who are already here? What can I add, but what can I learn, and what's useful, in terms of knowledge and wisdom from other people?" I think that that would have just reflected a completely different kind of approach than what happened. Using what's there, partnering with community organizations that have probably been doing this kind of work for ten-plus years, instead of just barging in saying, "All right. We've got all these Ivy League kids. We're going to bring them in, because they are smart, so they can fix it."

I am particularly interested in issues of race and gender and how they impact Black girls in public schools. For example, not too long ago there was a video of a school safety officer throwing a Black girl out of her chair and onto the floor. Just thinking about both the ridiculousness of a grown man in a school tossing Black children across classrooms and the race and gender implications of that is crazy. But we tend to ignore the fact that Black girls have educational problems because we graduate from college at a higher rate and there's a higher percentage of us getting advanced degrees. But there are things that are being ignored like mental health issues, sexual assault, and the serious silencing around the sexual assault of Black girls in schools.

My goal is not only to develop curriculum that empowers Black girls to achieve academically within whatever school system and environment they're in, but also to come up with radical solutions to change the schools too. That's what I'm thinking about now: how to change things in schools so that when someone tosses you across the classroom, which is insane, you understand what happened, advocate for yourself, and demand justice for yourself. I want to empower Black girls to do those things for ourselves, instead of this sort of really masculine rhetoric of, "You tossed a

Black girl across the classroom, so the fruit of Islam is going to come march outside the school, and as Black men, we have to protect you."

I feel that too often we think in narrow ways about what's happening in schools and don't think about what's also happening in the communities around the schools. I think our solutions right now are things like how we need to change the curriculum, or hire more teachers of color, or bring back arts programs. But there's no simple fix. We have to make a full-throated commitment to enhancing education for students of color and for poor students. But on the same note, we also have to make a commitment to enhancing the cultural education of white students. We don't tend to say white students need culturally responsive teaching. We're not saying white students need to learn about Black and brown issues. We're saying, "We're going to teach the Black people about themselves." That has to change.

ACKNOWLEDGMENTS

If ever asked to offer advice about what is required for an idea to become a published book, I would say that faith, luck, and grace are a too rarely acknowledged publishing trinity. Faith that the ideas undergirding the project are worthy and real, luck in finding others who believe in you as much as in the project, and grace from the universe that opens doors and makes connections that one cannot really plan for or count on. Faith, luck, and grace are every single bit as necessary for a book to "become" as is an intriguing premise, an engaging idea, or wordsmithing skill. For me, during the course of writing this book, this "trinity" sometimes took human form, appearing as angels at particular moments with necessary advice, perspective, help, door opening, and support when I knew I needed it, and even when I didn't. These are my angels.

I arrived at Cornell the same year I began to seriously think that the research I had been doing on race, segregation, and education for the previous few years was actually the beginning of a book project. I wasn't sure. Sabine Haenni, in her role as director of American Studies, asked me to teach the Rabinor Seminar during the fall semester of 2013 and to reflect on the subject matter of the course by delivering the Rabinor Lecture at the end of the class. The course and lecture became this book. Sabine, thank you.

One of the audience members in attendance that day was Michael Jones-Correa, a colleague in the government department who in the week following the lecture asked if we could meet for coffee to chat about my talk. The advice he gave me about paying some mind to the realities of electoral politics was invaluable and led to a productive rethinking of a number of chapters. Michael, thank you.

Leslie Mitchner, the editor in chief and associate director of Rutgers University Press, was the editor of my first two books. Over coffee while we were catching up I told her about *Cutting School*. She told me she might have an interest in the project but immediately encouraged me to find an agent and a larger press. Over the next few years, she checked in to see how the thinking and writing were going and consistently offered her help and advice. Her belief that this was a book I should write became mine too. Leslie, thank you.

From the moment she first read the early version of the book proposal, my agent, Diana Finch, became a tireless supporter for the project. She gently nudged me forward when I needed it, was thoughtful about a strategy for finding the book a home, and is one of the most responsive people with whom I have ever worked in any capacity. Diana, thank you.

As I began to take on the task of turning the original book proposal into the first solid chapter, my friend and Spelman sister Tayari Jones was working on her fourth novel. Though hundreds of miles apart, we took to writing before the sun was up for a few hours before the day's responsibilities started. Though the writing mornings waxed and waned, we completed our manuscripts within a few months of each other. More important, we cemented a friendship. Tayari, thank you.

When *Cutting School* found a home at The New Press, it was due to the enthusiastic support of my editor, Tara Grove. She immediately and completely understood the concept and had a level of enthusiasm that could only be described as unflagging, even as she sweetly suggested editorial changes for one section or another. This is a much better book because of her efforts. Tara, thank you.

To my family: my mother, Belvie Rooks, my son, Jelani Rooks, and my husband, Bill Gaskins. You are my everything. Thank you is not nearly enough. I love you.

NOTES

Introduction: The Segrenomics of American Education

1. Kimberly Johnson, "We Are Not Quitters: Capturing Obama's Attention Was Just the Beginning of a Complicated Story," *Aljazeera* (2014).

2. Ibid.

3. Emma Brown, "Obama Administration Spent Billions to Fix Failing Schools, and it Didn't Work," *Washington Post*, January 19, 2017.

4. Kimberly Johnson, "Verdict Looms for Education in South Carolina's 'Corridor of Shame,'" *Aljazeera* (2014).

5. Carolyn Click and Dawn Hinshaw, "SC Supreme Court Finds for Poor Districts in 20-year-old School Equity Suit," *The State*, November 12, 2014.

6. National Visionary Leadership Project interviews and conference collection (AFC 2004/007), Archive of Folk Culture, American Folklife Center, Library of Congress, Washington, D.C., https://lccn.loc.gov/2004695153.

7. David Kirp, "Making Schools Work," *New York Times*, May 19, 2012.

8. United States, National Commission on Excellence in Education. *A Nation at Risk: The Imperative for Educational Reform: A Report to the Nation and the Secretary of Education, United States Department of Education.* Washington, D.C.: The Commission, 1983. See also Erica Frankenberg and Rebecca Jacobsen, "Trends School Integration Polls," *Public Opinion Quarterly* 75, no. 4 (2011).

9. *A Nation at Risk.*

10. Lesley Bartlett, Marla Frederick, Thaddeus Gulbrandsen, and Enrique Murillo, "The Marketization of Education: Public Schools for Private Ends," *Anthropology and Education Quarterly* 33, no. 1 (Mar. 2002): 5–29.

11. Ibid.

12. Jens Krogstad and Richard Fry, "Dept. of Ed. Projects Public Schools Will Be 'Majority-Minority' This Fall," August 18, 2014, www.pewresearch.org/fact-tank/2014/08/18/u-s-public-schools-expected-to-be-majority-minority-starting-this-fall/.

13. Johnson, "We Are Not Quitters."

1. Rich College Students, Poor Public Schools

1. Race to the Top Fund, "Program Description," U.S. Department of Education, www2.ed.gov/programs/racetothetop/index.html.

2. George Joseph, "Astroturf Activism: Who Is Behind Students for Education Reform?" *The Nation*, January 11, 2013.

3. Walton Family Foundation, "Walton Family Foundation Grants," *Walton Family Foundation*, www.waltonfamilyfoundation.org/who-we-are/grant-reports-financials.

4. Students for Education Reform, Inc. "990 Returns," *ProPublica*, https://projects.propublica.org/nonprofits/organizations/450647583.

5. Diane Ravitch, "Public Education, Who Are the Corporate Reformers?" *Moyers & Company*, March 28, 2014.

6. J.A. Fromm and R.V. Kern, "Investment Opportunities in Education: Making a Profit While Making a Difference," *Journal of Private Equity* (Fall 2000): 38–51.

7. Kenneth J. Saltman, *The Edison Schools: Corporate Schooling and the Assault on Public Education* (Burlington, MA: Taylor and Francis, 2005), location 104–17, Kindle edition.

8. Samuel E. Abrams, *Education and the Commercial Mindset* (Cambridge, MA: Harvard University Press, 2016), location 421–24, Kindle edition.

9. Ibid., location 1170.

10. Ibid., location 3039.

11. Fromm and Kern, "Investment Opportunities in Education, 38–51.

12. Rockefeller Foundation, "Innovative Finance: Shaping the Next Generation of Financing Solutions to Unlock Private Capital for Social Good," www.rockefellerfoundation.org/our-work/initiatives/innovative-finance/.

13. Fred Hechinger, "Education, About Education," *New York Times*, December 6, 1989: 22.

14. Wendy Kopp, *One Day, All Children: The Unlikely Triumph of Teach for America and What I Learned Along the Way* (New York: Public Affairs, 2008), location 137, Kindle edition.

15. Rachel Cohen, "The True Cost of Teach for America's Impact on Urban Schools," *American Prospect*, January 5, 2015.

16. Whitney Tilson, Address to the Value Investing Congress, "An Analysis of K–12 Education and Why It's My Largest Short Position" (September 17, 2013), http://docplayer.net/5359657-An-analysis-of-k12-lrn-and-why-it-is-my-largest-short-position.html.

17. Justin Miller, "Hedging Education: How Hedge Funders Spurred the Pro Charter Political Network," *American Prospect*, May 6, 2016.

18. Ibid.

19. Ibid.

20. Frederick Hess, "Our Achievement Gap Mania," *National Affairs*, no. 9 (Fall 2011).

21. Nikole Hannah-Jones, "The Problem We All Live With," *This American Life* (2015), radio archive.

22. Gary Orfield, John Kucsera, and Genevieve Siegel-Hawley, "E Pluribus . . . Separation: Deepening Double Segregation for More Students," *Civil Right Project, K–12 Education, Integration and Diversity*, September 19, 2012, http://civilrights project.ucla.edu/research/k-12-education/integration-and-diversity/mlk-national /e-pluribus . . . separation-deepening-double-segregation-for-more-students/.

23. Teach for America, "2015 Supporters and Financials," https://teachfor america.app.box.com/s/c88nvda3jrezmy91o9cuy2pukbu24fv5.

24. Martin Biddy, Amherst College Presidential Commencement Address, May 2013, www.amherst.edu/news/specialevents/commencement/speeches_mul timedia/2013/presidential_address.

25. Hannah Schwarz and Amy Wang, "TFA Popularity Rises," *Yale Daily News*, January 22, 2013.

2. White Philanthropy, Black Education

1. Quoted in James Anderson, *The Education of Blacks in the South, 1860–1935* (Chapel Hill and London: UNC Press, 1996), 162.

2. W.E.B DuBois, *The Negro Common School*, no. 6 (Atlanta: Atlanta University Publications, 1901), 38.

3. Horace Mann Bond, *Negro Education in Alabama: A Study in Cotton and Steel* (Tuscaloosa: University of Alabama Press, 1994), 142, citing H. Paul Douglass, *Christian Reconstruction in the South* (Boston: Pilgrim Press, 1909), 122–23.

4. Bond, *Negro Education in Alabama*.

5. Mary S. Hoffschwelle, *The Rosenwald Schools of the American South* (Gainesville, FL: University Press of Florida, 2006), 16.

6. Bond, *Negro Education in Alabama*,162.

7. The Equal Justice Initiative, "Lynching in America: Confronting the History of Racial Terror: Report Summary," 2015, http://eji.org/sites/default/files /lynching-in-america-second-edition-summary.pdf.

8. Ibid.

9. Earl Black and Merl Black, *Politics and Society in the South* (Cambridge: Harvard University Press, 1989), 88.

10. Charles Dabney, "The Negro in the Schools," *Proceedings of the Annual Conference for Education in the South*, Capon Springs, West Virginia (1901): 61.

11. George Winston, "Industrial Training in Relation to the Negro Problem," *Proceedings of the Annual Conference for Education in the South*, Capon Springs, West Virginia (1901): 101.

12. Anderson, *Education of Blacks*, 88–89.

13. Douglas A. Blackmon, *Slavery by Another Name: The Re-enslavement of Black People in America from the Civil War to World War II* (New York: Doubleday, 2008), 40.

14. *Fourth Conference for Education in the South, Proceedings* (Winston-Salem, NC, 1901): 6.

15. Cited in Adam Fairclough, *Better Day Coming: Blacks and Equality, 1890–2000* (New York: Penguin Books, 2002), 51.

16. Ibid.

17. Cited in Bond, *Negro Education in Alabama*, Kindle location 5266–267.

18. Ibid.

19. Anderson, *Education of Blacks*, 90.

20. Brian Jones, "The Struggle for Black Education," in *Education and Capitalism: Struggles for Learning and Liberation,* ed. Jeff Bale and Sarah Knopp (San Francisco: Haymarket Books, 2012), 51.

21. Frederick T. Gates, "The Country School of Tomorrow," Occasional Papers, no.1 (New York: General Education Board, 1913), p. 2.

22. Ibid., 6.

23. General Education Board, *An Account of Its Activities, 1902–1914,* New York: General Education Board (1915), 194

24. Ibid., 193.

25. "Virginia Randolph Teaching Pioneer," *African American Registry*, www.aaregistry.org/historic_events/view/virginia-e-randolph-teaching-pioneer.

26. General Education Board, *Occasional Papers*, 192–96.

27. Edwin Embree and Julia Waxman, *Investment in People: The Story of the Julius Rosenwald Fund* (New York: Harper & Brothers, 1949), 49.

28. M.H. Griffin, 1921, quoted in Anderson, *Education of Blacks*, 162.

29. Embree and Waxman, *Investment in People*, 11.

30. Ibid.

31. Carol Anderson, *White Rage: The Unspoken Truth of Our Racial Divide* (New York: Bloomsbury Publishing, 2016), 71.

32. Daniel Aaronson and Bhash Mazumder, "The Impact of Rosenwald Schools on Black Achievement," Chicago: Federal Reserve Bank of Chicago, Working Paper No. 2009-26, December 2009.

33. Quoted in Anderson, *White Rage*, 71–72.

34. Hoffschwelle, *The Rosenwald Schools*, 40–41.

35. Ibid.

36. Bond, *Negro Education in Alabama*, Kindle location 5185–5288.

37. Department of the Interior, Bureau of Education, "An Educational Study of Alabama," no. 41 (1919): 192.

38. Bond, *Negro Education in Alabama*, Kindle location 5242–248.

39. Claire Zilman, "IBM Defends the Radical 6-Year High School It Founded to Get Young Minorities into Tech," *Fortune,* March 18, 2016.

3. *Brown* Children, White Retribution

1. Ian Millhiser, " 'Brown v. Board of Education' Didn't End Segregation, Big Government Did," *The Nation,* May 24, 2014.

2. Tony Badger, "Southerners Who Refused to Sign the Southern Manifesto," *Historical Journal* 42(2): 524.

3. Christopher Bonastia, "White Justifications for School Closings in Prince Edward County, Virginia, 1959–1964," *Du Bois Review* (Fall 2009): 314.

4. PBS.org, "Landmark Cases: *Plessy v. Ferguson* (1896)," www.pbs.org/wnet /supremecourt/antebellum/landmark_plessy.html.

5. Richard Kluger, *Simple Justice: The History of Brown v. Board of Education and Black America's Struggle for Equality* (New York: Knopf Doubleday Publishing Group, 2011): 434–37.

6. Ibid.

7. Brown Foundation, "Brown Case—Belton v. Gebhart," http://brownv board.org/content/brown-case-belton-v-gebhart.

8. Kluger, *Simple Justice*, 514–15.

9. Ibid., 542.

10. Joan Johns Cobb, "Eyewitness to Jim Crow," *Jim Crow History*, https://web .archive.org/web/20070301120537/http://www.jimcrowhistory.org/resources /narratives/Joan_Johns_Cobb.htm.

11. Kristen Green, *Something Must Be Done About Prince Edward County: A Family, a Virginia Town, a Civil Rights Battle* (New York: HarperCollins, 2015), location 751–97, Kindle edition.

12. Ibid.

13. O.D. Gona, "When the Busses Came: A Daughter's Recollection of Reverend Joseph A. De Laine's Role in Briggs v. Elliott," *Teachers College Record* 107, no. 3 (March 2005). See also http://brownvboard.org/content/brown-case-briggs -v-elliott.

14. James Patterson, *Brown v. Board of Education: A Civil Rights Milestone and Its Troubled Legacy* (New York: Oxford University Press, 2001), 27.

15. Quoted in Kluger, *Simple Justice*, 25.

16. Kluger, *Simple Justice*, 22.

17. Ibid., 23

18. Ibid., 23–24.

19. Erin Adamson, "Breaking Barriers: Topekans Reflect on Role in Desegregating Nation's Schools," *Topeka Capital Journal*, May 11, 2003.

20. Bill Kurtis, "Brown v, Board of Education," *PBS Newshour*, May 12, 2004.

21. *Brown v. Board of Education*, 98 F. Supp. 797, 798 (D. Kan. 1951), rev'd, 347 U.S. 483 (1954).

22. Melba Patillo Beals, *Warriors Don't Cry* (New York and London: Washington Square Press, 1994), 25–27.

23. Joseph Kamp, *Behind the Plot to Sovietize the South* (New York: Headlines Press, 1956).

24. The Lost Year Project, www.thelostyear.com/.

25. Sondra Gordy, *Finding the Lost Year: What Happened When Little Rock Closed Its Public Schools* (Fayetteville: University of Arkansas Press, 2010), 28–29.

26. Ibid., *The Lost Year Project*, 43–45

27. Ibid.

28. H.M. Alexander, *The Little Rock Recall Election* (New York: McGraw-Hill, 1960).

29. Ben Muse, *Virginia's Massive Resistance* (Bloomington: Indiana University Press, 1961), 30–32.

30. Ibid.

31. Green, *Something Must Be Done*, Kindle location 1461–472.

32. Ibid., Kindle location 1517.

33. Ibid., Kindle location 1528.

34. Ibid., Millhiser, "'Brown v. Board of Education' Didn't End Segregation."

35. Noliwe Rooks, "Why It's Time for a Second Emancipation Proclamation," *Time Ideas*, January 21, 2013, http://ideas.time.com/2013/01/21/mlk-day-its-time -for-a-second-emancipation-proclamation/.

36. Nikole Hannah-Jones, "School Segregation, the Continuing Tragedy of Ferguson," *Pro Publica*, December 19, 2014.

37. Ibid.

4. How the North Wasn't One

1. Lee Sustar, "The Struggle for Busing," *Socialist Worker*, March 29, 2013, https://socialistworker.org/2013/03/29/struggle-for-busing.

2. Matthew F. Delmont, *Why Busing Failed: Race, Media, and the National Resistance to School Desegregation* (Berkeley: University of California Press, 2016), Kindle location 482–86.

3. Ibid.

4. Edward McClelland, "How Mayor Daley Outfoxed Martin Luther King," NBC News Chicago, www.nbcchicago.com/blogs/ward-room/How-Mayor-Daley -Outfoxed-Martin-Luther-King-113881699.html.

5. Ibid.

6. Baltimore City Public School System, "From the Old Order to the New Order—Reasons and Results, 1957–1997," *Internet Archive Wayback Machine*, archived from the original on January 2, 2004, web.archive.org/web/20040102 085255/http://www.baltimorecityschools.org/About/History/From_the_oldor derl.asp. See also Charles T. Clotfelter, *After Brown: The Rise and Retreat of School Desegregation* (Princeton, NJ: Princeton University Press, 2004), 101–9.

7. United States Kerner Commission, *Report of the National Advisory Commission on Civil Disorders* (Washington: United States Kerner Commission, 1968), 65–71.

8. Ibid.

9. Dan Baum, *Smoke and Mirrors: The War on Drugs and the Politics of Failure* (Seattle: Back Bay Books, 1997), 18.

10. Jason Sokol, "How a Young Joe Biden Turned Liberals Against Integration," *Politico*, August 4, 2015.

11. Ibid.

12. Lorraine Hansberry, "The Scars of the Ghetto," *Monthly Review*, 67, no. 01 (May 2015).

13. Ibid.

14. Tammerlin Drummond, "Black Panther School a Legend in Its Time," *East Bay Times*, October 6, 2016.

15. Ibid.

16. National Visionary Leadership Project interviews and conference collection (AFC 2004/007), Archive of Folk Culture, American Folklife Center, Library of Congress, Washington, D.C., https://lccn.loc.gov/2004695153.

17. Marva Collins and Civia Tamarkin, *Marva Collins' Way: Returning to Excellence in Education* (New York: Penguin Publishing Company, 1982), 80.

18. Mikel Kweku Osei Holt, "Marva Collins, the Mother of Black Academic Excellence," *Milwaukee Community Journal*, July 10, 2015, http://community journal.net/marva-collins-the-mother-of-Black-academic-excellence/.

19. Ronald Ferguson, "Teachers' Perceptions and Expectations and the Black-White Test Score Gap," *Urban Education* 38, no. 4 (July 2003): 485–93.

20. Collins, Oral history interview.

21. Jody Temkin, "Beidler Faculty Welcomes New Partner," *Chicago Reporter*, July 26, 2005.

22. Marva Collins interviews, Library of Congress, *National Visionary Leadership Project*.

23. Jonathan Rowe, "Ivy Leaf Preschool Nurtures Reading," *Christian Science Monitor*, March 28, 1986; See also Lindsey Gruson, "Education; Private Schools for Blacks," *New York Times*, October 21, 1986.

24. Gruson, "Education."

25. Walter Naedele, "New Strategies Urged for Blacks at a Federal Civil Rights Hearing," *Philadelphia Inquirer*, May 6, 1996, 6b.

26. Rod Godwyn, "Learning Self-Appreciation," *Philadelphia Daily News*, February 6, 1996.

27. Ansley T. Erickson, *Making the Unequal Metropolis: School Desegregation and Its Limits* (Chicago: University of Chicago Press, 2016), Kindle location 650–52.

28. Milton Friedman, "The Role of Government in Education" in Robert A. Solo (ed.), *Economics and the Public Interest* (New Brunswick, NJ: Rutgers University Press, 1955), 123-44.

29. Brendan Fischer, "Cashing in on Kids: 172 ALEC Bills Push Privatization in 2015," *PR Watch,* March 8, 2016, www.prwatch.org/news/2016/03/13054 /cashing-kids-172-alec-education-bills-2015#sthash.3E6Xe3ja.dpuf.

30. Bruce Murphy, "The Legacy of Annette Polly Williams," *Urban Milwaukee,* November 11, 2014.

31. George Clowes, "The Model for the Nation: An Exclusive Interview with Polly Williams," Heartland Institute, August 30, 2002, www.heartland.org/news-opinion /news/the-model-for-the-nation-an-exclusive-interview-with-annette-polly-williams.

32. Ibid.

33. Murphy, "Legacy of Annette Polly Williams."

34. Ibid.

35. Diane Ravitch, *The Death and Life of the Great American School System: How Testing and Choice Are Undermining Education* (New York: Basic Books, 2011), 117.

36. James Ryan, *Five Miles Away, A World Apart: One City, Two Schools, and the Story of Educational Opportunity in Modern America* (London and New York: Oxford University Press, 2010), 14.

37. Stephen Henderson, "Betsy DeVos and the Twilight of Public Education," *Detroit Free Press,* December 3, 2016.

5. Education Dreams and Virtual Nightmares

1. Rebecca Mead, "Betsy DeVos and the Plan to Break Public Schools," *New Yorker,* December, 14, 2016.

2. Valerie Strauss, "To Trump's Education Pick, The US Public School System Is a Dead End," *Washington Post,* December 21, 2016. See also, Betsy DeVos speech, American Federation for Children, March 13, 2015, www.youtube.com /watch?v=f_2nH4aLLDc.

3. Matt Barnes, "Betsy DeVos, Trump's EdSec Pick Promoted Virtual Schools Despite Dismal Results," *The 74,* December 1, 2016, www.the74million .org/article/betsy-devos-trumps-edsec-pick-promoted-virtual-schools-despite -dismal-results. See also *A Call to Action to Improve the Quality of Virtual Charter Public Schools,* June 2016, www.publiccharters.org/wp-content/uploads/2016/06 /VirtualReport_Web614.pdf.

4. Sheryl Gay Stolberg, Michael D. Shear, and Alan Blinder, "In Obama Era, G.O.P. Bolsters Grip in the States," *New York Times,* November 12, 2015.

5. "Corroding the Classroom: Republican Gubernatorial Candidates' Devastating Cuts to Education," *American Bridge*, September 29, 2014, https://americanbridgepac.org/corroding-the-classroom-republican-gubernatorial-candidates-devastating-cuts-to-education/.

6. Diane Ravitch, "Public Education: Who Are the Corporate Reformers?" *Moyers & Company*, March 28, 2014.

7. Mike Carson, "Virtual Schools Coming to Every Alabama District by 2016–2017," *AL.com*, April 26, 2015, www.al.com/news/index.ssf/2015/04/virtual_schools_coming_to_ever.html.

8. Brendan Fischer and Zachary Peters, "Cashing in on Kids: 172 ALEC Education Bills Push Privatization in 2015," *PR Watch*, March 8, 2016.

9. Noel Gallagher, "Maine's New Virtual Charter School Sees 25% Enrollment Drop Since Opening," *Portland Press Herald*, January 6, 2016.

10. Daniel Denvir, "Who's Killing Philly Public Schools?" *Philadelphia City Paper*, May 2, 2012.

11. Kevin McCorry, "All Cyber School Applications Denied in Pennsylvania," *Newsworks*, January 28, 2014.

12. Andre Perry and Rani Weingarten, "Gov. Tom Corbett Has Slashed Funding for Pennsylvania's Neediest Students. Fixing Schools Means Voting Him Out," *Washington Post*, October 24, 2014.

13. NPR, "The Cold Realities of Education in a Poor Pennsylvania School District," April 24, 2016.

14. Aaron Case, "Indescribably Insane: A Public School System from Hell," *Salon*, August 19, 2013.

15. Stephanie Saul, "Profits and Questions at Online Charter Schools," *New York Times* December 13, 2011.

16. Greg Toppo, "Online Schools Spend Millions to Attract Students," *USA Today*, November 28, 2012.

17. Benjamin Wermund, "Will Shareholders Shine a Light on Virtual Charters?" *Politico*, December, 15, 2016.

18. Pennsylvania School Boards Association, "PSBA Special Report: Charter School Revenues, Expenditures and Transparency," www.psba.org/wp-content/uploads/2016/08/Charter-School-RtK-08172016.pdf.

19. Melanie Bavaria, "Districts' Only Link to Cyber Charters: Money," *Philadelphia Public School Notebook*, June 7, 2016.

20. Ibid.

21. Matt Richtel, "In Classroom of the Future, Stagnant Scores," *New York Times*, September 3, 2011.

22. Eloise Quintanilla, "Cellphones Helping Minorities Close Gap on Internet Access?" *Christian Science Monitor*, February 10, 2011.

23. Seanna Adcox, "SC Expanding Students' Online Course Offerings," *South Carolina Now*, July 10, 2013, www.scnow.com/news/state/article_37da45c8-e962 -11e2-a835-001a4bcf6878.html.

24. Report of the National Education Policy Center, "Virtual Schools in the U.S. 2015: Politics, Performance, Policy, and Research Evidence," 2015, http:// nepc.colorado.edu/publication/virtual-schools-annual-2015.

25. "Governor Nikki Haley Announces K–12 Education Reform Initiative," *GWD Today*, January 9, 2014, www.gwdtoday.com/main.asp?SectionID=2&Sub SectionID=27&ArticleID=28147.

26. Jeff Bryant, "The Big Jeb Bush Charter School Lie: How Florida Became a Cautionary Tale for the Rest of the Country" *Salon*, August 12, 2015.

27. Alec MacGillis, "Testing Time: Jeb Bush's Educational Experiment," *New Yorker*, January, 26, 2015.

28. Stephanie Mencimer, "Jeb Bush's Cyber Attack on Public Schools," *Mother Jones*, November/December 2011.

29. Digital Learning Now, "Report Card 2014," http://excelined.org/2014 DLNReportCard/.

30. James Williams, "DeVos Set for Confirmation Hearings with Support from Jeb Bush," *News Talk Florida*, January 17, 2017, www.newstalkflorida.com /featured/devos-set-confirmation-hearings-support-jeb-bush/.

31. Laura Herrera, "In Florida, Virtual Classrooms with No Teachers," *New York Times*, January 17, 2011.

32. Mencimer, "Jeb Bush's Cyber Attack."

33. Wisconsin Department of Public Instruction, "An Evaluation: Virtual Charter Schools," February 2010, www.documentcloud.org/documents/256077 -wisconsin-audit.html.

34. Molly Beck, "National Report Card: Wisconsin's Achievement Gap Worst in Nation," *Wisconsin State Journal*, November 8, 2013.

35. "Connect Ed," Department of Education: Office of Educational Technology, June 6, 2013, https://tech.ed.gov/connected/.

6. Stealing School

1. Kyle Spencer, "Can You Steal an Education?" *Hechinger Report*, May 18, 2015.

2. Michael Flaherty, "The Latest Crime Wave: Sending Your Child to a Better School," *Wall Street Journal*, October 1, 2011.

3. Naomi Nix, "Connecticut's Shame: In One of America's Richest Counties, a High School Has Been Failing for 50 Years," *The 74*, May 15, 2016.

4. Ibid.

5. Motoko Rich, Amanda Cox, and Matthew Bloch, "Money, Race and Success: How Your School District Compares," *New York Times*, April 29, 2016.

6. David Gurliacci, "Moccia says that contrary to other reports, a homeless woman decided to move her child from a Norwalk to a Bridgeport school, and that she isn't even homeless," *Norwalk Patch*, May 10, 2011, http://patch.com/connecticut/norwalk/mayor-i-dont-believe-mcdowell#video-5795088.

7. Jen Roesch, "Sent to Jail for 'Stealing' School," *Socialist Worker*, March 7, 2012.

8. Khadijah Z. Ali-Coleman, "Mom Jailed for Enrolling Kids in School Tells Her Story in New Book, Film," *Ebony*, March 20, 2014.

9. Julianne Hing, "Kelley Williams-Bolar's Long, Winding Fight to Educate Her Daughters," *Colorlines*, May 16, 2012.

10. Soledad O'Brien, "How Stealing a Better Education for Your Kids Can Land You in Jail," *Aljazeera America*, January 20, 2014.

11. Smith Richards, "Family's Latest Gambit Wins Bexley Schooling," *Columbus Post-Dispatch*, December 2, 2010.

12. Eddy Ramirez, "Schools Crack Down on Boundary Hopping," *US News*, March 2, 2009.

13. Ibid.

14. Molly Bloom, "Atlanta Charter School Reports $600,000 Missing," *Atlanta Journal-Constitution*, October 20, 2015.

15. Ibid.

16. Heather Leigh, "Charter School Management Accused of Theft, Other Crimes," *News 4 Jacksonville*, May 26, 2016.

17. Stephanie Mencimer, "School for Scoundrels," *Mother Jones*, November/December 2011.

18. Preston C. Green, Bruce D. Baker, Joseph Oluwole, and Julie F. Mead, "Are We Heading Toward a Charter School 'Bubble'?: Lessons from the Subprime Mortgage Crisis," *University of Richmond Law Review*, 50, no. 783 (2016).

19. Erin Richards and Jim McLaughlin, "Schools Get Creative to Attract Milwaukee Students; Public, Charter, Voucher Schools All Vying for Education Dollars," *Milwaukee-Wisconsin Journal Sentinel*, August 16, 2012.

20. Mencimer, "School for Scoundrels."

21. Ruth Coniff, "FBI Tracks Charter Schools," *The Progressive*, August 20, 2014.

22. Jennifer Dixon, "5 Stories of Dubious Decisions, Wasteful Spending, a Deal for Swampland," *Detroit Free Press*, June 22, 2014.

23. Green et al., "Charter School 'Bubble.'"

24. Ibid.

7. The Age of Resistance

1. Yana Kunichoff, "Chicago Parents Enter Week 2 of Hunger Strike Protesting Corporate Ed Reform and Dyett HS Closure," *In These Times*, August 24, 2015.

2. Elizabeth Harris, "20% of New York State Students Opted Out of Standardized Tests This Year," *New York Times*, August 12, 2015.

3. LDF, "LDF and Others File Complaint Against New York City Specialized High Schools Challenging Admissions Process," NAACP LDF, September 27, 2012.

4. Sean Reardon, "The Widening Academic Achievement Gap Between the Rich and the Poor: New Evidence and Possible Explanations," Greg Duncan and Richard Murnane, eds., Whither Opportunity?: Rising Inequality, Schools and Children's Life Chances, New York: Russell Sage Foundation (2011): 91–117.

5. Noliwe Rooks, "Why It's Time to Get Rid of Standardized Tests," *Time*, October 11, 2012.

6. The National Center for Fair and Open Testing, "National Resolution on High Stakes Testing," December 17, 2015, http://fairtest.org/national-resolution-highstakes-testing.

7. *Washington Post*, "Text: George W. Bush's Speech to the NAACP," NAACP 91st Annual Conference, July 10, 2000.

8. Kelly Wallace, "Parents All Over U.S. 'Opting Out' of Standardized Student Testing," CNN, April, 17 2015.

9. Derek Beigh, "Students Organize Screening of Anti-Testing Film," *Pantagraph*, April 2, 2015, www.pantagraph.com/news/local/students-organize -screening-of-anti-testing-film/article_dda5a78d-6a78-572f-88d8-0d306 f833f74.html.

10. Carla Shedd, *Unequal City: Race, Schools, and Perceptions of Injustice* (New York: Russell Sage Foundation, 2015), Kindle location 264–69.

11. Maia Bloomfield Cucchiara, *Marketing Schools, Marketing Cities: Who Wins and Who Loses When Schools Become Urban Amenities* (Chicago and London: University of Chicago Press, 2013), 50–51.

12. Sarah Jaffe, "When Students Go on Strike for Their School," *The Progressive*, January 2, 2015.

13. Bill Wichert, "Thousands of Newark Students Leave School in Protest, Block Major Intersection," *New Jersey.com*, May 22, 2015.

14. Ibid.

15. Julie Bowman, "Crumbling, Destitute Schools Threaten Detroit's Recovery," *New York Times*, January 21, 2016.

16. Nancy Hanover, "Detroit Public Schools Students Launch Protests to Demand Quality Education," *World Socialist Web Site*, February 11, 2016.

17. Jaffe, "When Students Go on Strike."

18. "Education Justice," *Coleman Advocates for Children and Youth*, http:// colemanadvocates.org/what-we-do/policy-campaigns/.

19. "Mayor de Blasio Announces Roadmap to Reduce Punitive School Discipline and Make Schools Safer," Press Release, November 2, 2015, www1.nyc .gov/office-of-the-mayor/news/779-15/mayor-de-blasio-roadmap-reduce-punitive -school-discipline-make-schools-safer.

20. Eva Moskowitz, "Turning Schools into Fight Clubs," *Wall Street Journal*, April 1, 2015.

21. Jershua Connor and Kelly Welch, "The Other School Bathroom Issue," *US News*, May 26, 2016.

22. Leo Casey, "Student Discipline, Race and Eva Moskowitz's Success Academy Charter Schools," Albert Shanker Institute, October 19, 2015, www.shanker institute.org/blog/student-discipline-race-and-eva-moskowitz%E2%80%99s-suc cess-academy-charter-schools.

23. Jaffe, "When Students Go on Strike."

24. Sam Newhouse, "Students, Supporters Protest Philly School Cops' Use of Force on a High Schooler," *Metro*, May 17, 2016.

25. "Ending the School-to-Prison Pipeline," *Urban Youth Collective*, www.urbanyouthcollaborative.org/ending-school-to-prison-pipeline/.

26. Jessica Huseman, "The Rise of Homeschooling Among Black Families," *The Atlantic*, February 2015.

27. Ibid. See also, Ama Mazama, "African American Homeschooling as Racial Protection," *Journal of Black Studies* 43, no. 7 (October 2012): 723–48.

Coda: Trickle-Up Education

1. Dale Russakoff, "Schooled," *New Yorker*, May 19, 2014.

2. Terri Gross, "Assessing the 100 Million Upheaval of Newark's Public Schools," NPR, September 21, 2015.

3. Dale Russakoff, *The Prize* (New York: Houghton Mifflin Harcourt, 2015), 212–13.

4. Russakoff, "Schooled."

5. George Joseph, "Teach for America Has Gone Global, and Its Board Has Strange Ideas About What Poor Kids Need," *The Nation*, July 1, 2016.

6. Kovid Gupta and Shaheen Mistri, *Redrawing India: The Teach for India Story* (Haryana: Random House Publishers India Pvt. Ltd., 2014), Kindle location 246–49.

7. Ibid., Kindle location 1365–366.

8. Joseph, "Teach for America."

INDEX

About the Author

Noliwe Rooks is the director of American Studies at Cornell University and was for ten years the associate director of African American studies at Princeton University. The author of *White Money/Black Power* and *Hair Raising*, she lives in Ithaca, New York.

Celebrating 25 Years of Independent Publishing

Thank you for reading this book published by The New Press. The New Press is a nonprofit, public interest publisher celebrating its twenty-fifth anniversary in 2017. New Press books and authors play a crucial role in sparking conversations about the key political and social issues of our day.

We hope you enjoyed this book and that you will stay in touch with The New Press. Here are a few ways to stay up to date with our books, events, and the issues we cover:

- Sign up at www.thenewpress.com/subscribe to receive updates on New Press authors and issues and to be notified about local events
- Like us on Facebook: www.facebook.com /newpressbooks
- Follow us on Twitter: www.twitter.com /thenewpress

Please consider buying New Press books for yourself; for friends and family; and to donate to schools, libraries, community centers, prison libraries, and other organizations involved with the issues our authors write about.

The New Press is a 501(c)(3) nonprofit organization. You can also support our work with a tax-deductible gift by visiting www.thenewpress.com/donate.